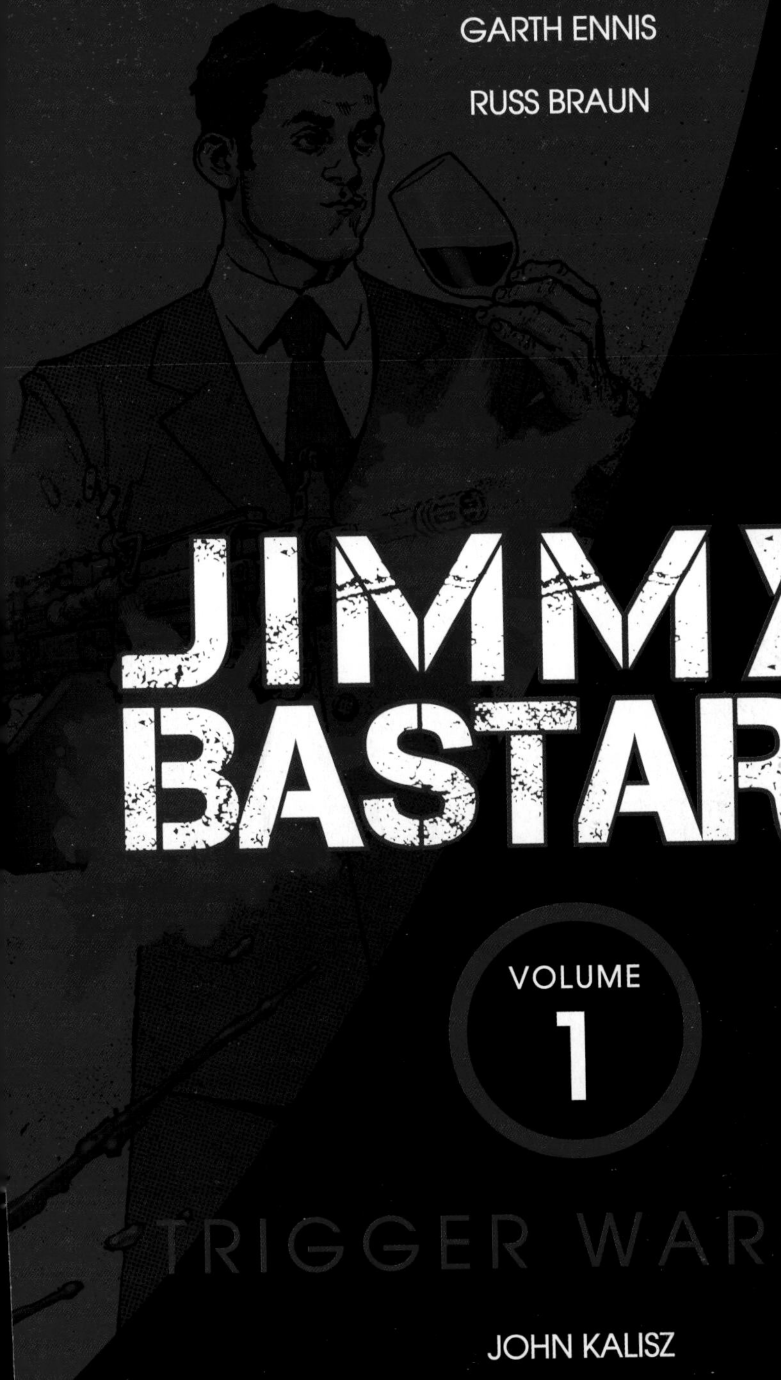

GARTH ENNIS

RUSS BRAUN

JIMMY'S BASTARDS

VOLUME 1

TRIGGER WARNING

JOHN KALISZ

ROB STEEN

DAVE JOHNSON

ANDY CLARKE

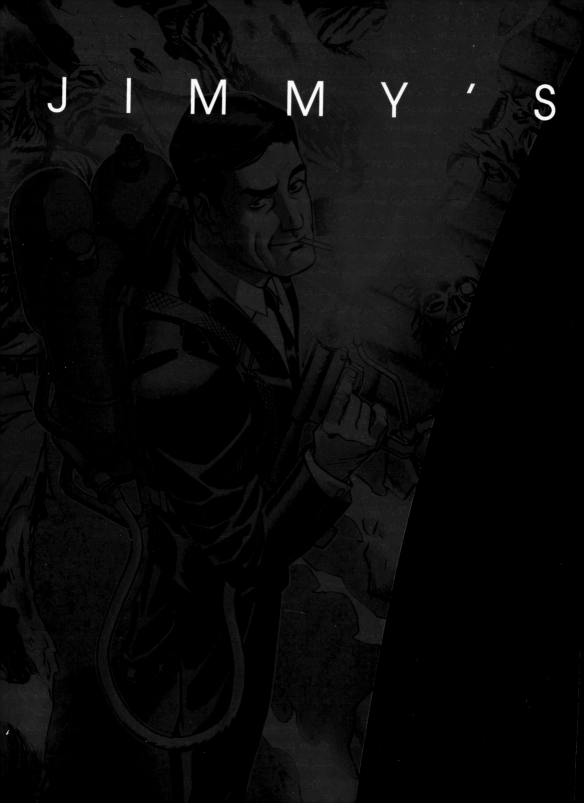

JIMMY'S

BASTARDS VOLUME 1

TRIGGER WARNING

GARTH ENNIS co-creator & writer

RUSS BRAUN co-creator & artist

JOHN KALISZ (issues #1-#4) **with GUY MAJOR** (issue #5) colorists

ROB STEEN letterer

DAVE JOHNSON front cover

JOE JUSKO variant cover

DAVE JOHNSON (issues #1-#4) **& ANDY CLARKE with JOSE VILLARRUBIA** (issue #5) original covers

RUSS BRAUN with JOHN KALISZ, TERRY & RACHEL DODSON, CULLY HAMNER, PHIL HESTER with MIKE SPICER, ANDREW ROBINSON, MIKE ROOTH & ELIZABETH TORQUE
original variant covers

JOHN J. HILL logo designer

JOHN J. HILL & COREY BREEN book designers

MIKE MARTS editor

AFTERSHOCK

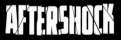

MIKE MARTS - Editor-in-Chief • JOE PRUETT - Publisher/ Chief Creative Officer • LEE KRAMER - President
JAWAD QURESHI - SVP, Investor Relations • JON KRAMER - Chief Executive Officer • MIKE ZAGARI - SVP, Brand
JAY BEHLING - Chief Financial Officer • STEPHAN NILSON - Publishing Operations Manager
LISA Y. WU - Retailer/Fan Relations Manager • ASHLEY WYATT - Publishing Assistant

AfterShock Trade Dress and Interior Design by JOHN J. HILL • AfterShock Logo Design by COMICRAFT
Original series production (issues 1-5) by CHARLES PRITCHETT • Proofreading by DOCTOR Z.
Publicity: contact AARON MARION (aaron@publichausagency.com) & RYAN CROY (ryan@publichausagency.com)
Special thanks to TEDDY LEO & LISA MOODY

JIMMY'S BASTARDS VOLUME 1: TRIGGER WARNING Published by AfterShock Comics, LLC, 15300 Ventura Boulevard Suite 507, Sherman Oaks, CA 91403. Originally published as Jimmy's Bastards #1-5. PRINTED IN KOREA.
First Printing: January 2018. 10 9 8 7 6 5 4 3 2 1

AFTERSHOCKCOMICS.COM Follow us on social media

JIMMY'S BASTARDS

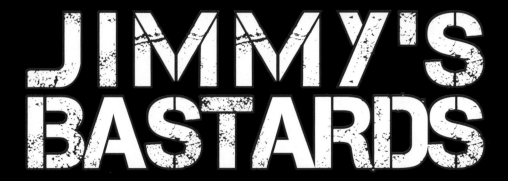

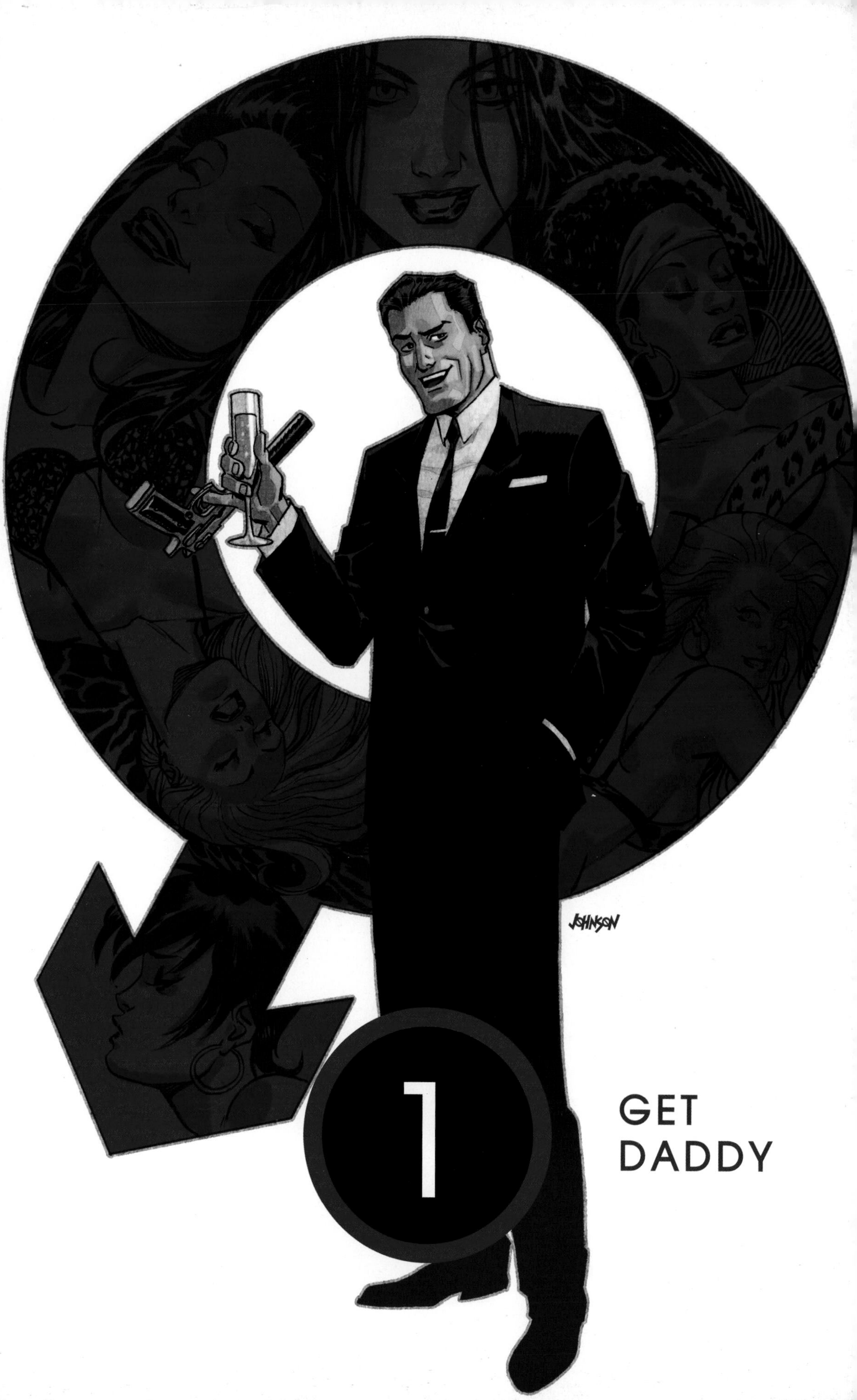
JOHNSON

1

GET DADDY

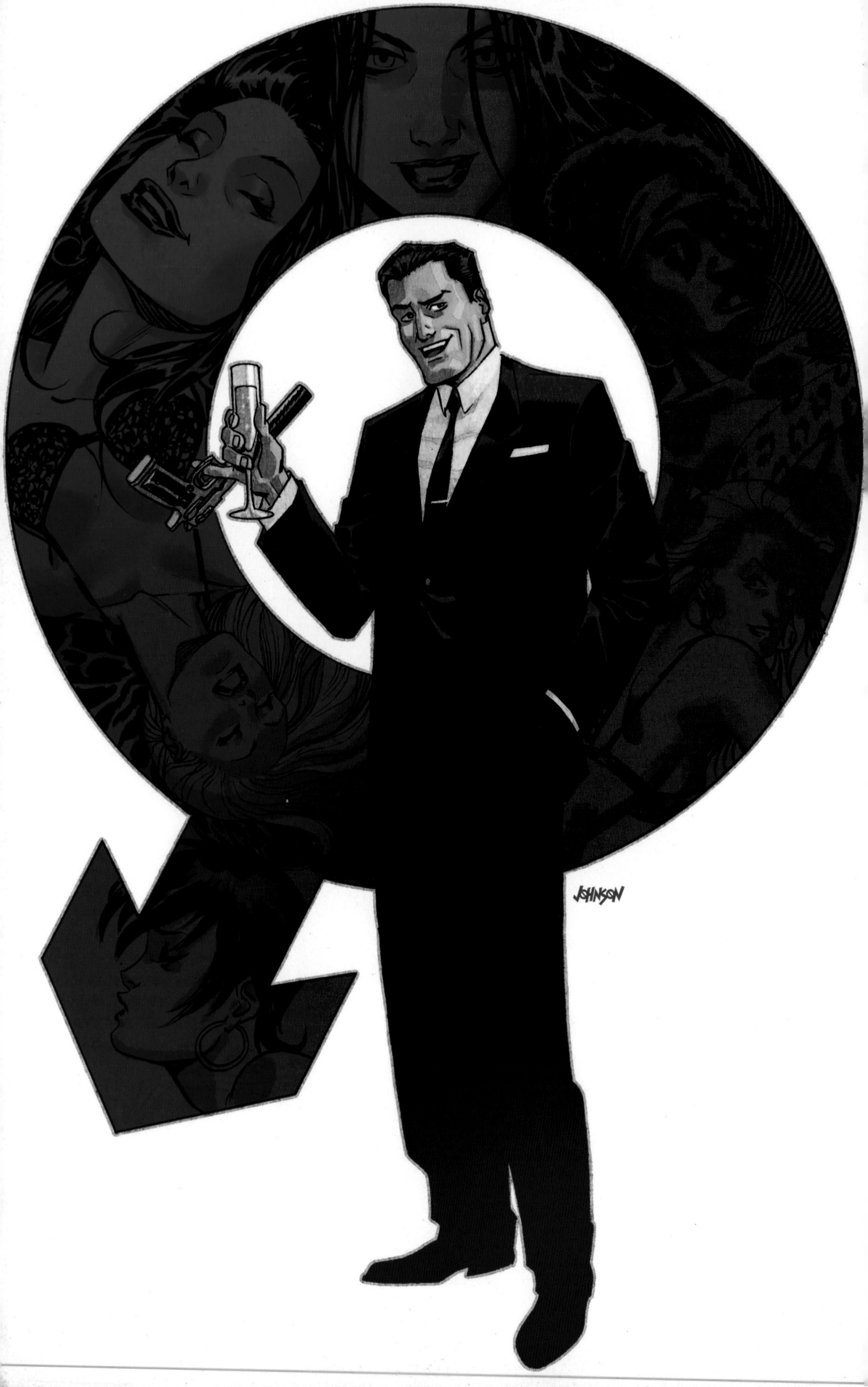
JOHNSON

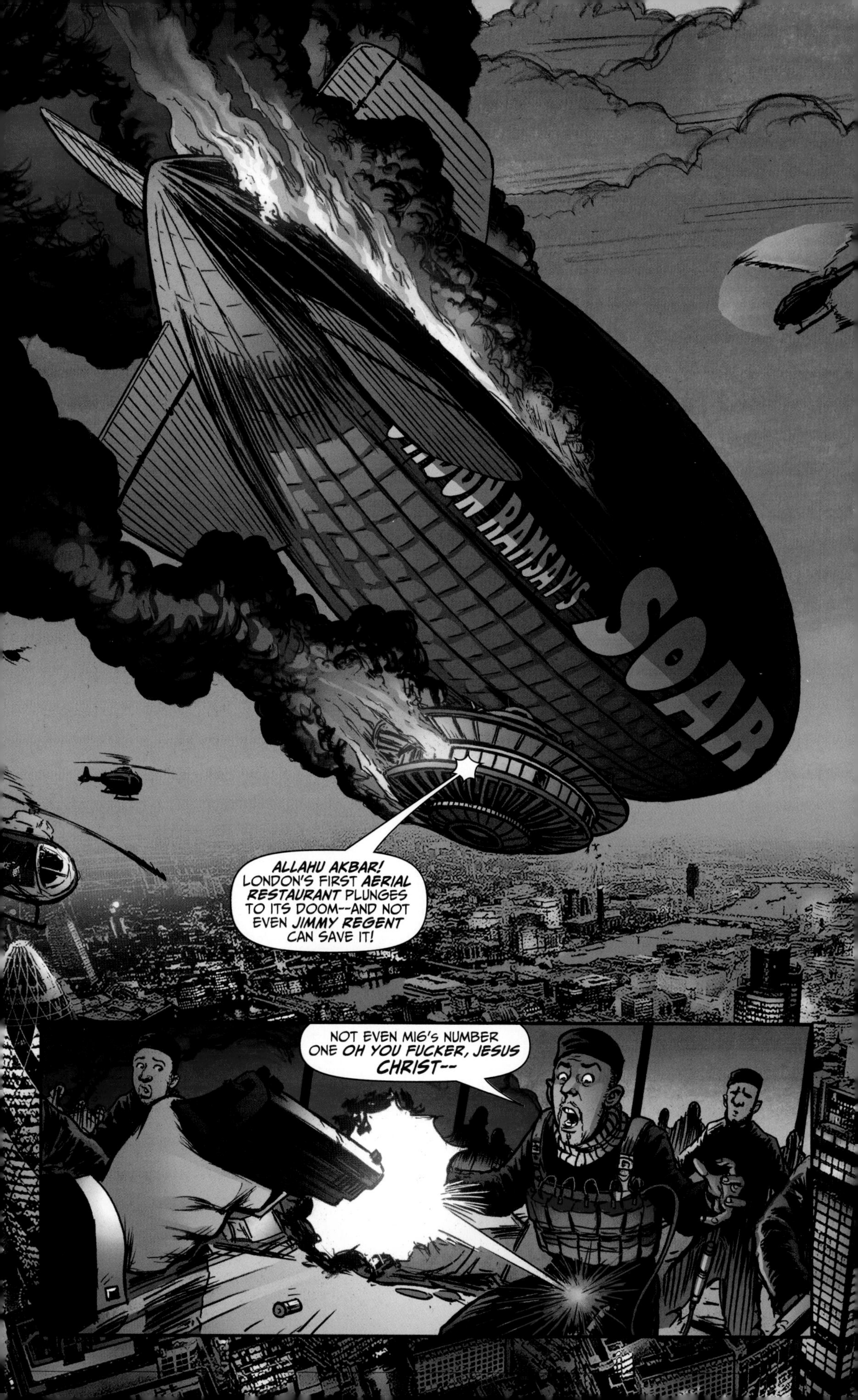
RAMSAY'S
SOAR
ALLAHU AKBAR! LONDON'S FIRST AERIAL RESTAURANT PLUNGES TO ITS DOOM--AND NOT EVEN JIMMY REGENT CAN SAVE IT!
NOT EVEN MI6'S NUMBER ONE OH YOU FUCKER, JESUS CHRIST--

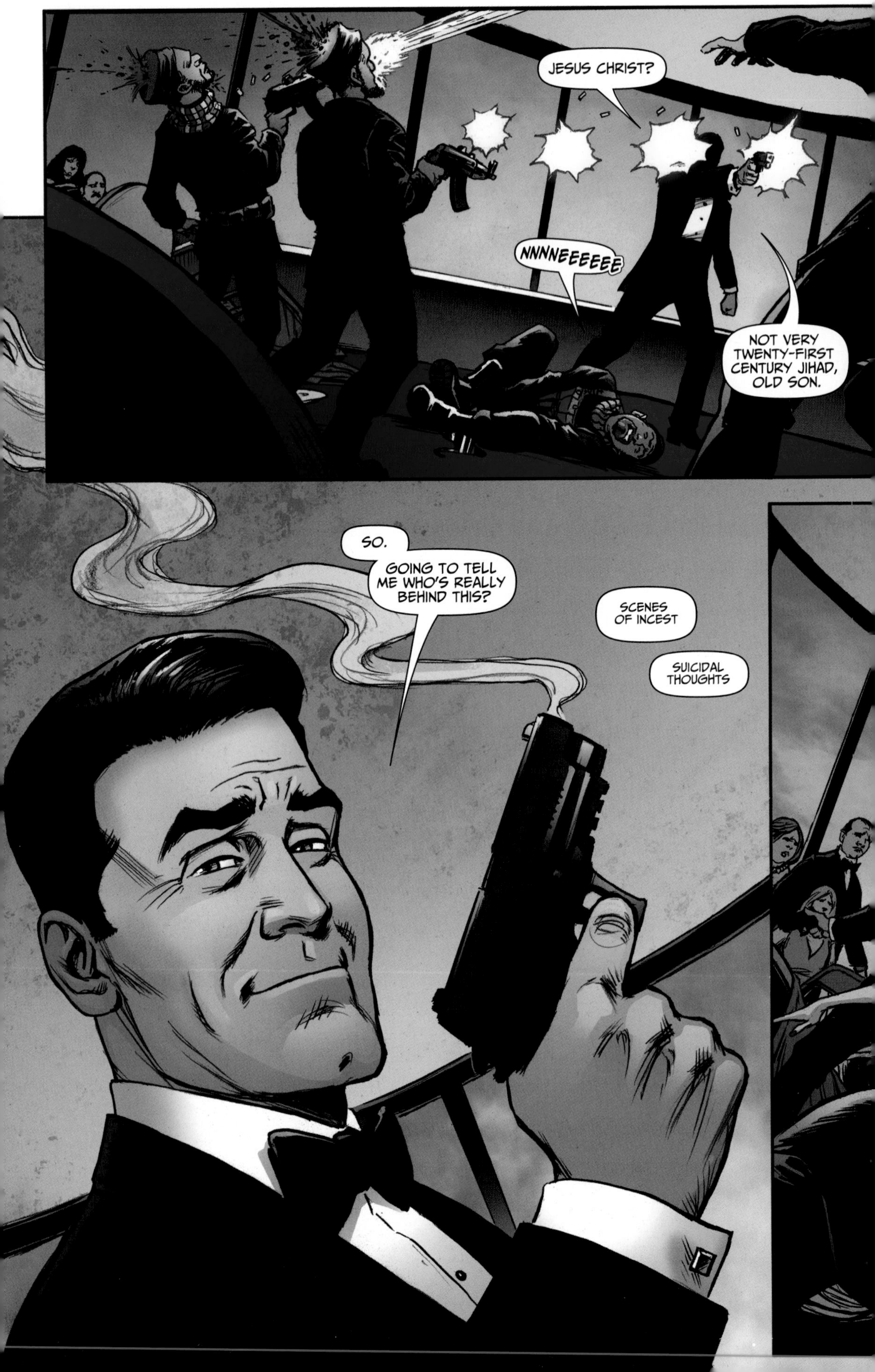
JESUS CHRIST?
NNNNEEEEEE
NOT VERY TWENTY-FIRST CENTURY JIHAD, OLD SON.
SO.
GOING TO TELL ME WHO'S REALLY BEHIND THIS?
SCENES OF INCEST
SUICIDAL THOUGHTS

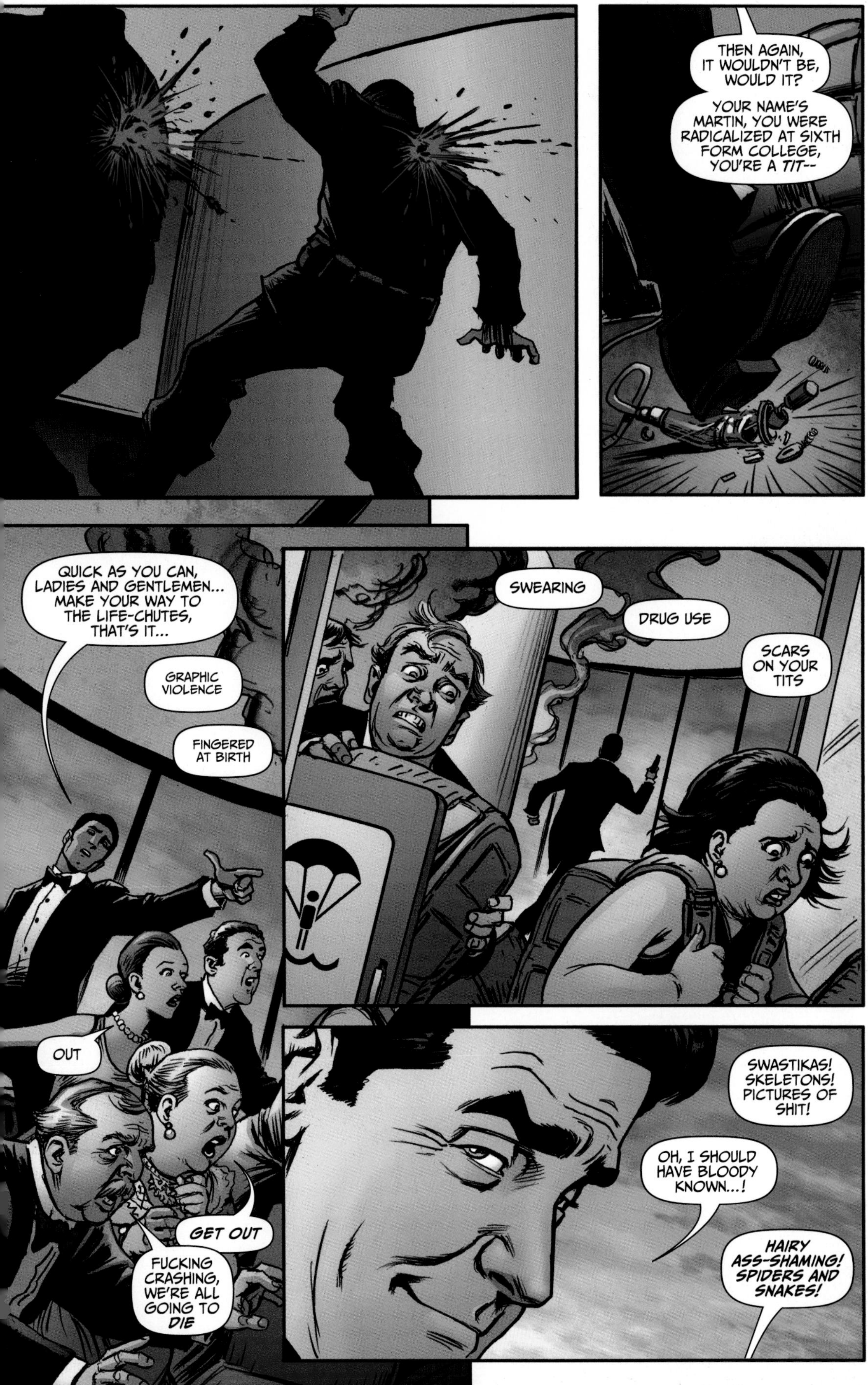
THEN AGAIN, IT WOULDN'T BE, WOULD IT?
YOUR NAME'S MARTIN, YOU WERE RADICALIZED AT SIXTH FORM COLLEGE, YOU'RE A TIT--
QUICK AS YOU CAN, LADIES AND GENTLEMEN... MAKE YOUR WAY TO THE LIFE-CHUTES, THAT'S IT...
GRAPHIC VIOLENCE
FINGERED AT BIRTH
OUT
GET OUT
FUCKING CRASHING, WE'RE ALL GOING TO DIE
SWEARING
DRUG USE
SCARS ON YOUR TITS
SWASTIKAS! SKELETONS! PICTURES OF SHIT!
OH, I SHOULD HAVE BLOODY KNOWN...!
HAIRY ASS-SHAMING! SPIDERS AND SNAKES!

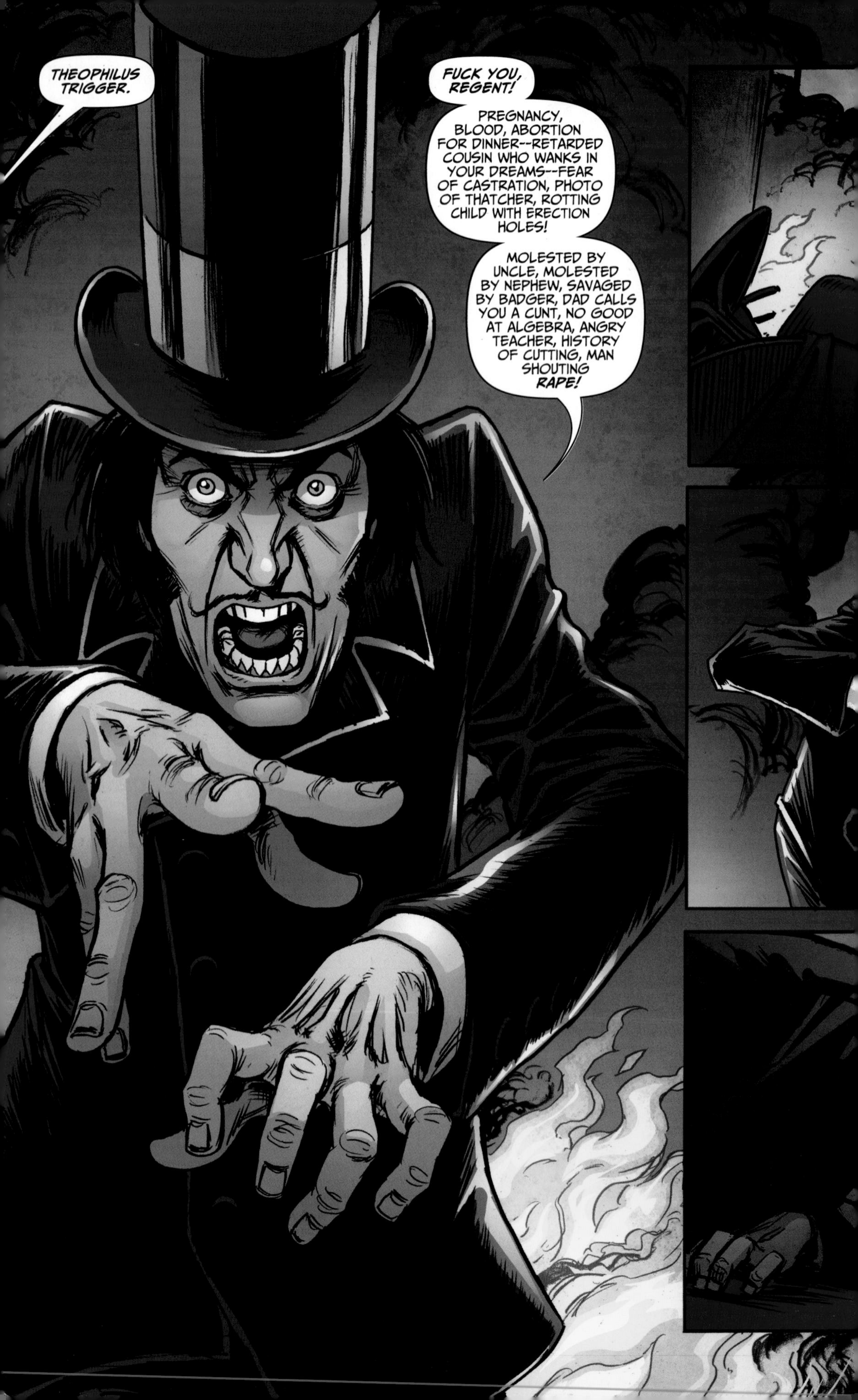
THEOPHILUS TRIGGER.
FUCK YOU, REGENT!
PREGNANCY, BLOOD, ABORTION FOR DINNER--RETARDED COUSIN WHO WANKS IN YOUR DREAMS--FEAR OF CASTRATION, PHOTO OF THATCHER, ROTTING CHILD WITH ERECTION HOLES!
MOLESTED BY UNCLE, MOLESTED BY NEPHEW, SAVAGED BY BADGER, DAD CALLS YOU A CUNT, NO GOOD AT ALGEBRA, ANGRY TEACHER, HISTORY OF CUTTING, MAN SHOUTING RAPE!

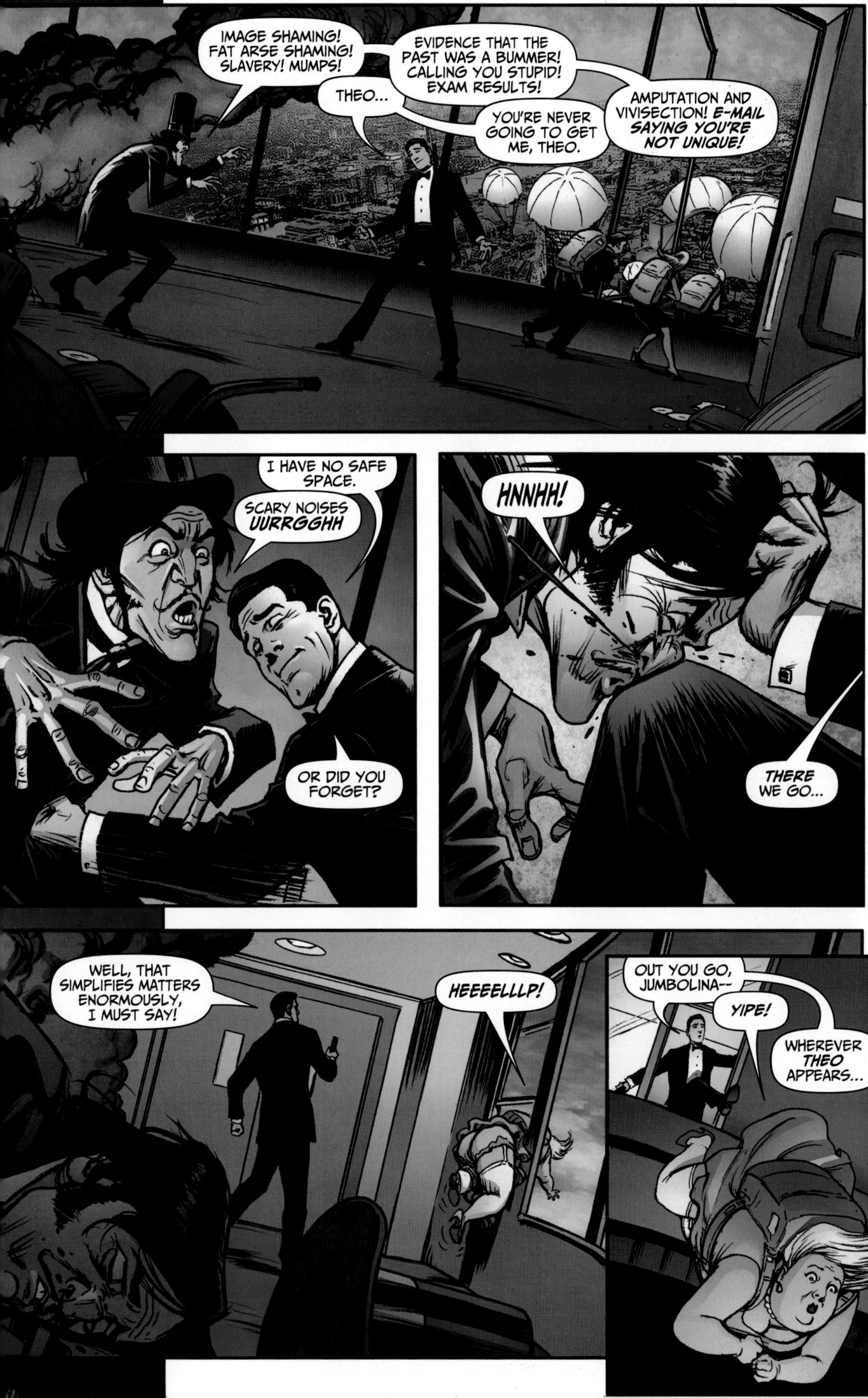
IMAGE SHAMING! FAT ARSE SHAMING! SLAVERY! MUMPS!
EVIDENCE THAT THE PAST WAS A BUMMER! CALLING YOU STUPID! EXAM RESULTS!
THEO...
YOU'RE NEVER GOING TO GET ME, THEO.
AMPUTATION AND VIVISECTION! E-MAIL SAYING YOU'RE NOT UNIQUE!
I HAVE NO SAFE SPACE.
SCARY NOISES UURRGGHH
OR DID YOU FORGET?
HNNHH!
THERE WE GO...
WELL, THAT SIMPLIFIES MATTERS ENORMOUSLY, I MUST SAY!
HEEEELLLP!
OUT YOU GO, JUMBOLINA--
YIPE!
WHEREVER THEO APPEARS...

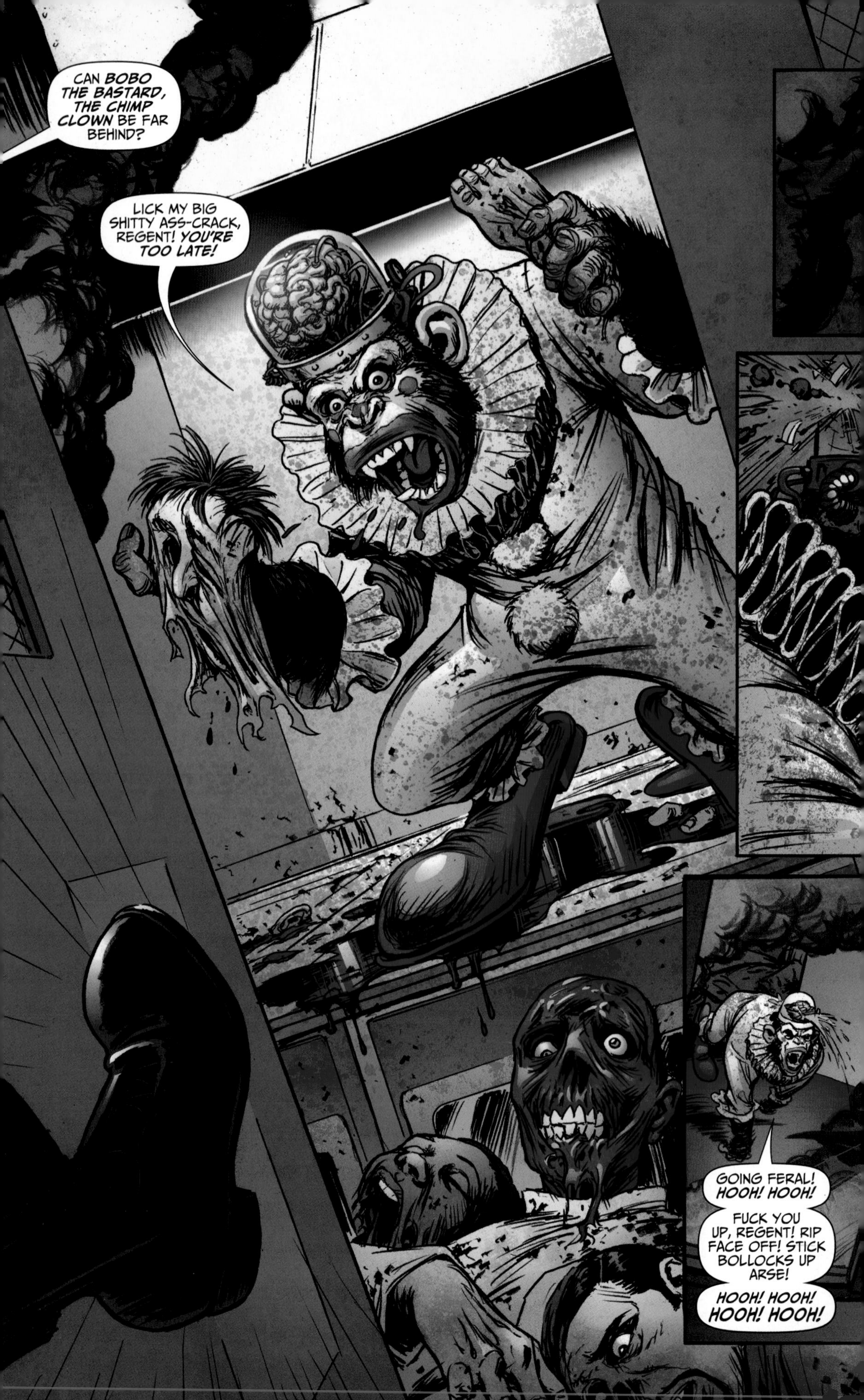
CAN ***BOBO THE BASTARD, THE CHIMP CLOWN*** BE FAR BEHIND?
LICK MY BIG SHITTY ASS-CRACK, REGENT! ***YOU'RE TOO LATE!***
GOING FERAL! ***HOOH! HOOH!***
FUCK YOU UP, REGENT! RIP FACE OFF! STICK BOLLOCKS UP ARSE!
HOOH! HOOH! HOOH! HOOH!

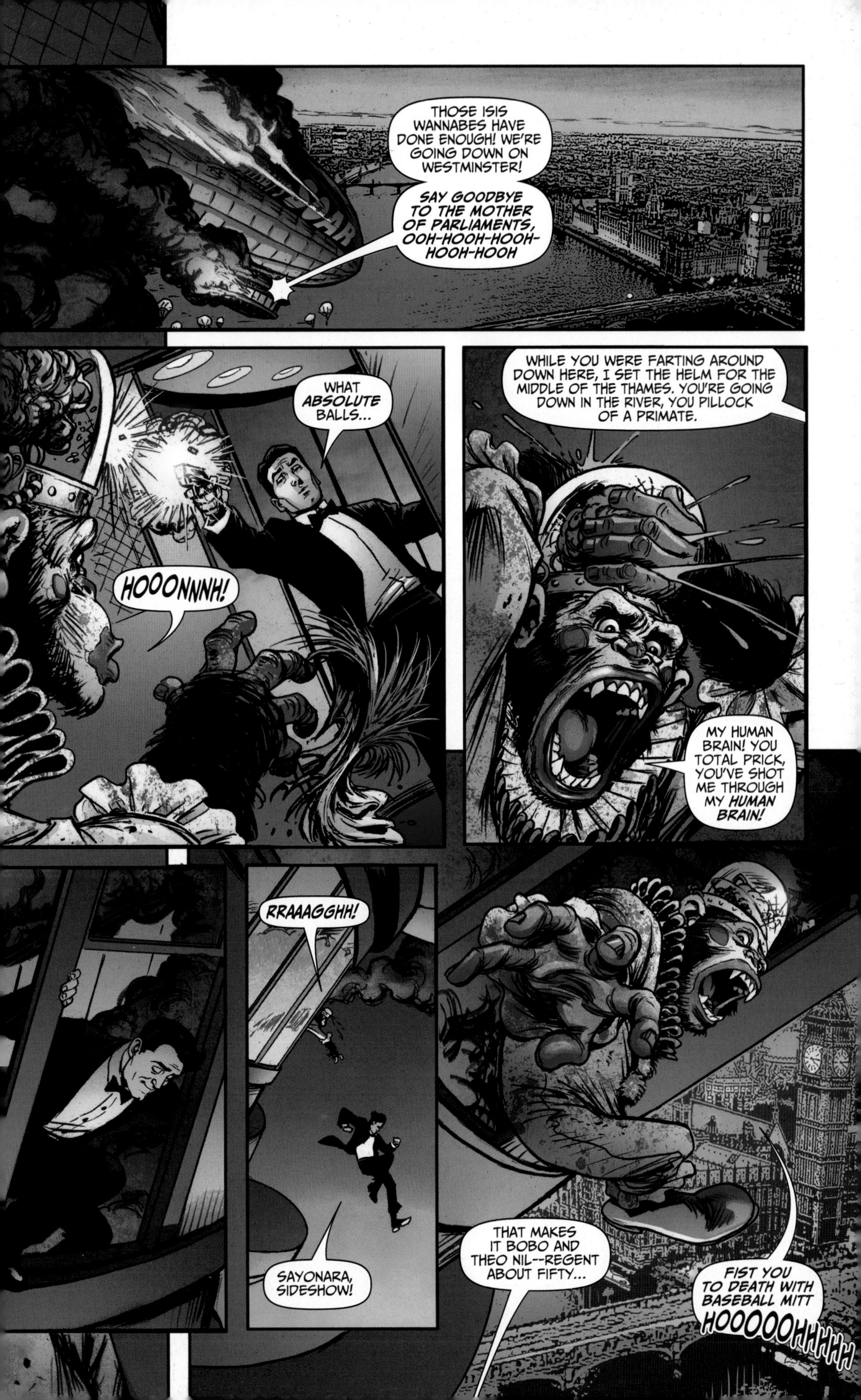
THOSE ISIS WANNABES HAVE DONE ENOUGH! WE'RE GOING DOWN ON WESTMINSTER!
SAY GOODBYE TO THE MOTHER OF PARLIAMENTS, OOH-HOOH-HOOH-HOOH-HOOH
WHAT ABSOLUTE BALLS...
HOOONNNH!
WHILE YOU WERE FARTING AROUND DOWN HERE, I SET THE HELM FOR THE MIDDLE OF THE THAMES. YOU'RE GOING DOWN IN THE RIVER, YOU PILLOCK OF A PRIMATE.
MY HUMAN BRAIN! YOU TOTAL PRICK, YOU'VE SHOT ME THROUGH MY HUMAN BRAIN!
RRAAAGGHH!
SAYONARA, SIDESHOW!
THAT MAKES IT BOBO AND THEO NIL--REGENT ABOUT FIFTY...
FIST YOU TO DEATH WITH BASEBALL MITT
HOOOOOHHHHHH

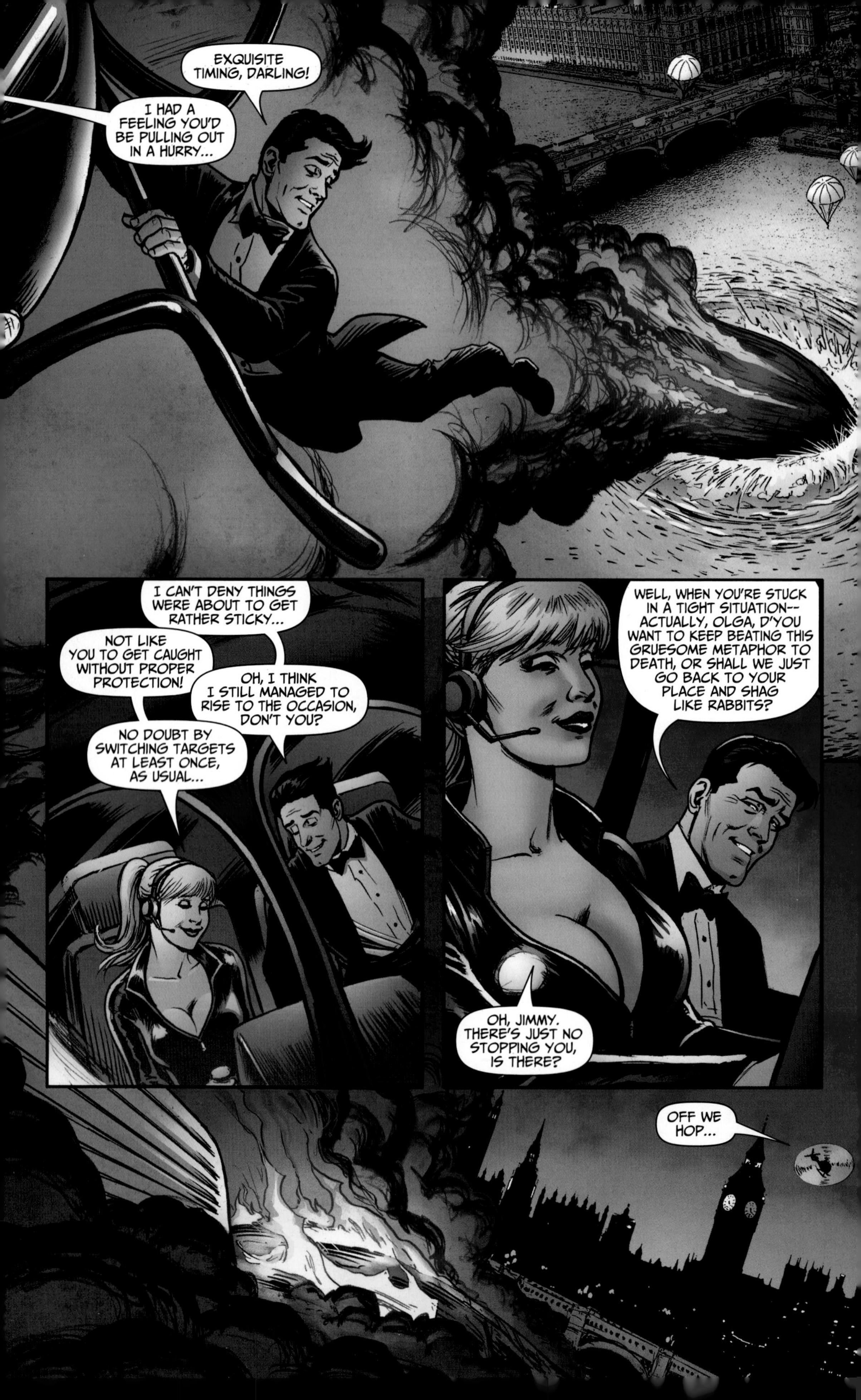
EXQUISITE TIMING, DARLING!
I HAD A FEELING YOU'D BE PULLING OUT IN A HURRY...
I CAN'T DENY THINGS WERE ABOUT TO GET RATHER STICKY...
NOT LIKE YOU TO GET CAUGHT WITHOUT PROPER PROTECTION!
OH, I THINK I STILL MANAGED TO RISE TO THE OCCASION, DON'T YOU?
NO DOUBT BY SWITCHING TARGETS AT LEAST ONCE, AS USUAL...
WELL, WHEN YOU'RE STUCK IN A TIGHT SITUATION--ACTUALLY, OLGA, D'YOU WANT TO KEEP BEATING THIS GRUESOME METAPHOR TO DEATH, OR SHALL WE JUST GO BACK TO YOUR PLACE AND SHAG LIKE RABBITS?
OH, JIMMY. THERE'S JUST NO STOPPING YOU, IS THERE?
OFF WE HOP...

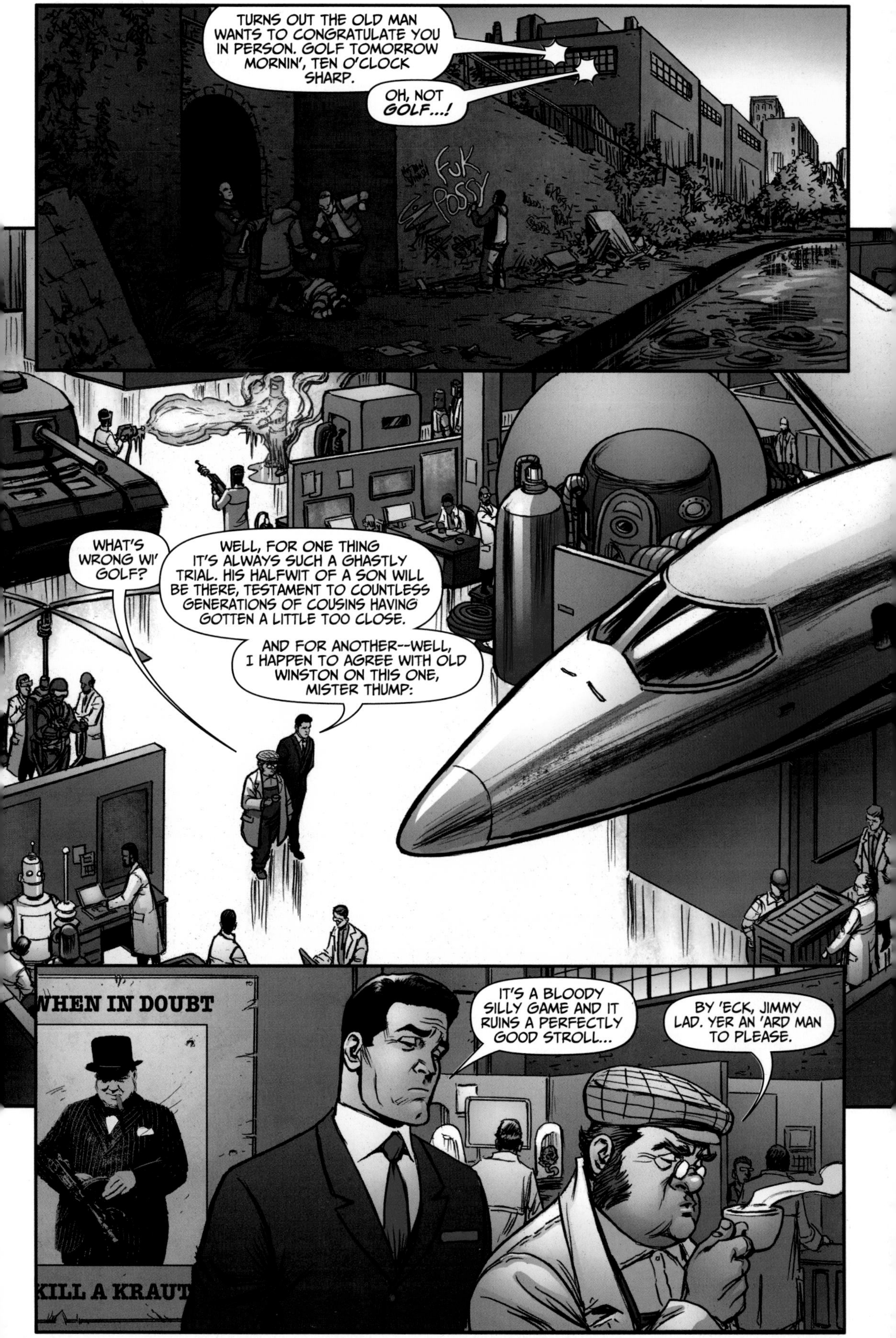

TURNS OUT THE OLD MAN WANTS TO CONGRATULATE YOU IN PERSON. GOLF TOMORROW MORNIN', TEN O'CLOCK SHARP.
OH, NOT GOLF...!
FUK POSSY
WHAT'S WRONG WI' GOLF?
WELL, FOR ONE THING IT'S ALWAYS SUCH A GHASTLY TRIAL. HIS HALFWIT OF A SON WILL BE THERE, TESTAMENT TO COUNTLESS GENERATIONS OF COUSINS HAVING GOTTEN A LITTLE TOO CLOSE.
AND FOR ANOTHER--WELL, I HAPPEN TO AGREE WITH OLD WINSTON ON THIS ONE, MISTER THUMP:
WHEN IN DOUBT
KILL A KRAUT
IT'S A BLOODY SILLY GAME AND IT RUINS A PERFECTLY GOOD STROLL...
BY 'ECK, JIMMY LAD. YER AN 'ARD MAN TO PLEASE.

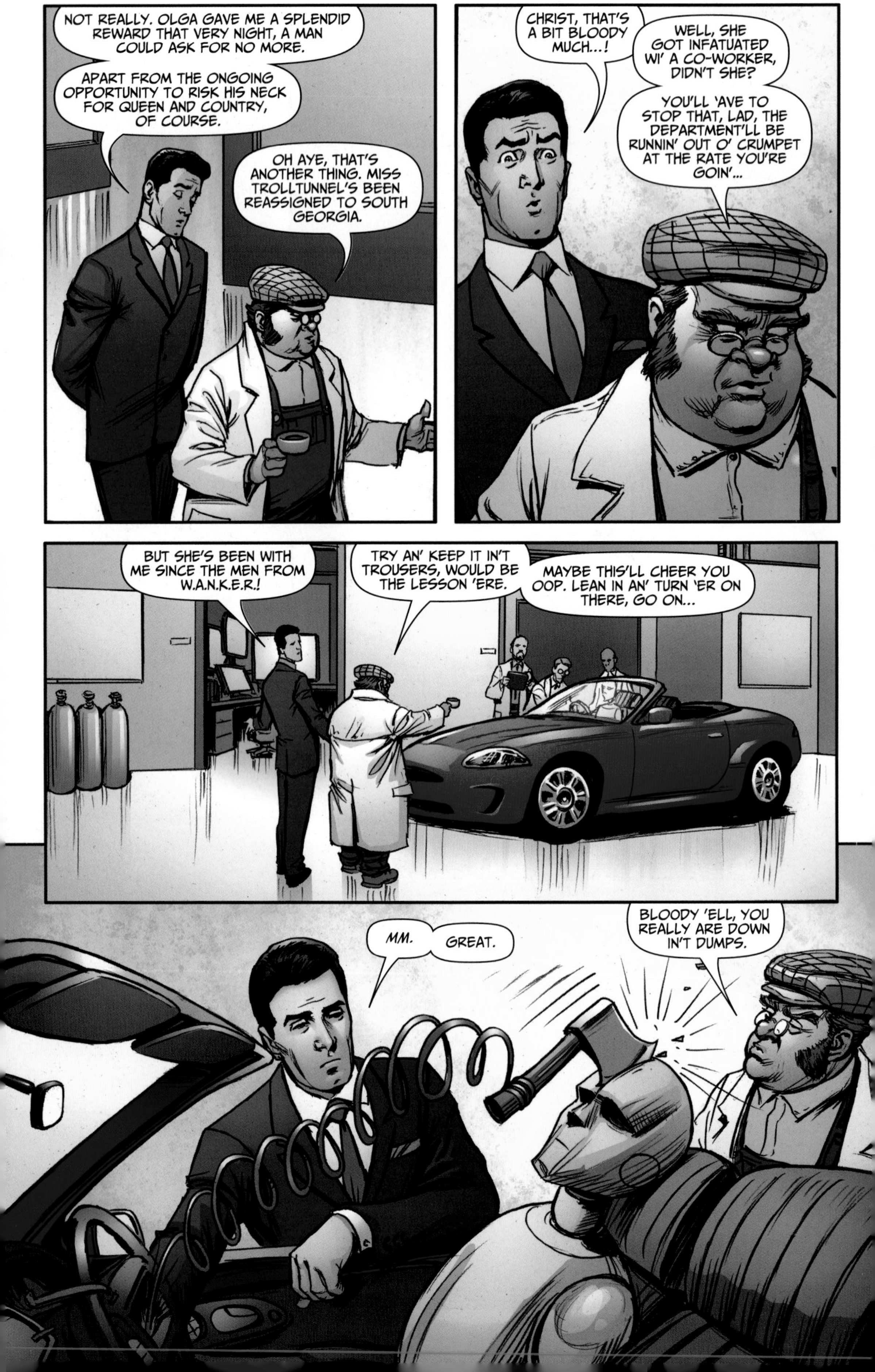
NOT REALLY. OLGA GAVE ME A SPLENDID REWARD THAT VERY NIGHT, A MAN COULD ASK FOR NO MORE.
APART FROM THE ONGOING OPPORTUNITY TO RISK HIS NECK FOR QUEEN AND COUNTRY, OF COURSE.
OH AYE, THAT'S ANOTHER THING. MISS TROLLTUNNEL'S BEEN REASSIGNED TO SOUTH GEORGIA.
CHRIST, THAT'S A BIT BLOODY MUCH...!
WELL, SHE GOT INFATUATED WI' A CO-WORKER, DIDN'T SHE?
YOU'LL 'AVE TO STOP THAT, LAD, THE DEPARTMENT'LL BE RUNNIN' OUT O' CRUMPET AT THE RATE YOU'RE GOIN'...
BUT SHE'S BEEN WITH ME SINCE THE MEN FROM W.A.N.K.E.R.!
TRY AN' KEEP IT IN'T TROUSERS, WOULD BE THE LESSON 'ERE.
MAYBE THIS'LL CHEER YOU OOP. LEAN IN AN' TURN 'ER ON THERE, GO ON...
MM.
GREAT.
BLOODY 'ELL, YOU REALLY ARE DOWN IN'T DUMPS.

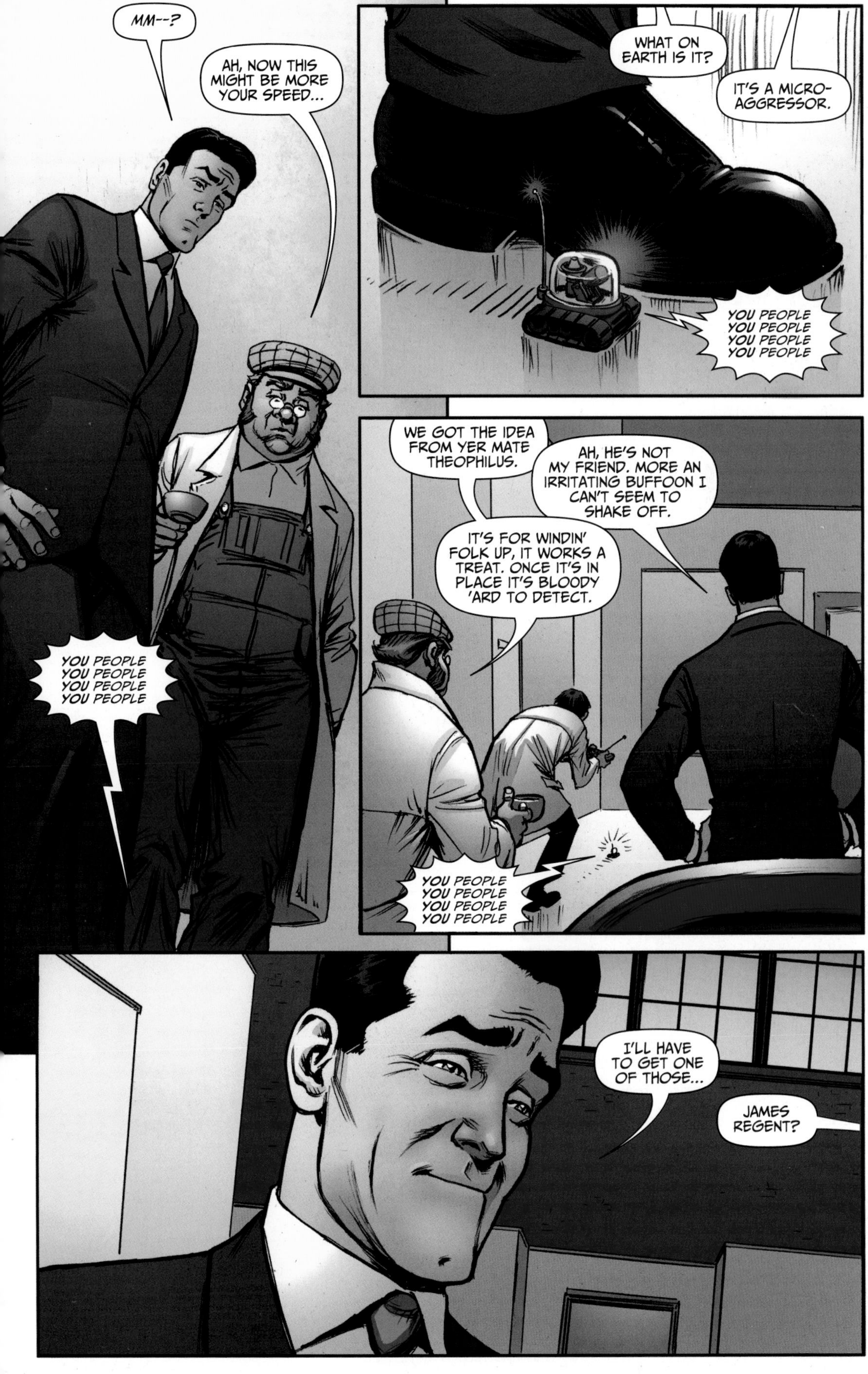
MM--?
AH, NOW THIS MIGHT BE MORE YOUR SPEED...
YOU PEOPLE YOU PEOPLE YOU PEOPLE YOU PEOPLE
WHAT ON EARTH IS IT?
IT'S A MICRO-AGGRESSOR.
YOU PEOPLE YOU PEOPLE YOU PEOPLE YOU PEOPLE
WE GOT THE IDEA FROM YER MATE THEOPHILUS.
AH, HE'S NOT MY FRIEND. MORE AN IRRITATING BUFFOON I CAN'T SEEM TO SHAKE OFF.
IT'S FOR WINDIN' FOLK UP, IT WORKS A TREAT. ONCE IT'S IN PLACE IT'S BLOODY 'ARD TO DETECT.
YOU PEOPLE YOU PEOPLE YOU PEOPLE YOU PEOPLE
I'LL HAVE TO GET ONE OF THOSE...
JAMES REGENT?

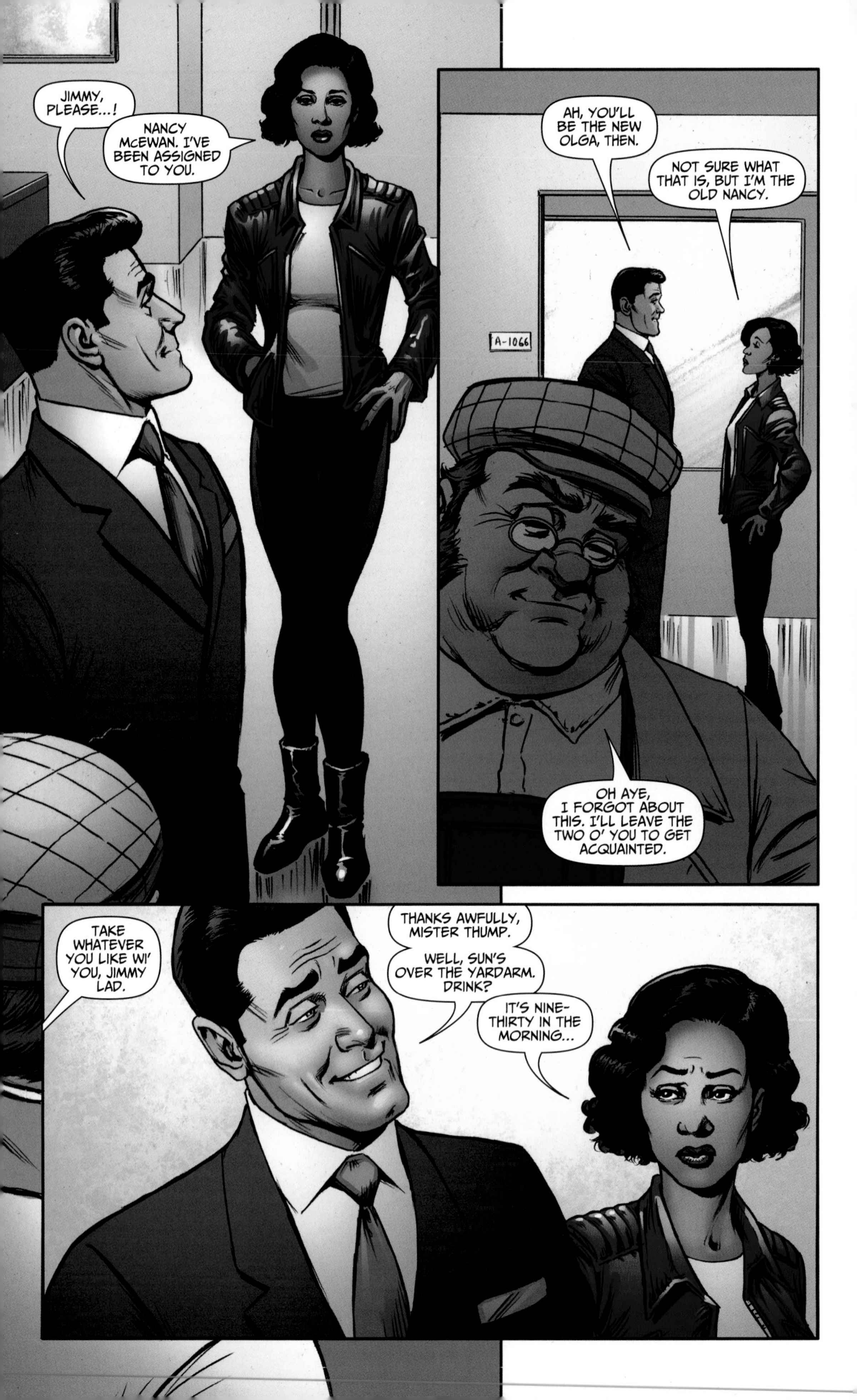
JIMMY, PLEASE...!
NANCY McEWAN. I'VE BEEN ASSIGNED TO YOU.
AH, YOU'LL BE THE NEW OLGA, THEN.
NOT SURE WHAT THAT IS, BUT I'M THE OLD NANCY.
A-1066
OH AYE, I FORGOT ABOUT THIS. I'LL LEAVE THE TWO O' YOU TO GET ACQUAINTED.
TAKE WHATEVER YOU LIKE WI' YOU, JIMMY LAD.
THANKS AWFULLY, MISTER THUMP.
WELL, SUN'S OVER THE YARDARM. DRINK?
IT'S NINE-THIRTY IN THE MORNING...

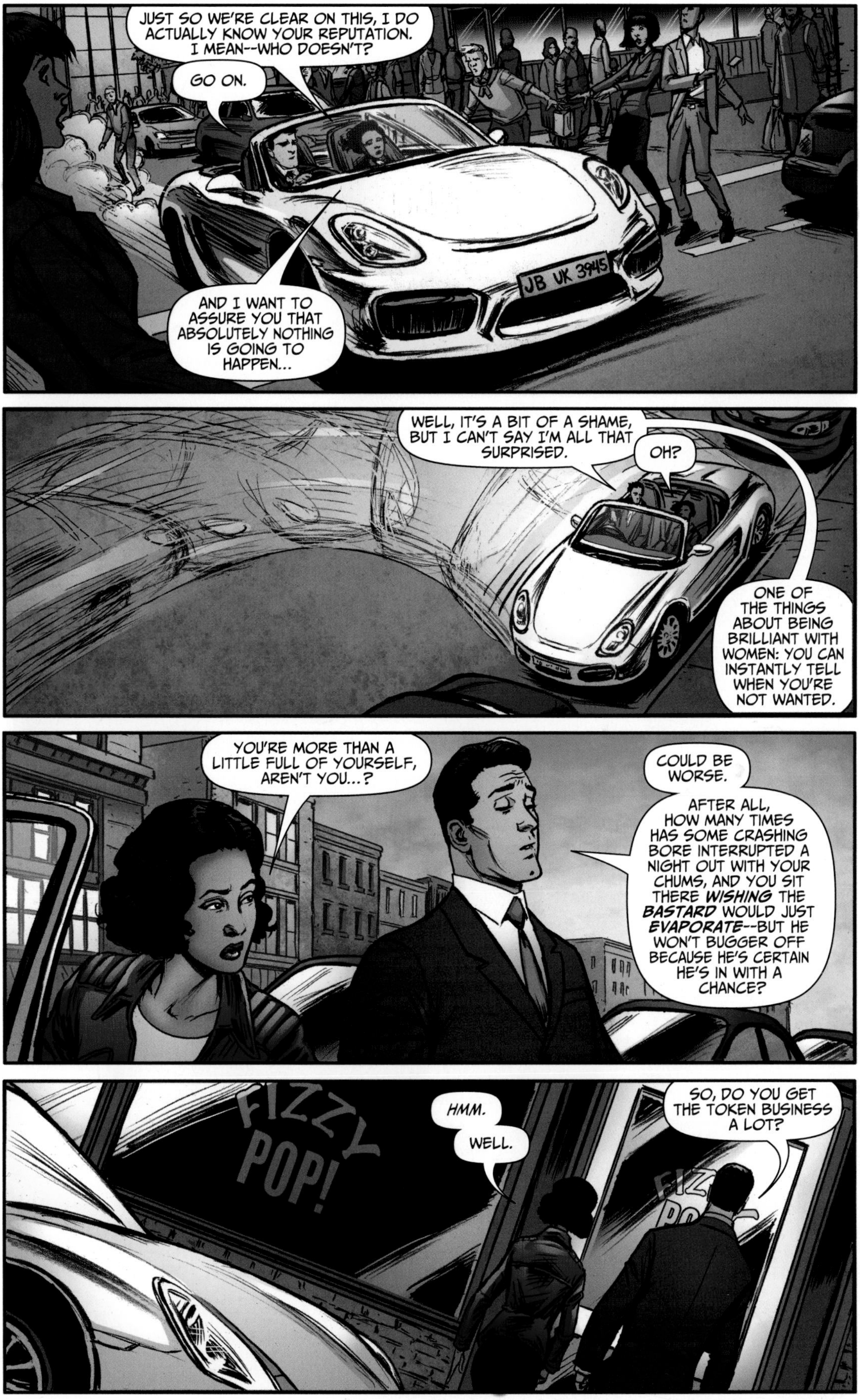

JUST SO WE'RE CLEAR ON THIS, I DO ACTUALLY KNOW YOUR REPUTATION. I MEAN--WHO DOESN'T?
GO ON.
AND I WANT TO ASSURE YOU THAT ABSOLUTELY NOTHING IS GOING TO HAPPEN...
JB UK 3945
WELL, IT'S A BIT OF A SHAME, BUT I CAN'T SAY I'M ALL THAT SURPRISED.
OH?
ONE OF THE THINGS ABOUT BEING BRILLIANT WITH WOMEN: YOU CAN INSTANTLY TELL WHEN YOU'RE NOT WANTED.
YOU'RE MORE THAN A LITTLE FULL OF YOURSELF, AREN'T YOU...?
COULD BE WORSE.
AFTER ALL, HOW MANY TIMES HAS SOME CRASHING BORE INTERRUPTED A NIGHT OUT WITH YOUR CHUMS, AND YOU SIT THERE *WISHING* THE *BASTARD* WOULD JUST *EVAPORATE*--BUT HE WON'T BUGGER OFF BECAUSE HE'S CERTAIN HE'S IN WITH A CHANCE?
FIZZY POP!
HMM.
WELL.
SO, DO YOU GET THE TOKEN BUSINESS A LOT?

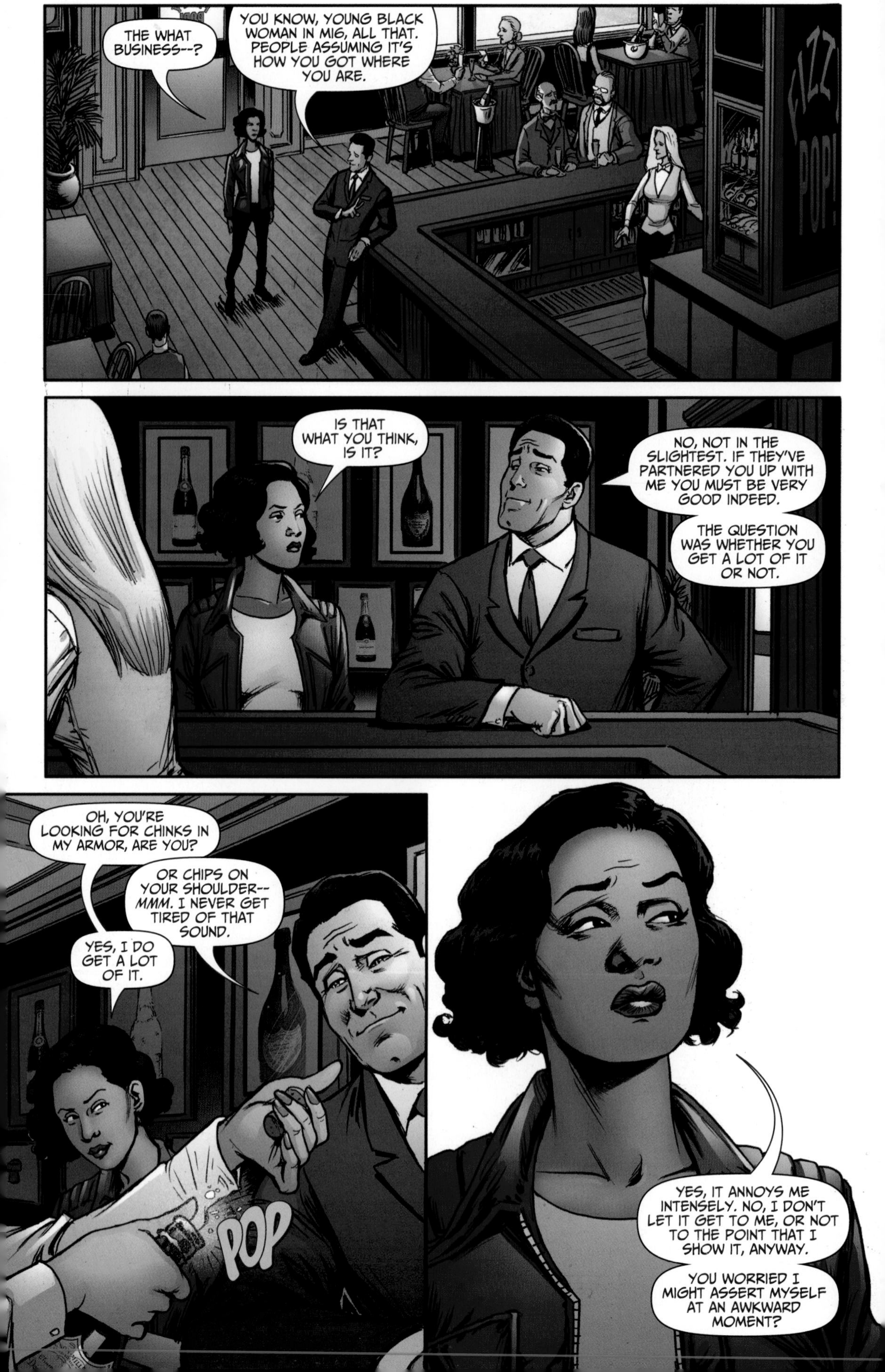
THE WHAT BUSINESS--?
YOU KNOW, YOUNG BLACK WOMAN IN MI6, ALL THAT. PEOPLE ASSUMING IT'S HOW YOU GOT WHERE YOU ARE.
POP!
IS THAT WHAT YOU THINK, IS IT?
NO, NOT IN THE SLIGHTEST. IF THEY'VE PARTNERED YOU UP WITH ME YOU MUST BE VERY GOOD INDEED.
THE QUESTION WAS WHETHER YOU GET A LOT OF IT OR NOT.
OH, YOU'RE LOOKING FOR CHINKS IN MY ARMOR, ARE YOU?
OR CHIPS ON YOUR SHOULDER--
YES, I DO GET A LOT OF IT.
MMM. I NEVER GET TIRED OF THAT SOUND.
POP
YES, IT ANNOYS ME INTENSELY. NO, I DON'T LET IT GET TO ME, OR NOT TO THE POINT THAT I SHOW IT, ANYWAY.
YOU WORRIED I MIGHT ASSERT MYSELF AT AN AWKWARD MOMENT?

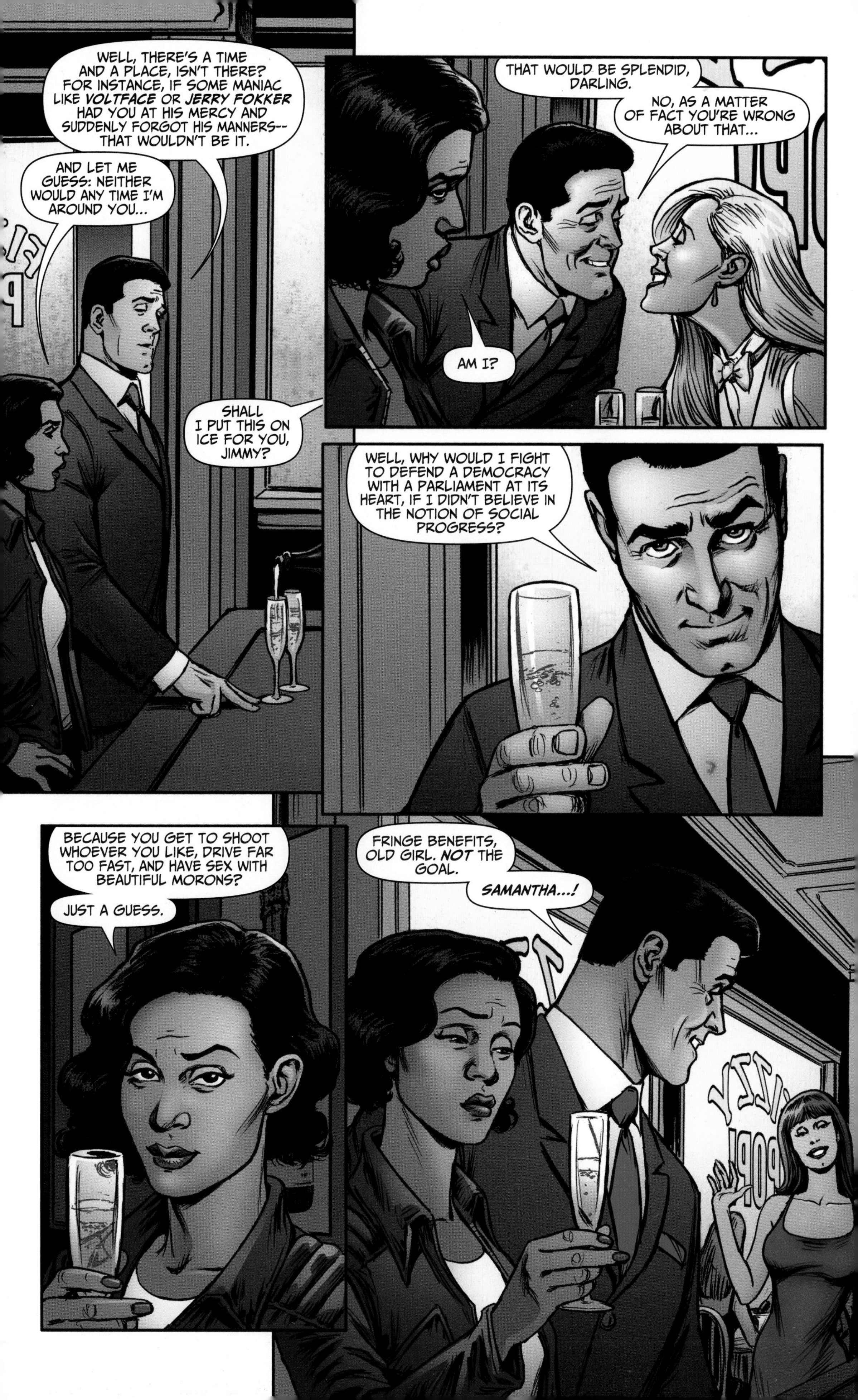
WELL, THERE'S A TIME AND A PLACE, ISN'T THERE? FOR INSTANCE, IF SOME MANIAC LIKE ***VOLTFACE*** OR ***JERRY FOKKER*** HAD YOU AT HIS MERCY AND SUDDENLY FORGOT HIS MANNERS-- THAT WOULDN'T BE IT.
AND LET ME GUESS: NEITHER WOULD ANY TIME I'M AROUND YOU...
SHALL I PUT THIS ON ICE FOR YOU, JIMMY?
THAT WOULD BE SPLENDID, DARLING.
NO, AS A MATTER OF FACT YOU'RE WRONG ABOUT THAT...
AM I?
WELL, WHY WOULD I FIGHT TO DEFEND A DEMOCRACY WITH A PARLIAMENT AT ITS HEART, IF I DIDN'T BELIEVE IN THE NOTION OF SOCIAL PROGRESS?
BECAUSE YOU GET TO SHOOT WHOEVER YOU LIKE, DRIVE FAR TOO FAST, AND HAVE SEX WITH BEAUTIFUL MORONS?
JUST A GUESS.
FRINGE BENEFITS, OLD GIRL. ***NOT*** THE GOAL.
SAMANTHA...!

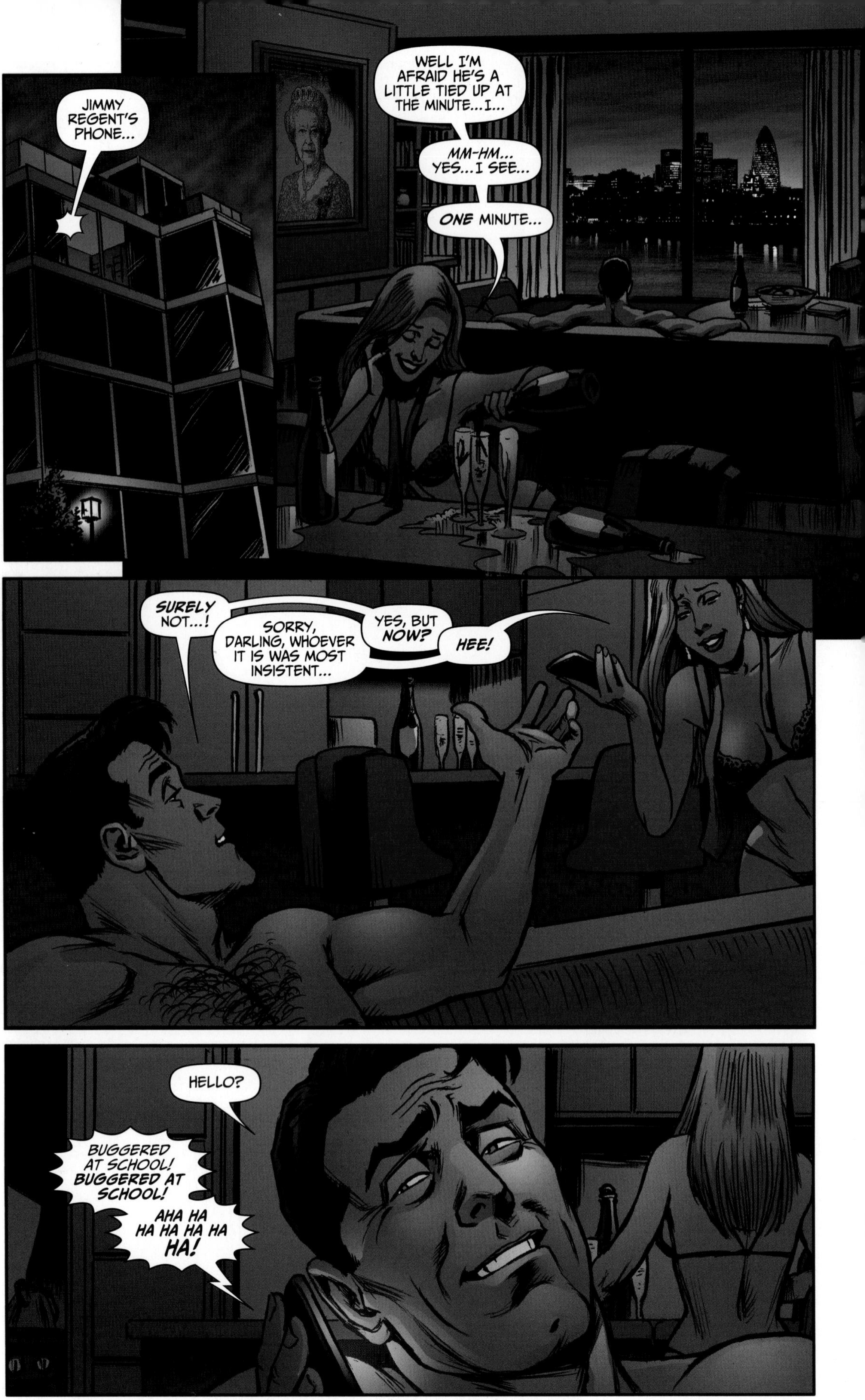
JIMMY REGENT'S PHONE...
WELL I'M AFRAID HE'S A LITTLE TIED UP AT THE MINUTE...I...
MM-HM... YES...I SEE...
ONE MINUTE...
SURELY NOT...!
SORRY, DARLING, WHOEVER IT IS WAS MOST INSISTENT...
YES, BUT NOW?
HEE!
HELLO?
BUGGERED AT SCHOOL! BUGGERED AT SCHOOL!
AHA HA HA HA HA HA HA!

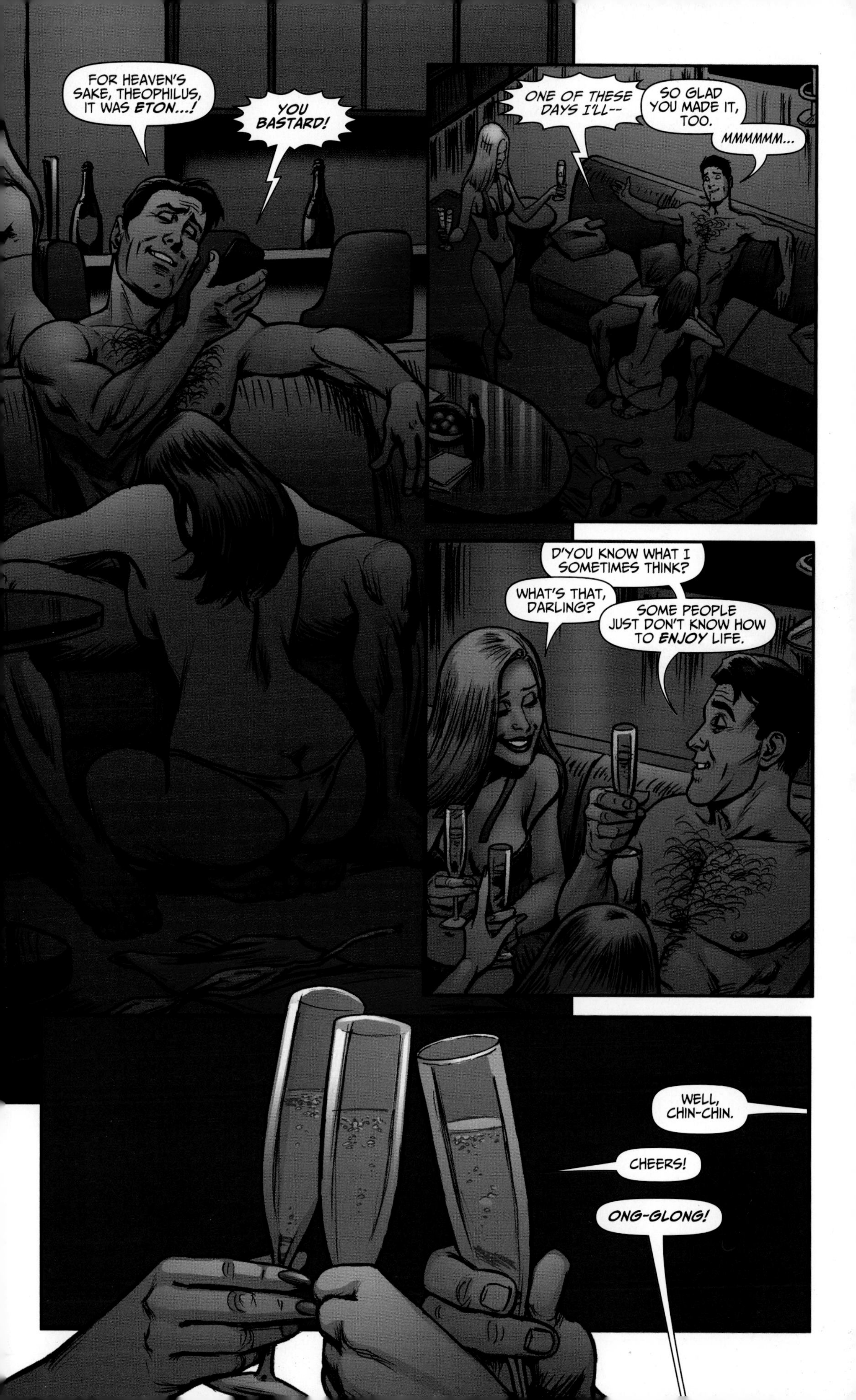
FOR HEAVEN'S SAKE, THEOPHILUS, IT WAS ETON...!
YOU BASTARD!
ONE OF THESE DAYS I'LL--
SO GLAD YOU MADE IT, TOO.
MMMMMM...
D'YOU KNOW WHAT I SOMETIMES THINK?
WHAT'S THAT, DARLING?
SOME PEOPLE JUST DON'T KNOW HOW TO ENJOY LIFE.
WELL, CHIN-CHIN.
CHEERS!
ONG-GLONG!

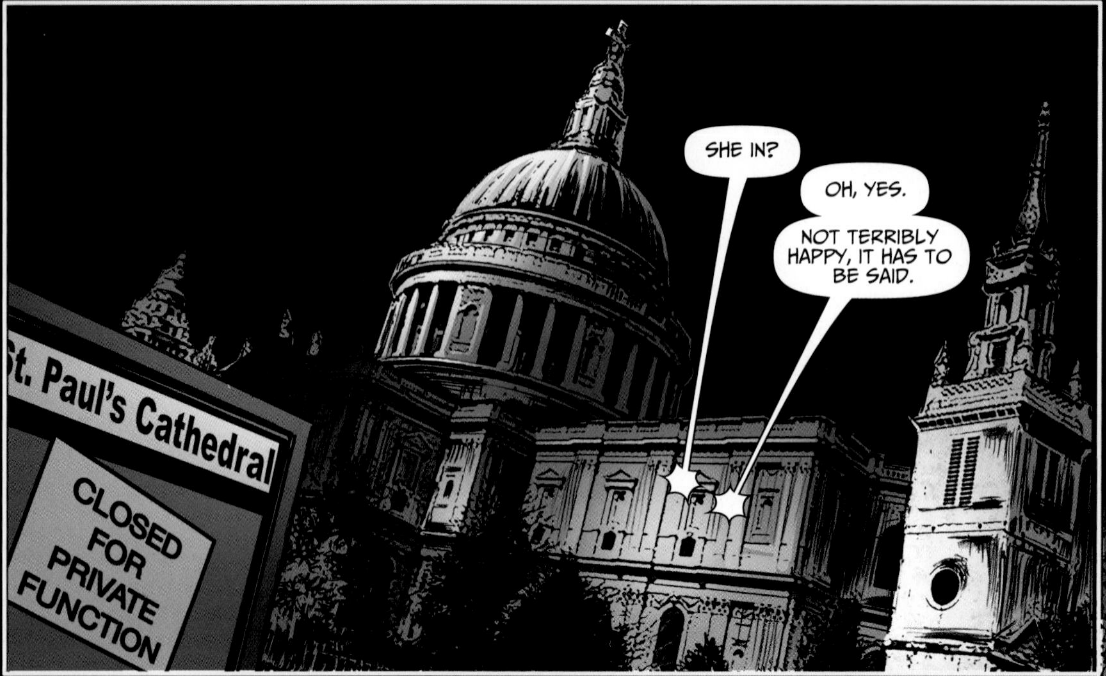
St. Paul's Cathedral
CLOSED FOR PRIVATE FUNCTION
SHE IN?
OH, YES.
NOT TERRIBLY HAPPY, IT HAS TO BE SAID.

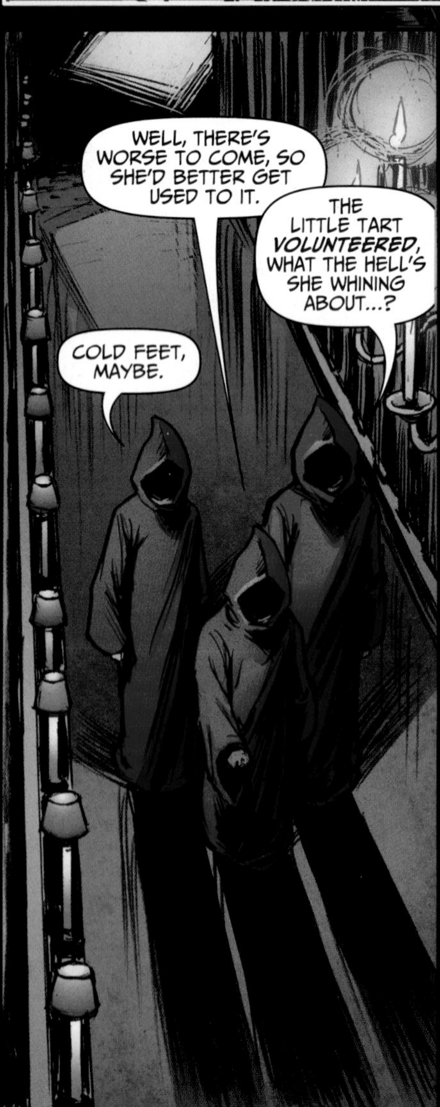
WELL, THERE'S WORSE TO COME, SO SHE'D BETTER GET USED TO IT.
THE LITTLE TART *VOLUNTEERED*, WHAT THE HELL'S SHE WHINING ABOUT...?
COLD FEET, MAYBE.

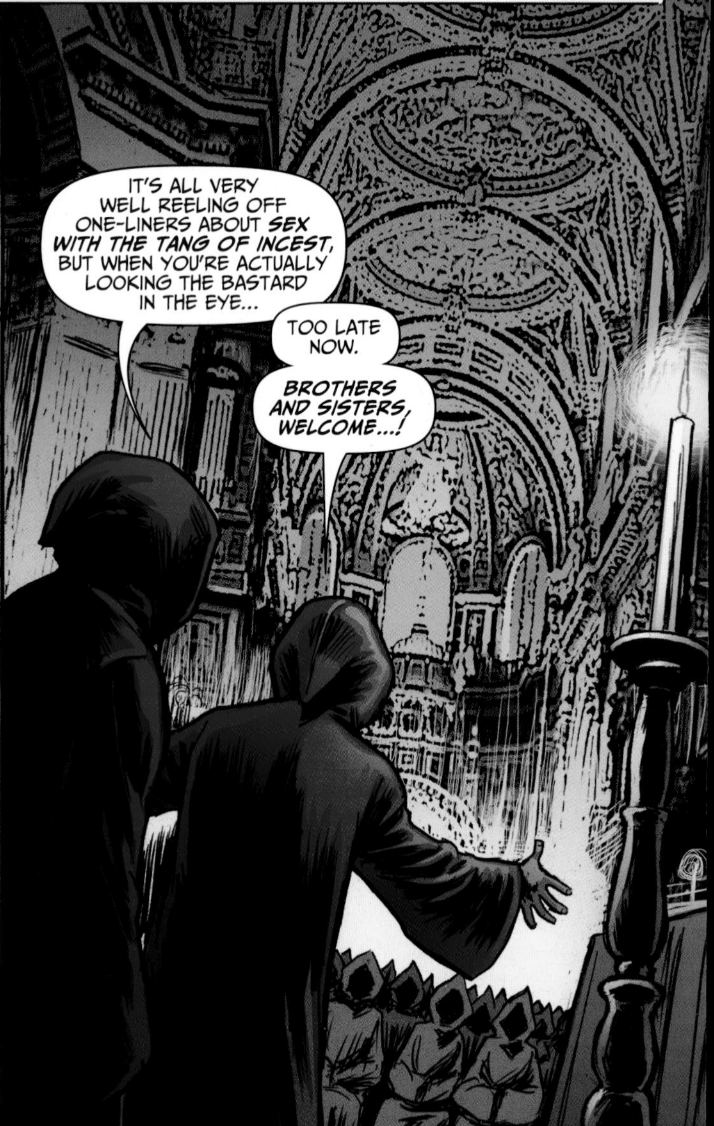
IT'S ALL VERY WELL REELING OFF ONE-LINERS ABOUT *SEX WITH THE TANG OF INCEST*, BUT WHEN YOU'RE ACTUALLY LOOKING THE BASTARD IN THE EYE...
TOO LATE NOW.
BROTHERS AND SISTERS, WELCOME...!

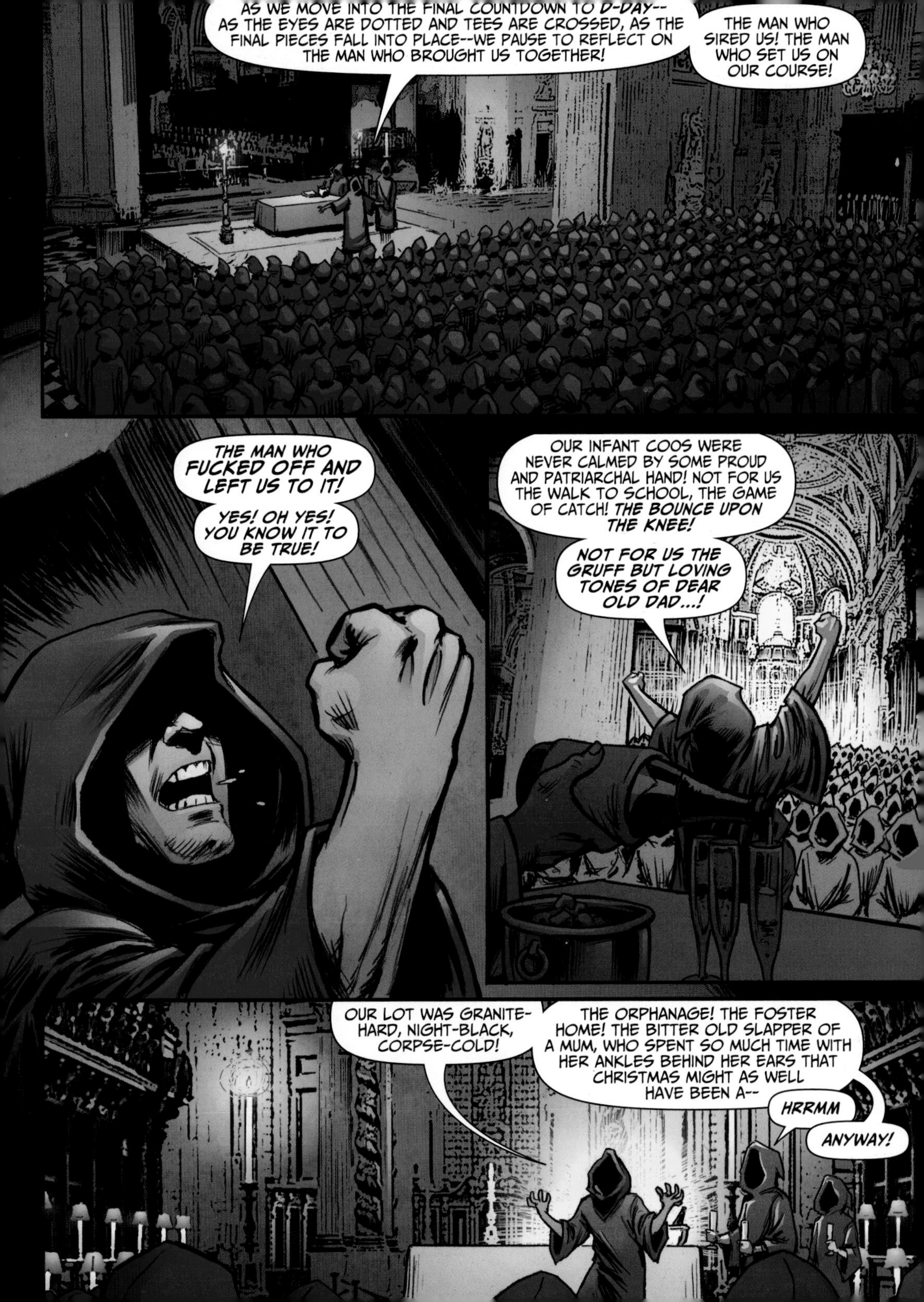
AS WE MOVE INTO THE FINAL COUNTDOWN TO D-DAY--AS THE EYES ARE DOTTED AND TEES ARE CROSSED, AS THE FINAL PIECES FALL INTO PLACE--WE PAUSE TO REFLECT ON THE MAN WHO BROUGHT US TOGETHER!
THE MAN WHO SIRED US! THE MAN WHO SET US ON OUR COURSE!
THE MAN WHO FUCKED OFF AND LEFT US TO IT!
YES! OH YES! YOU KNOW IT TO BE TRUE!
OUR INFANT COOS WERE NEVER CALMED BY SOME PROUD AND PATRIARCHAL HAND! NOT FOR US THE WALK TO SCHOOL, THE GAME OF CATCH! THE BOUNCE UPON THE KNEE!
NOT FOR US THE GRUFF BUT LOVING TONES OF DEAR OLD DAD...!
OUR LOT WAS GRANITE-HARD, NIGHT-BLACK, CORPSE-COLD!
THE ORPHANAGE! THE FOSTER HOME! THE BITTER OLD SLAPPER OF A MUM, WHO SPENT SO MUCH TIME WITH HER ANKLES BEHIND HER EARS THAT CHRISTMAS MIGHT AS WELL HAVE BEEN A--
HRRMM
ANYWAY!

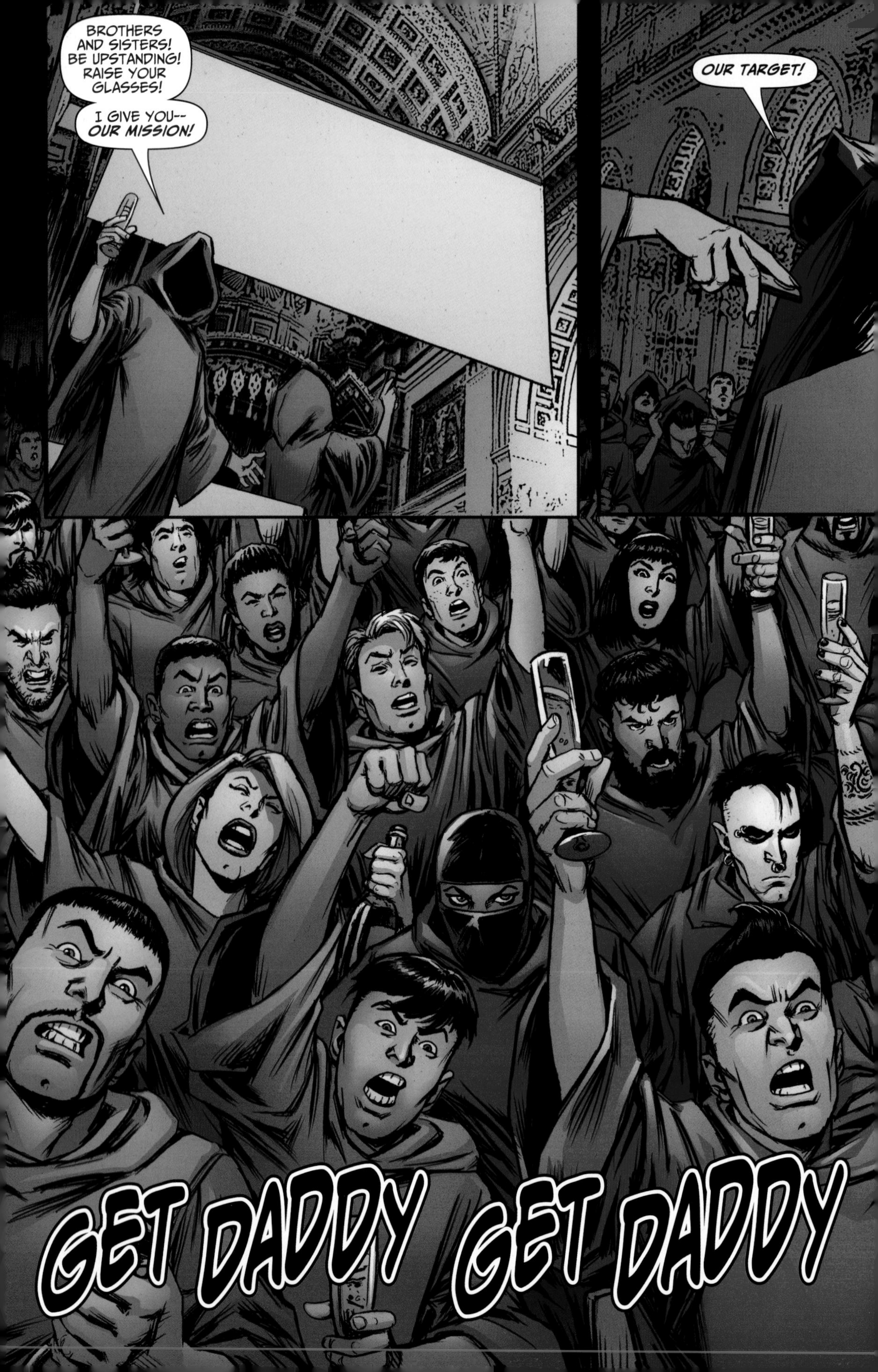
BROTHERS AND SISTERS! BE UPSTANDING! RAISE YOUR GLASSES!
I GIVE YOU-- OUR MISSION!
OUR TARGET!
GET DADDY GET DADDY

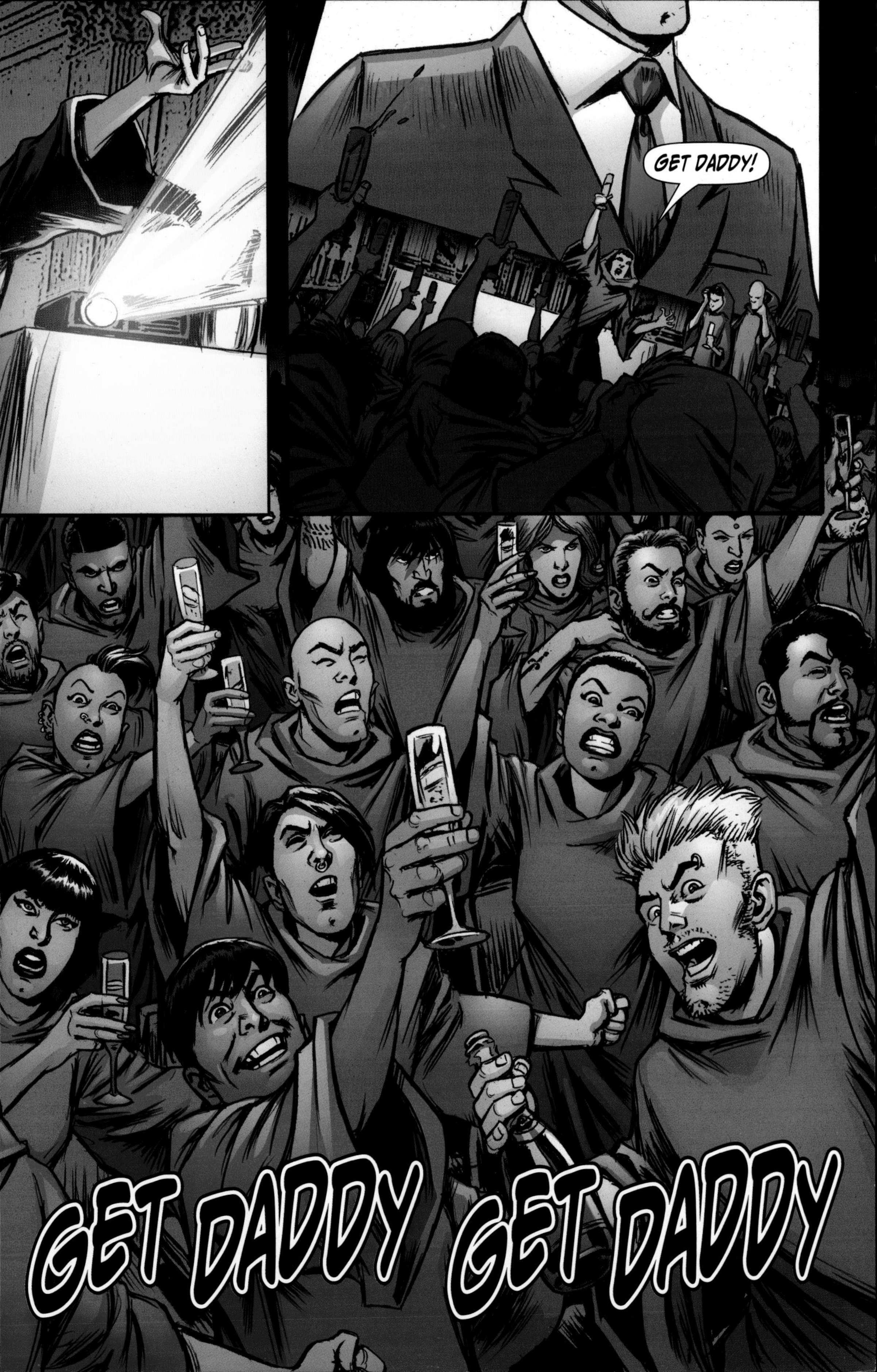
GET DADDY!
GET DADDY GET DADDY

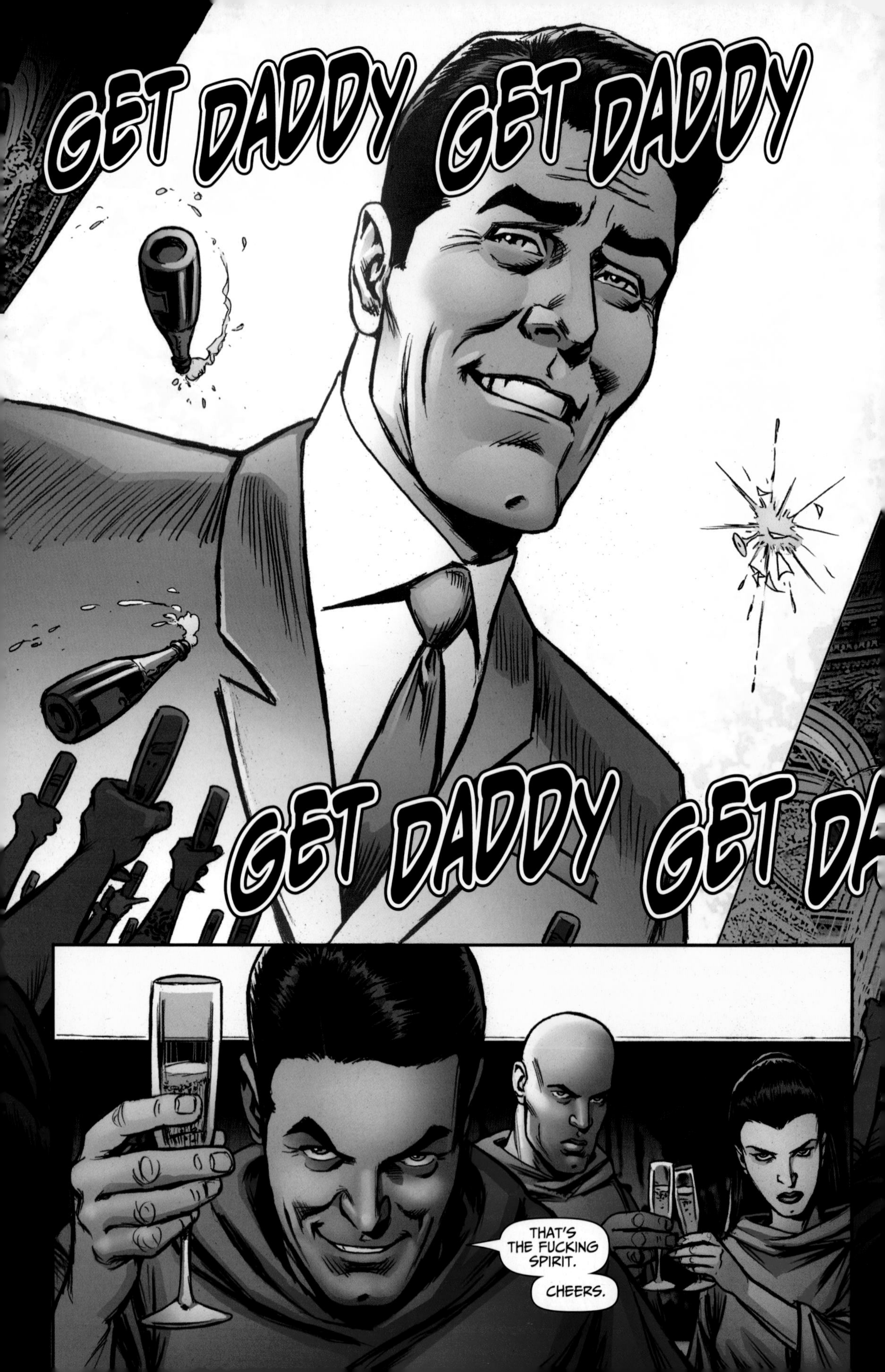
GET DADDY GET DADDY
GET DADDY GET DA
THAT'S THE FUCKING SPIRIT.
CHEERS.

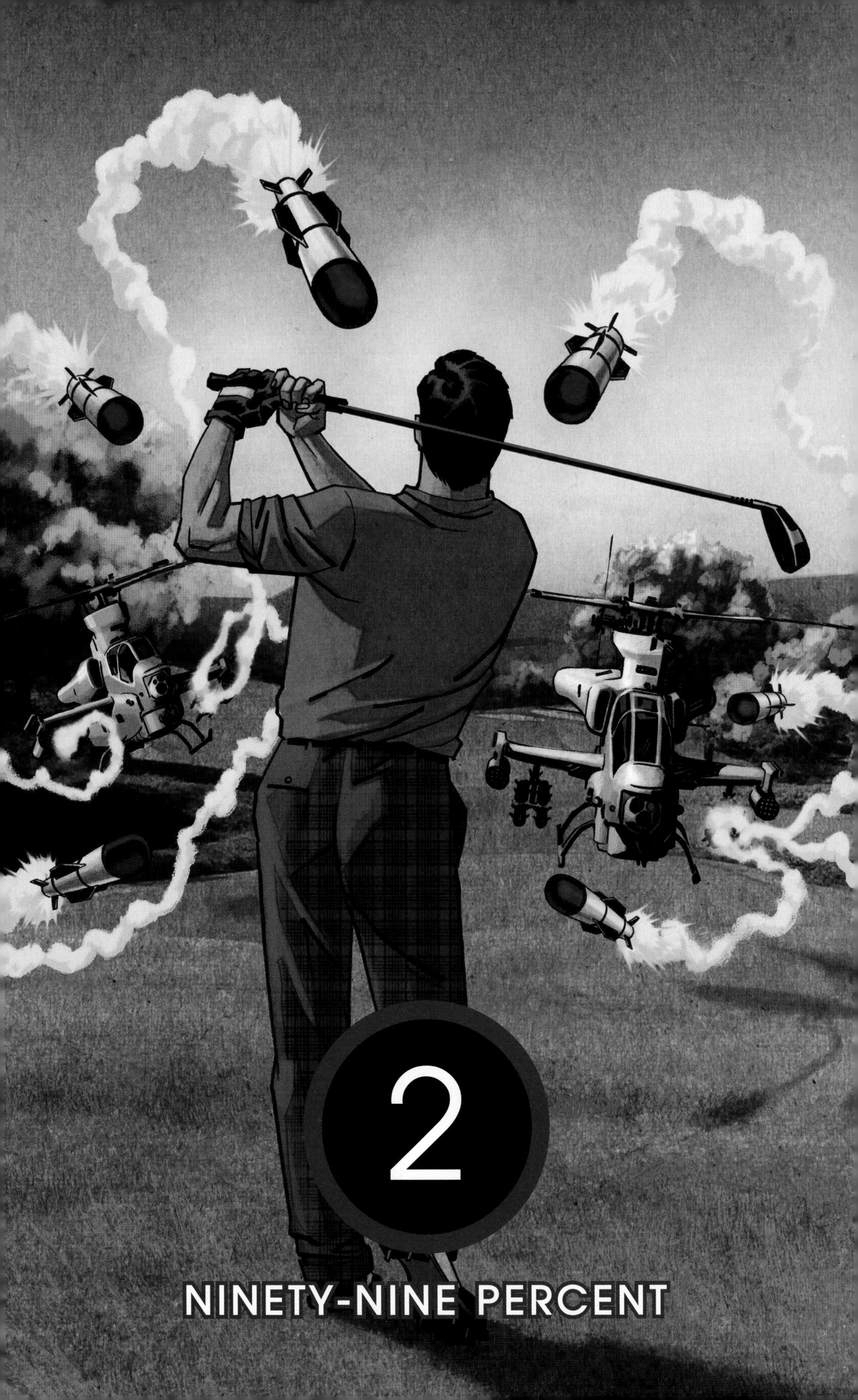

2

NINETY-NINE PERCENT

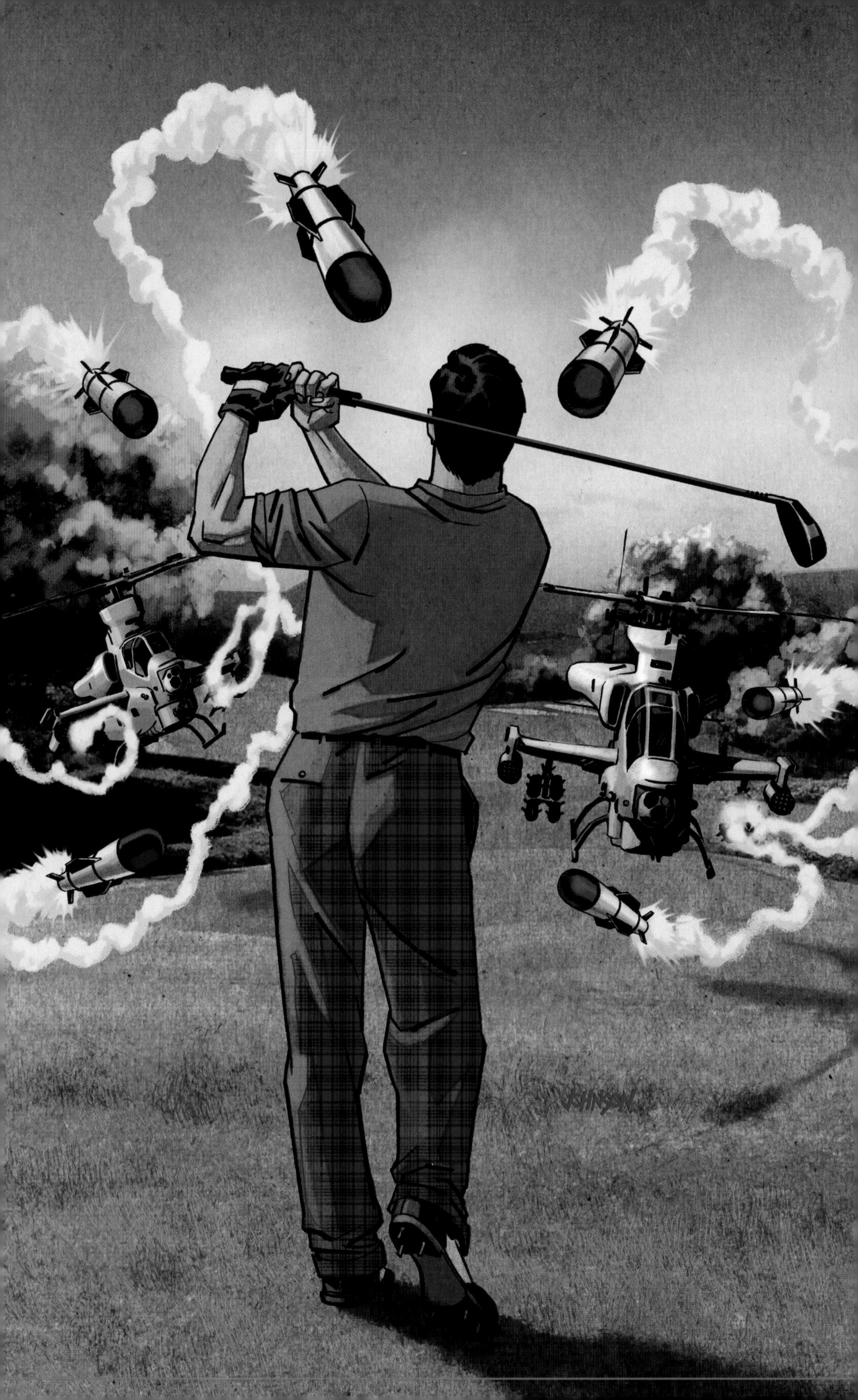
JOHNSON

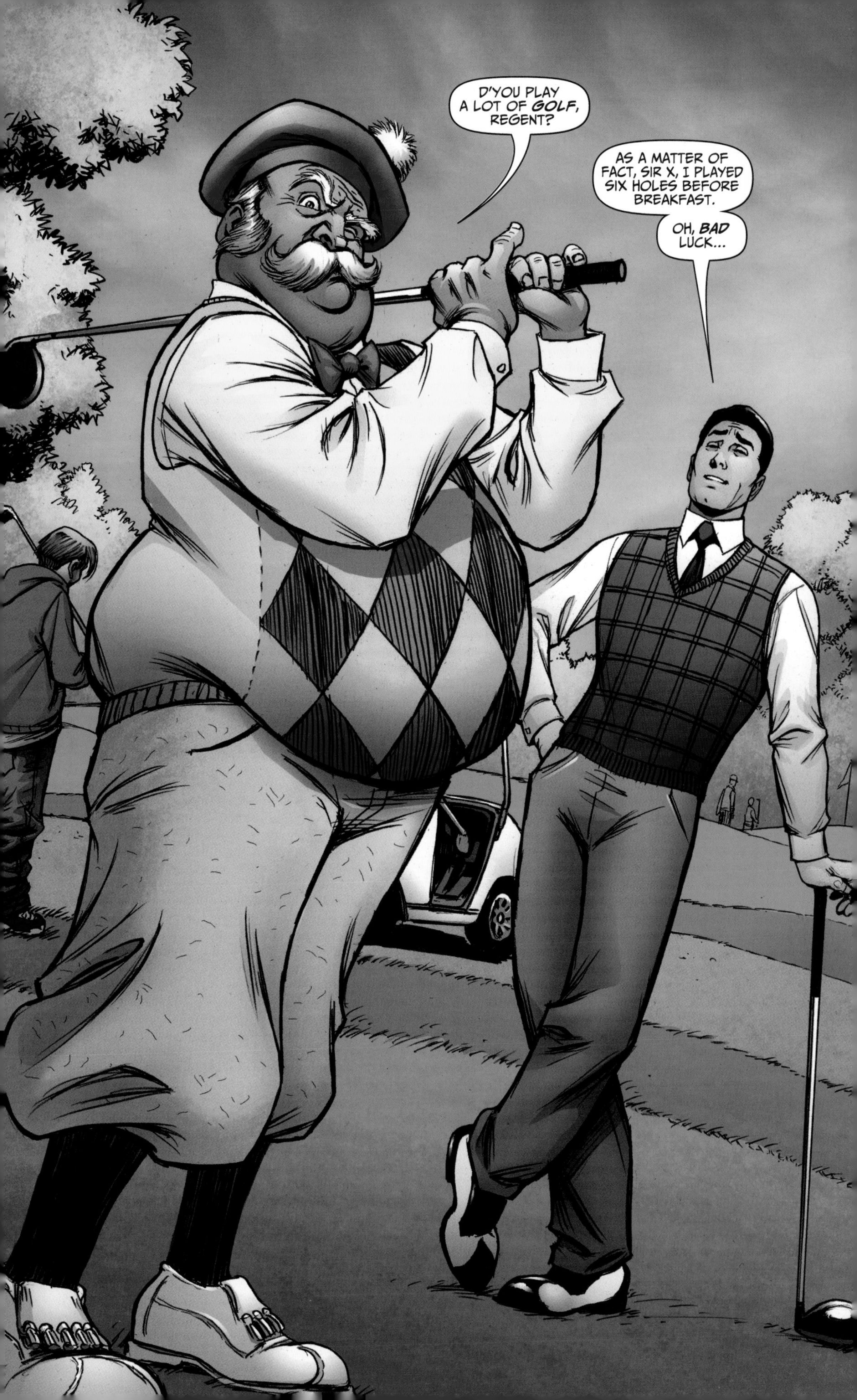
D'YOU PLAY A LOT OF GOLF, REGENT?
AS A MATTER OF FACT, SIR X, I PLAYED SIX HOLES BEFORE BREAKFAST.
OH, BAD LUCK...

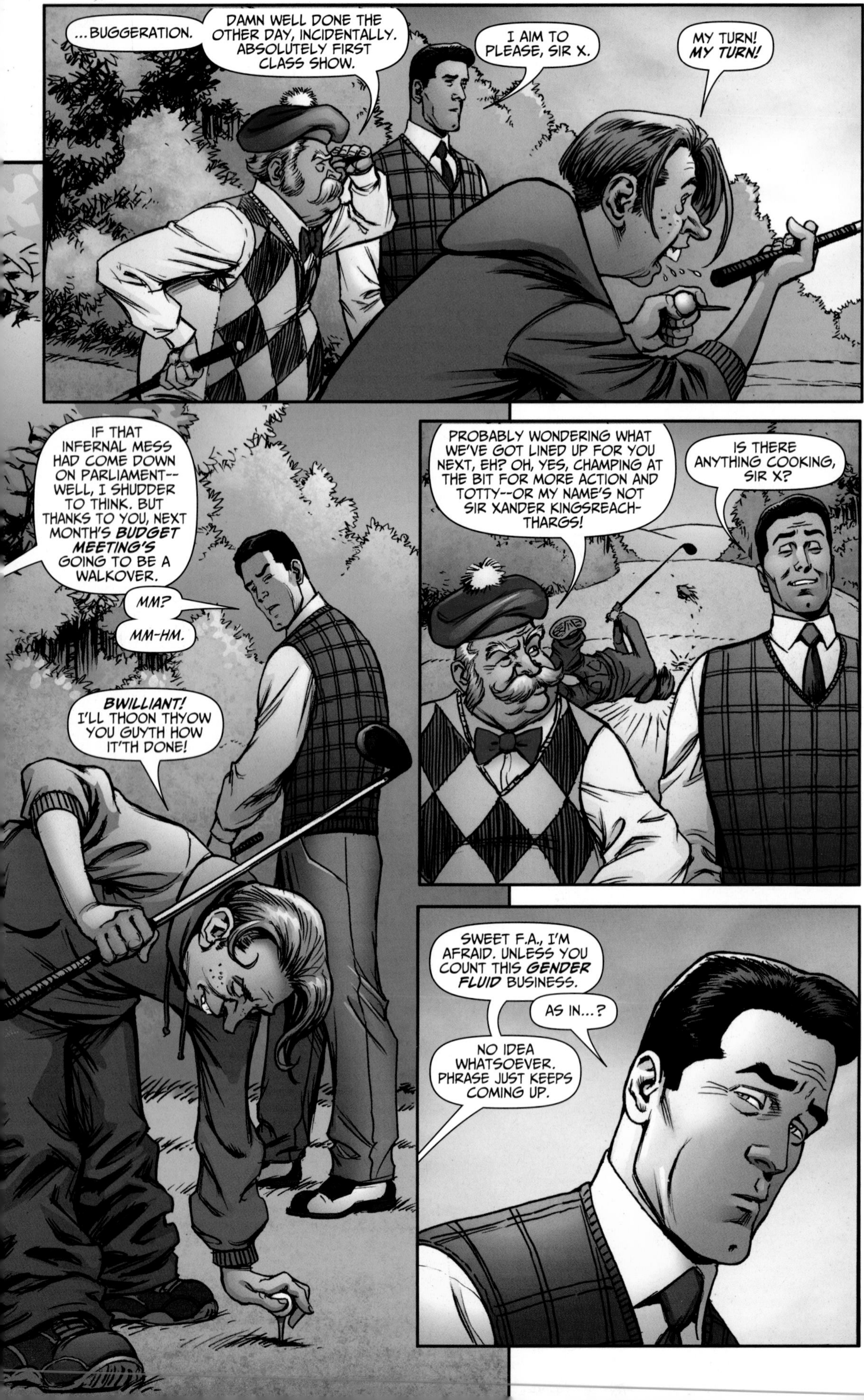

...BUGGERATION.
DAMN WELL DONE THE OTHER DAY, INCIDENTALLY. ABSOLUTELY FIRST CLASS SHOW.
I AIM TO PLEASE, SIR X.
MY TURN! *MY TURN!*
IF THAT INFERNAL MESS HAD COME DOWN ON PARLIAMENT--WELL, I SHUDDER TO THINK. BUT THANKS TO YOU, NEXT MONTH'S ***BUDGET MEETING'S*** GOING TO BE A WALKOVER.
MM?
MM-HM.
BWILLIANT! I'LL THOON THYOW YOU GUYTH HOW IT'TH DONE!
PROBABLY WONDERING WHAT WE'VE GOT LINED UP FOR YOU NEXT, EH? OH, YES, CHAMPING AT THE BIT FOR MORE ACTION AND TOTTY--OR MY NAME'S NOT SIR XANDER KINGSREACH-THARGS!
IS THERE ANYTHING COOKING, SIR X?
SWEET F.A., I'M AFRAID. UNLESS YOU COUNT THIS ***GENDER FLUID*** BUSINESS.
AS IN...?
NO IDEA WHATSOEVER. PHRASE JUST KEEPS COMING UP.

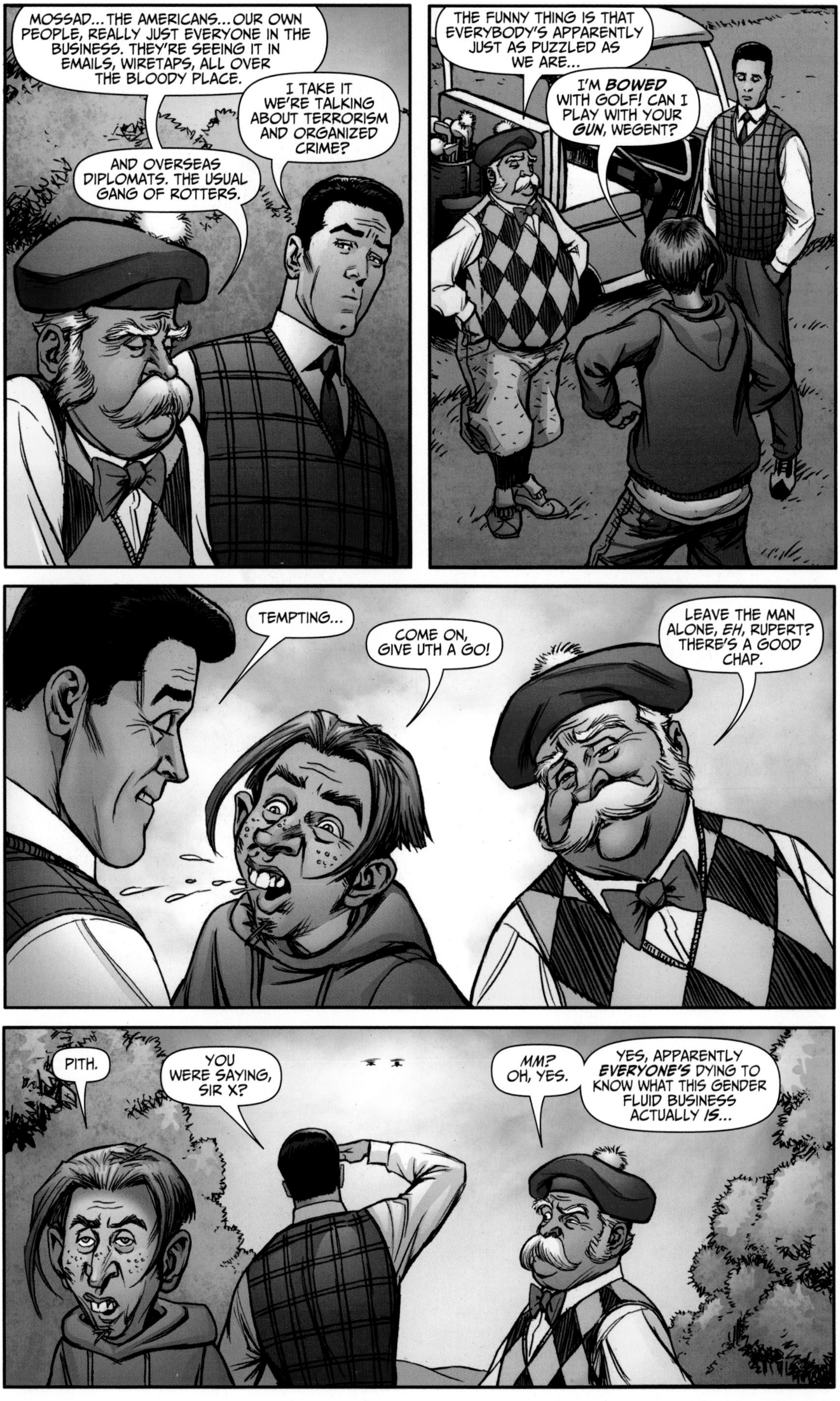
MOSSAD...THE AMERICANS...OUR OWN PEOPLE, REALLY JUST EVERYONE IN THE BUSINESS. THEY'RE SEEING IT IN EMAILS, WIRETAPS, ALL OVER THE BLOODY PLACE.
I TAKE IT WE'RE TALKING ABOUT TERRORISM AND ORGANIZED CRIME?
AND OVERSEAS DIPLOMATS. THE USUAL GANG OF ROTTERS.
THE FUNNY THING IS THAT EVERYBODY'S APPARENTLY JUST AS PUZZLED AS WE ARE...
I'M **BOWED** WITH GOLF! CAN I PLAY WITH YOUR ***GUN***, WEGENT?
TEMPTING...
COME ON, GIVE UTH A GO!
LEAVE THE MAN ALONE, *EH*, RUPERT? THERE'S A GOOD CHAP.
PITH.
YOU WERE SAYING, SIR X?
MM? OH, YES.
YES, APPARENTLY ***EVERYONE'S*** DYING TO KNOW WHAT THIS GENDER FLUID BUSINESS ACTUALLY *IS*...

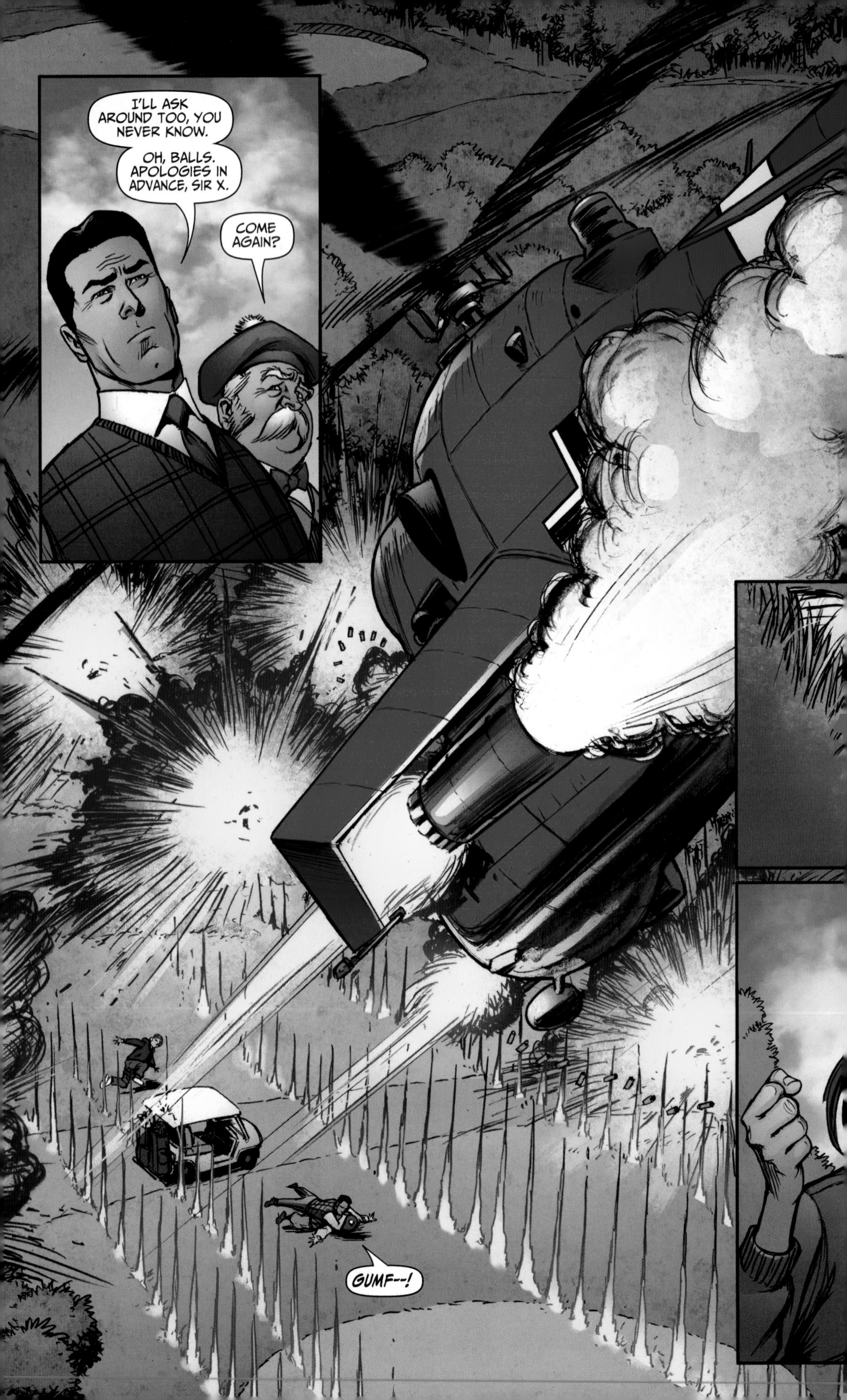
I'LL ASK AROUND TOO, YOU NEVER KNOW.
OH, BALLS. APOLOGIES IN ADVANCE, SIR X.
COME AGAIN?
GUMF--!

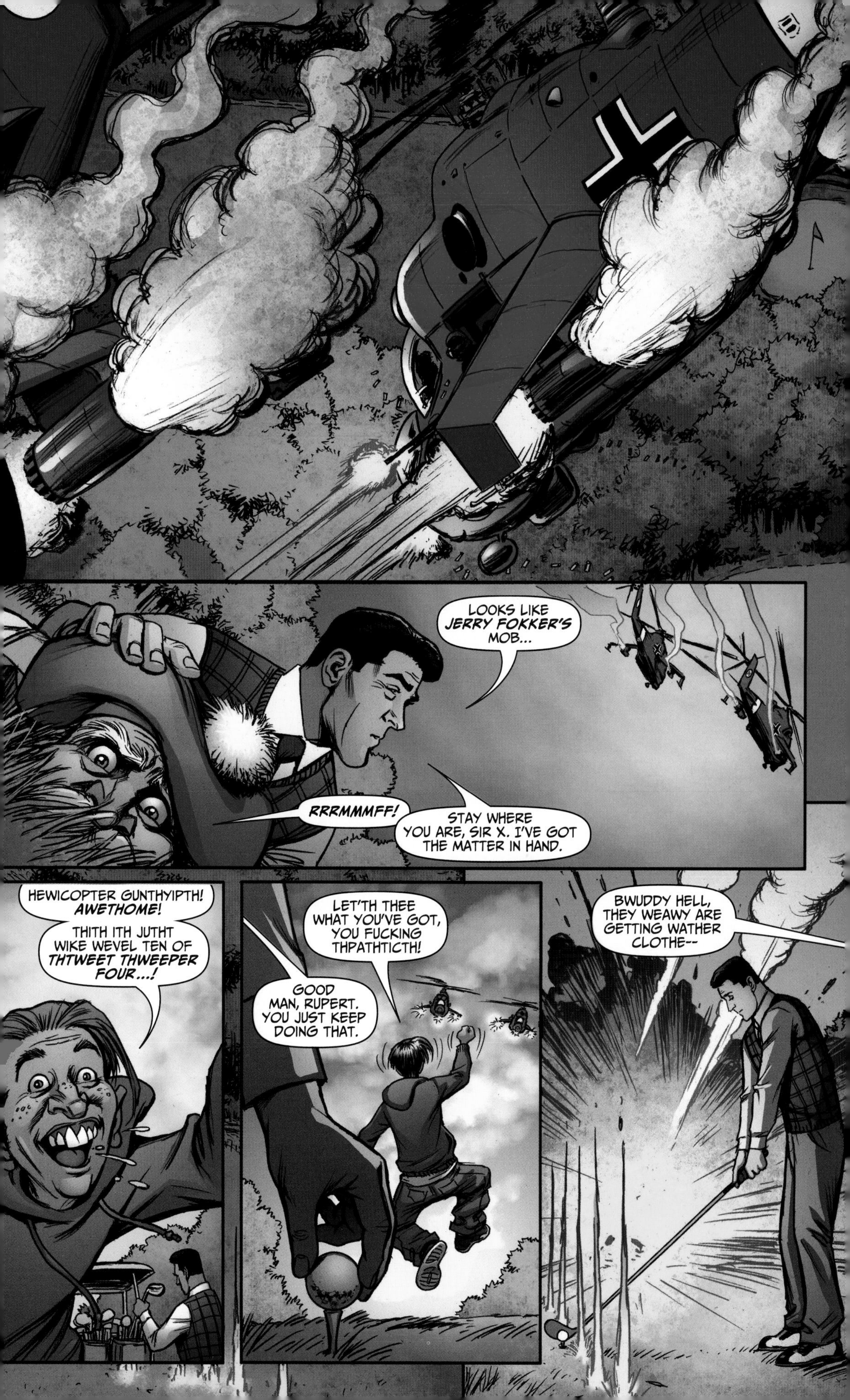
LOOKS LIKE *JERRY FOKKER'S* MOB...
RRRMMMFF!
STAY WHERE YOU ARE, SIR X. I'VE GOT THE MATTER IN HAND.
HEWICOPTER GUNTHYIPTH! ***AWETHOME!***
THITH ITH JUTHT WIKE WEVEL TEN OF ***THTWEET THWEEPER FOUR...!***
LET'TH THEE WHAT YOU'VE GOT, YOU FUCKING THPATHTICTH!
GOOD MAN, RUPERT. YOU JUST KEEP DOING THAT.
BWUDDY HELL, THEY WEAWY ARE GETTING WATHER CLOTHE--

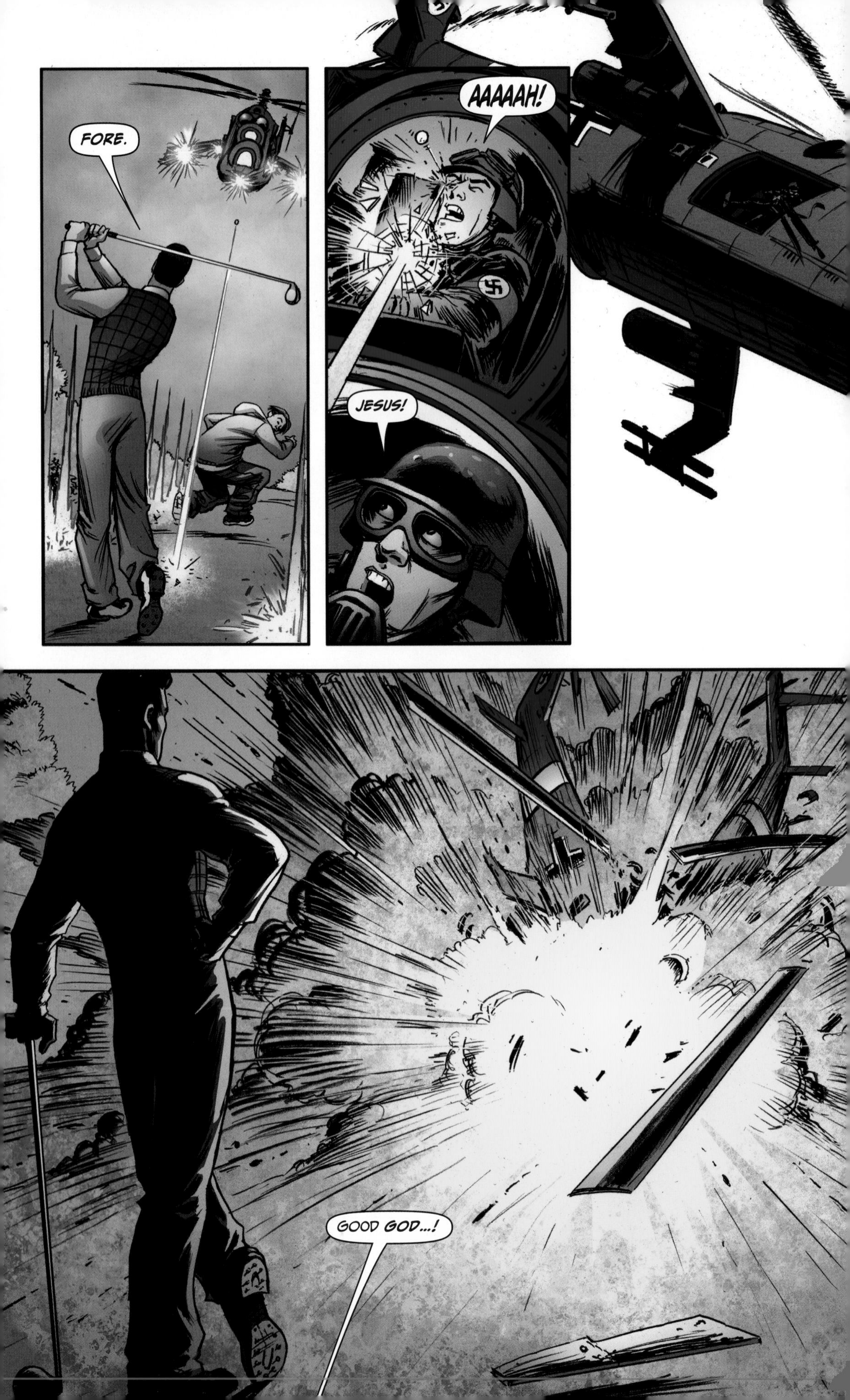
FORE.
AAAAAH!
JESUS!
GOOD GOD...!

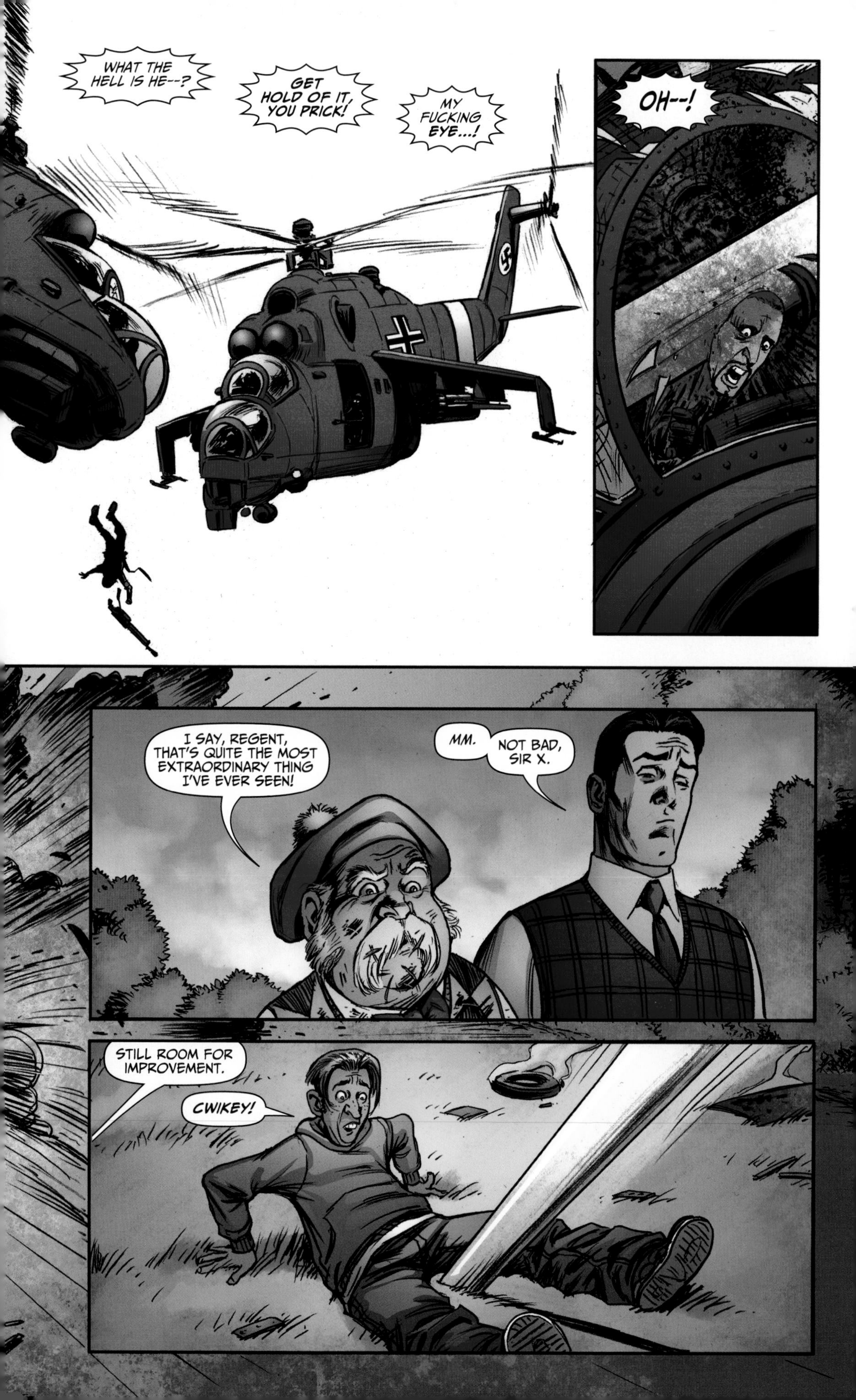
WHAT THE HELL IS HE--?
GET HOLD OF IT, YOU PRICK!
MY FUCKING EYE...!
OH--!
I SAY, REGENT, THAT'S QUITE THE MOST EXTRAORDINARY THING I'VE EVER SEEN!
MM.
NOT BAD, SIR X.
STILL ROOM FOR IMPROVEMENT.
CWIKEY!

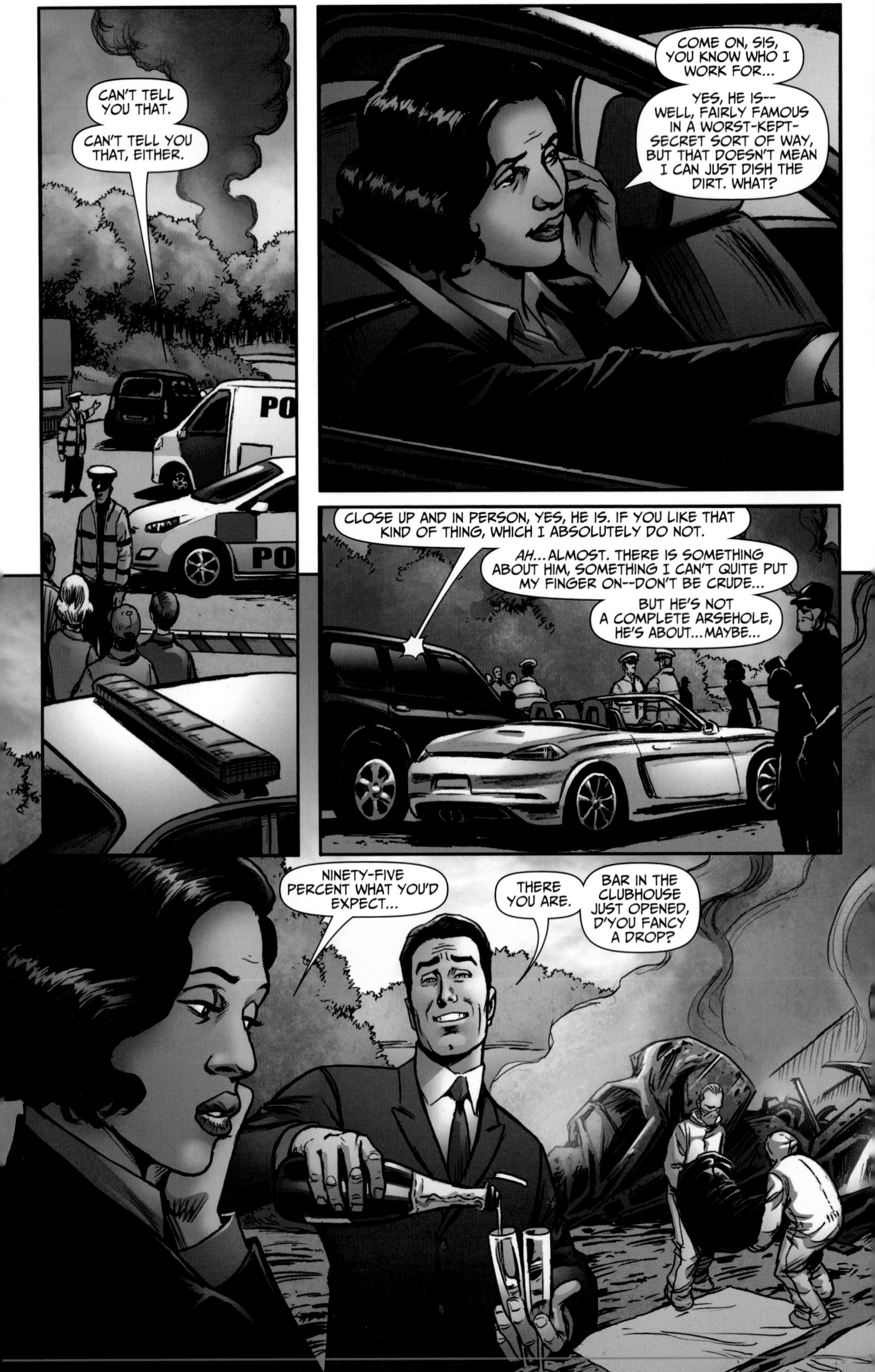
CAN'T TELL YOU THAT.
CAN'T TELL YOU THAT, EITHER.
POL
COME ON, SIS, YOU KNOW WHO I WORK FOR...
YES, HE IS-- WELL, FAIRLY FAMOUS IN A WORST-KEPT-SECRET SORT OF WAY, BUT THAT DOESN'T MEAN I CAN JUST DISH THE DIRT. WHAT?
CLOSE UP AND IN PERSON, YES, HE IS. IF YOU LIKE THAT KIND OF THING, WHICH I ABSOLUTELY DO NOT.
AH... ALMOST. THERE IS SOMETHING ABOUT HIM, SOMETHING I CAN'T QUITE PUT MY FINGER ON--DON'T BE CRUDE...
BUT HE'S NOT A COMPLETE ARSEHOLE, HE'S ABOUT... MAYBE...
NINETY-FIVE PERCENT WHAT YOU'D EXPECT...
THERE YOU ARE.
BAR IN THE CLUBHOUSE JUST OPENED, D'YOU FANCY A DROP?

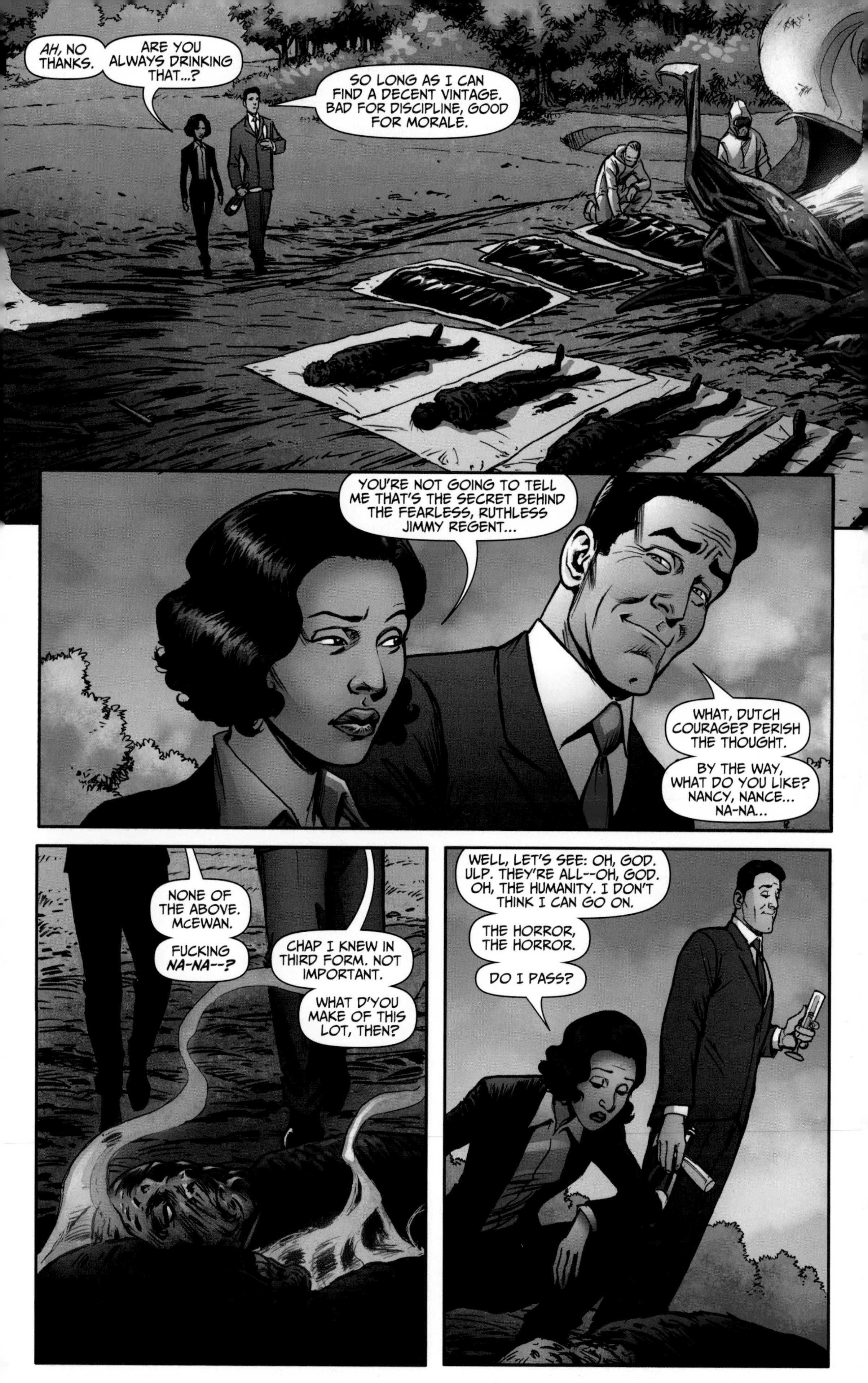
AH, NO THANKS.
ARE YOU ALWAYS DRINKING THAT...?
SO LONG AS I CAN FIND A DECENT VINTAGE. BAD FOR DISCIPLINE, GOOD FOR MORALE.
YOU'RE NOT GOING TO TELL ME THAT'S THE SECRET BEHIND THE FEARLESS, RUTHLESS JIMMY REGENT...
WHAT, DUTCH COURAGE? PERISH THE THOUGHT.
BY THE WAY, WHAT DO YOU LIKE? NANCY, NANCE... NA-NA...
NONE OF THE ABOVE. MCEWAN.
FUCKING *NA-NA--?*
CHAP I KNEW IN THIRD FORM. NOT IMPORTANT.
WHAT D'YOU MAKE OF THIS LOT, THEN?
WELL, LET'S SEE: OH, GOD. ULP. THEY'RE ALL--OH, GOD. OH, THE HUMANITY. I DON'T THINK I CAN GO ON.
THE HORROR, THE HORROR.
DO I PASS?

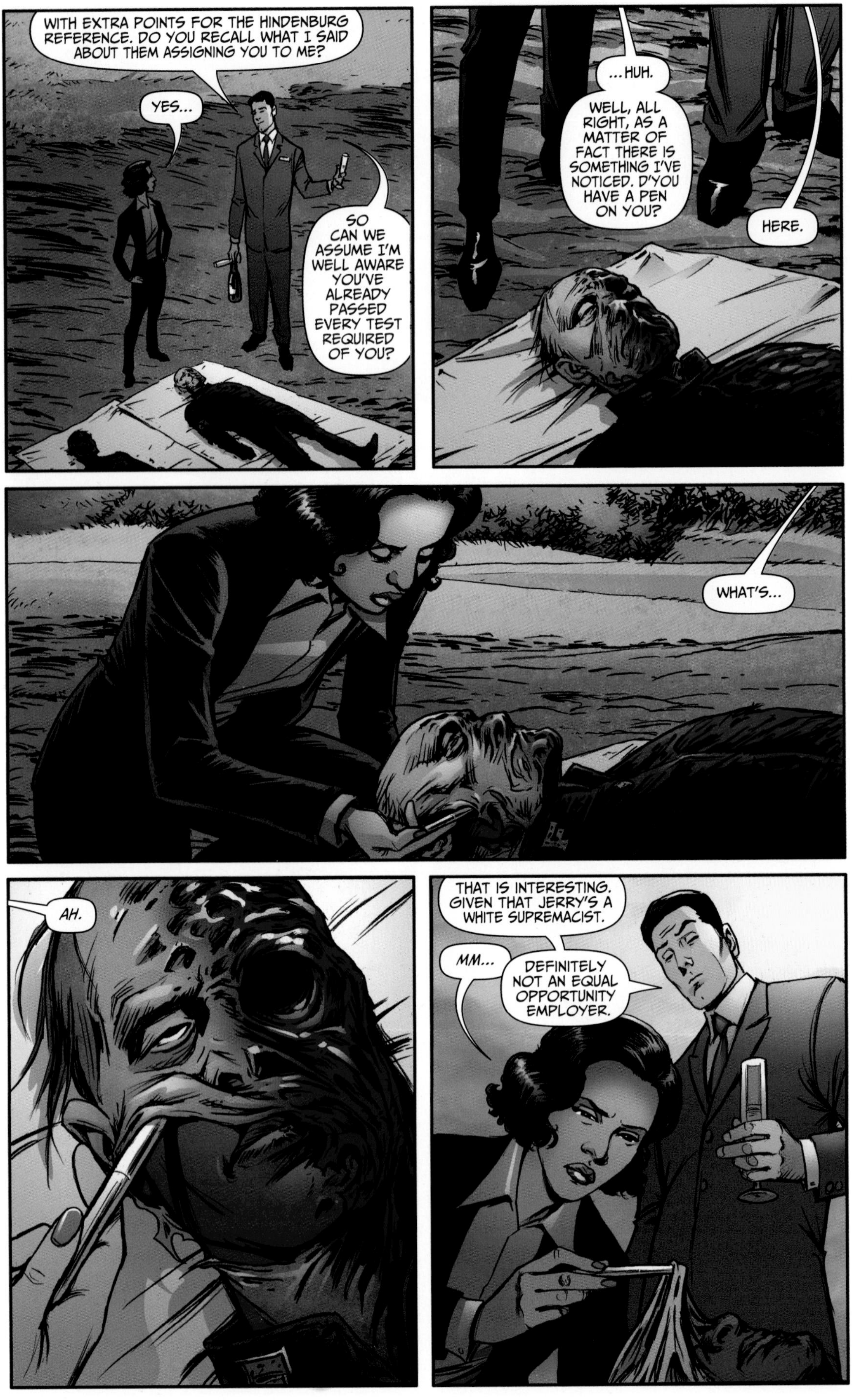

WITH EXTRA POINTS FOR THE HINDENBURG REFERENCE. DO YOU RECALL WHAT I SAID ABOUT THEM ASSIGNING YOU TO ME?
YES...
SO CAN WE ASSUME I'M WELL AWARE YOU'VE ALREADY PASSED EVERY TEST REQUIRED OF YOU?
...HUH.
WELL, ALL RIGHT, AS A MATTER OF FACT THERE IS SOMETHING I'VE NOTICED. D'YOU HAVE A PEN ON YOU?
HERE.
WHAT'S...
AH.
THAT IS INTERESTING. GIVEN THAT JERRY'S A WHITE SUPREMACIST.
MM...
DEFINITELY NOT AN EQUAL OPPORTUNITY EMPLOYER.

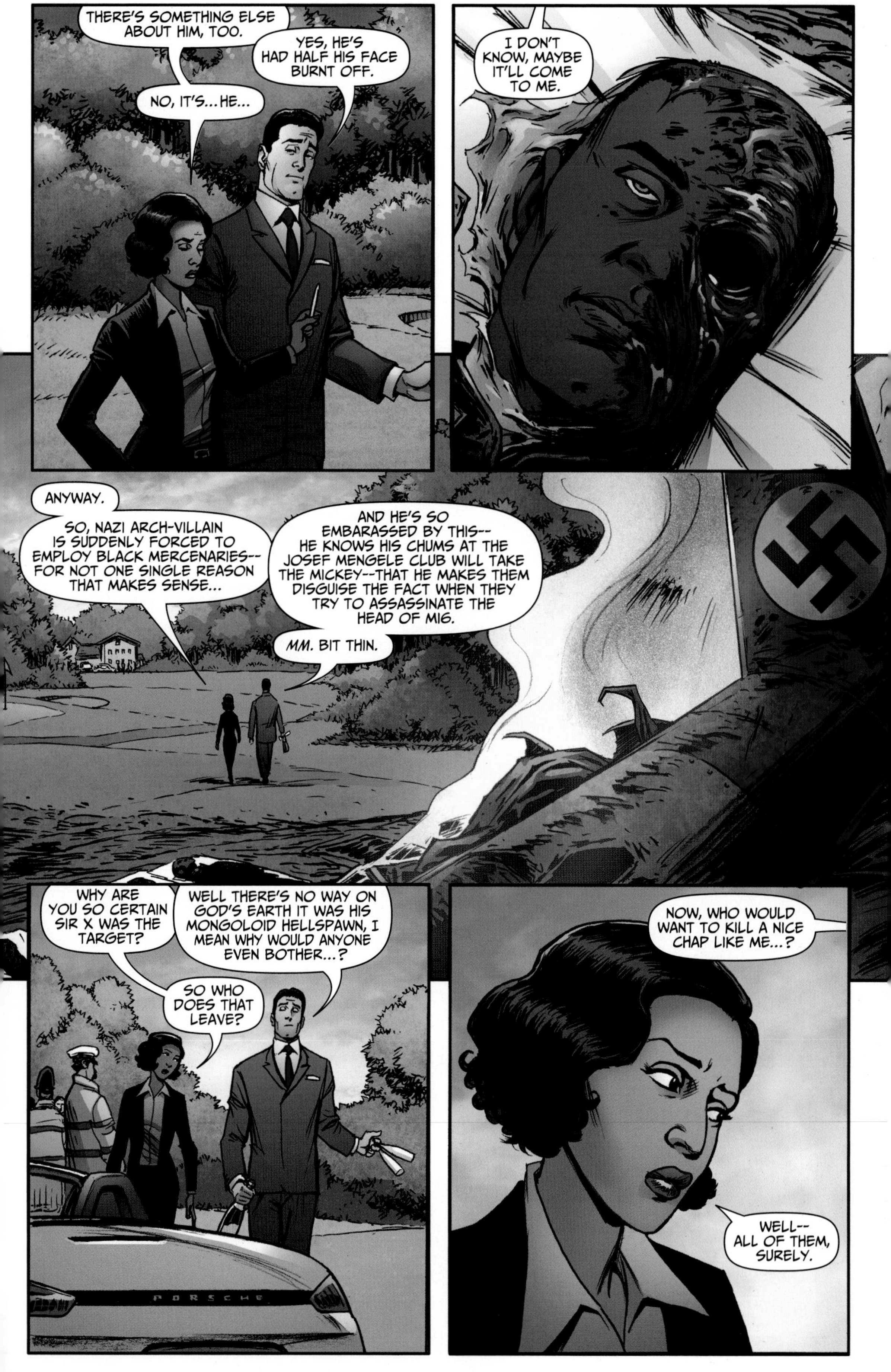
THERE'S SOMETHING ELSE ABOUT HIM, TOO.
YES, HE'S HAD HALF HIS FACE BURNT OFF.
NO, IT'S... HE...
I DON'T KNOW, MAYBE IT'LL COME TO ME.
ANYWAY.
SO, NAZI ARCH-VILLAIN IS SUDDENLY FORCED TO EMPLOY BLACK MERCENARIES--FOR NOT ONE SINGLE REASON THAT MAKES SENSE...
AND HE'S SO EMBARASSED BY THIS--HE KNOWS HIS CHUMS AT THE JOSEF MENGELE CLUB WILL TAKE THE MICKEY--THAT HE MAKES THEM DISGUISE THE FACT WHEN THEY TRY TO ASSASSINATE THE HEAD OF MI6.
MM. BIT THIN.
WHY ARE YOU SO CERTAIN SIR X WAS THE TARGET?
WELL THERE'S NO WAY ON GOD'S EARTH IT WAS HIS MONGOLOID HELLSPAWN, I MEAN WHY WOULD ANYONE EVEN BOTHER...?
SO WHO DOES THAT LEAVE?
PORSCHE
NOW, WHO WOULD WANT TO KILL A NICE CHAP LIKE ME...?
WELL--ALL OF THEM, SURELY.

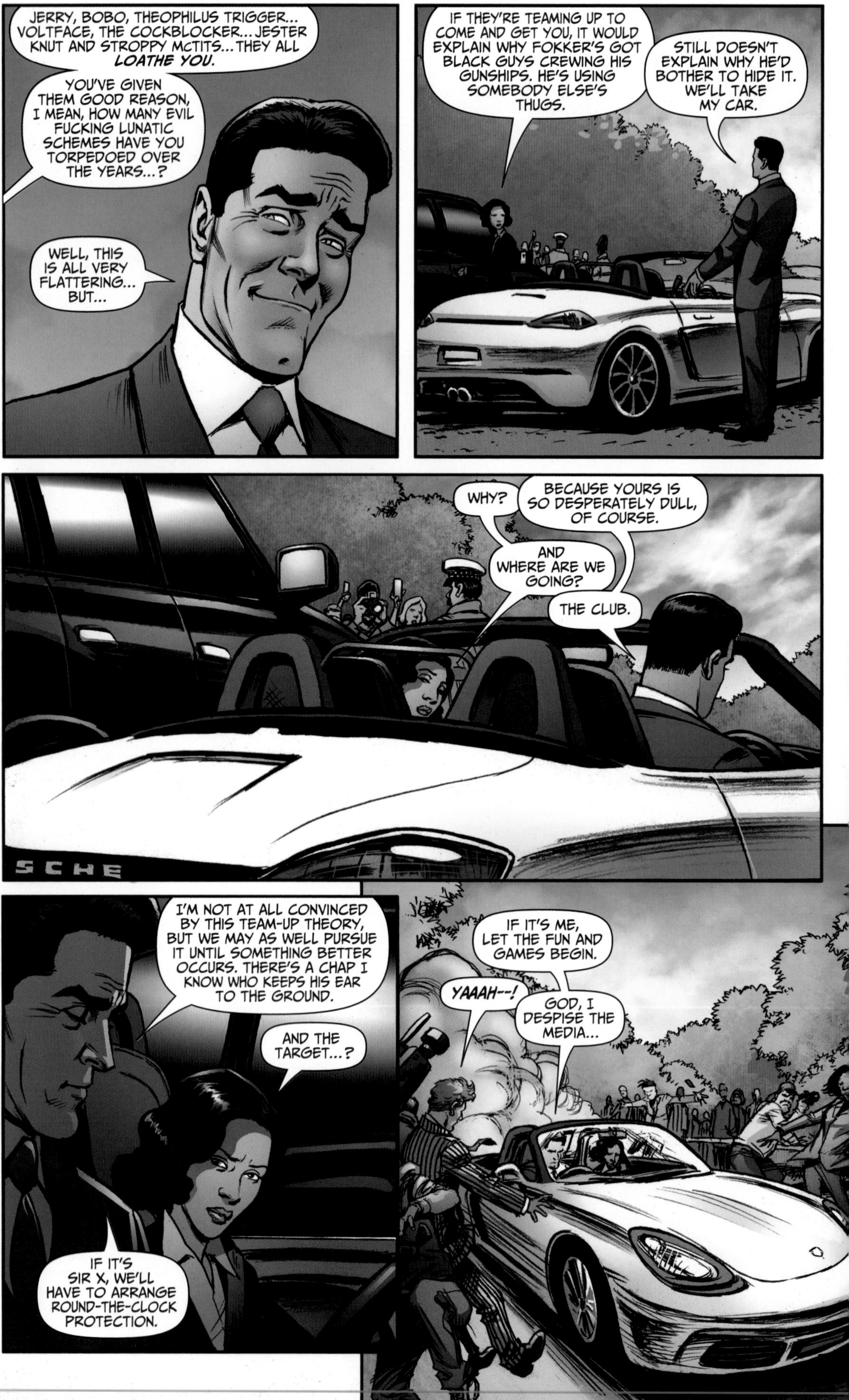
JERRY, BOBO, THEOPHILUS TRIGGER... VOLTFACE, THE COCKBLOCKER... JESTER KNUT AND STROPPY McTITS... THEY ALL *LOATHE YOU.*
YOU'VE GIVEN THEM GOOD REASON, I MEAN, HOW MANY EVIL FUCKING LUNATIC SCHEMES HAVE YOU TORPEDOED OVER THE YEARS...?
WELL, THIS IS ALL VERY FLATTERING... BUT...
IF THEY'RE TEAMING UP TO COME AND GET YOU, IT WOULD EXPLAIN WHY FOKKER'S GOT BLACK GUYS CREWING HIS GUNSHIPS. HE'S USING SOMEBODY ELSE'S THUGS.
STILL DOESN'T EXPLAIN WHY HE'D BOTHER TO HIDE IT. WE'LL TAKE MY CAR.
WHY?
BECAUSE YOURS IS SO DESPERATELY DULL, OF COURSE.
AND WHERE ARE WE GOING?
THE CLUB.
SCHE
I'M NOT AT ALL CONVINCED BY THIS TEAM-UP THEORY, BUT WE MAY AS WELL PURSUE IT UNTIL SOMETHING BETTER OCCURS. THERE'S A CHAP I KNOW WHO KEEPS HIS EAR TO THE GROUND.
AND THE TARGET...?
IF IT'S SIR X, WE'LL HAVE TO ARRANGE ROUND-THE-CLOCK PROTECTION.
IF IT'S ME, LET THE FUN AND GAMES BEGIN.
YAAAH--!
GOD, I DESPISE THE MEDIA...

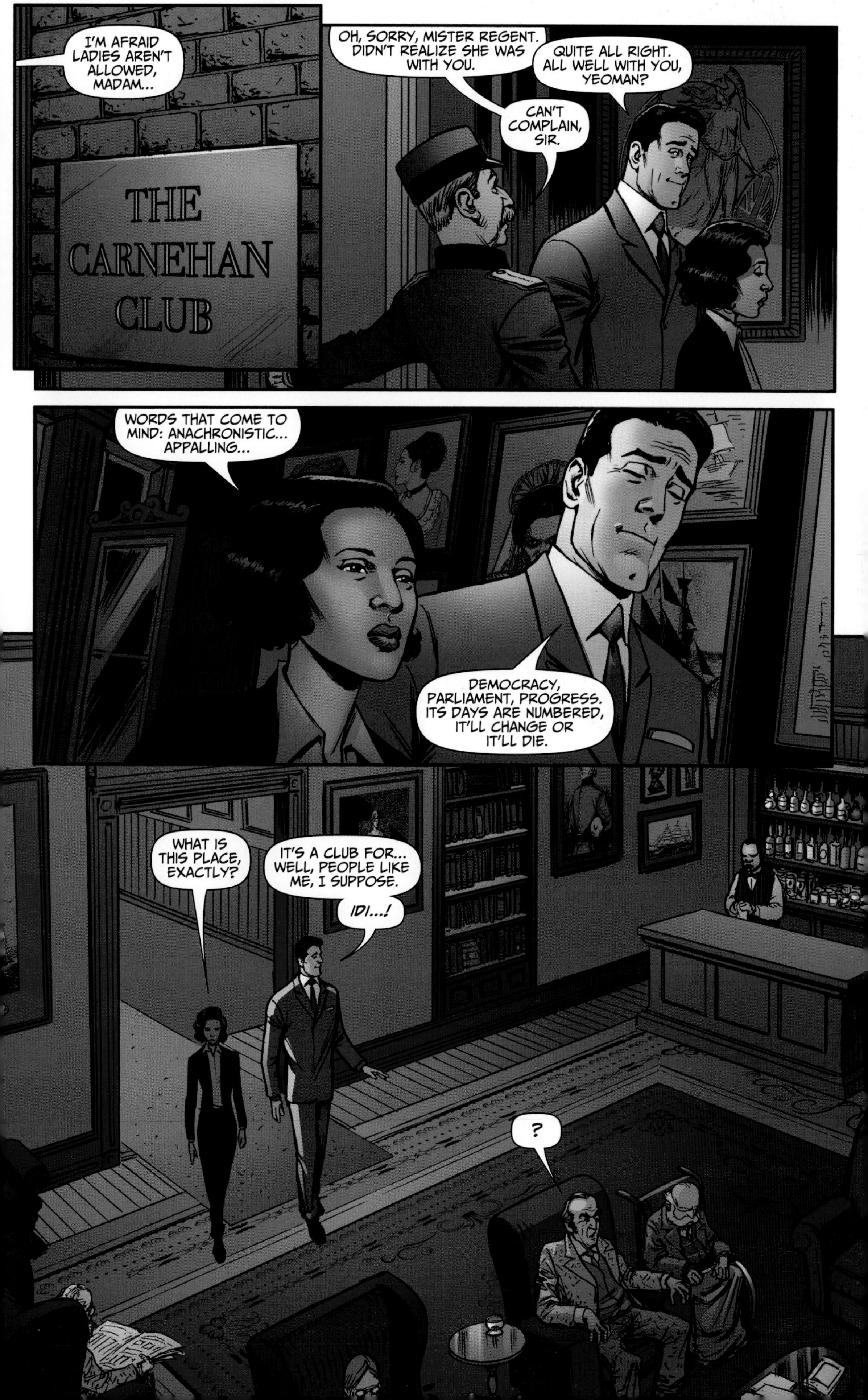
I'M AFRAID LADIES AREN'T ALLOWED, MADAM...
THE CARNEHAN CLUB
OH, SORRY, MISTER REGENT. DIDN'T REALIZE SHE WAS WITH YOU.
QUITE ALL RIGHT. ALL WELL WITH YOU, YEOMAN?
CAN'T COMPLAIN, SIR.
WORDS THAT COME TO MIND: ANACHRONISTIC... APPALLING...
DEMOCRACY, PARLIAMENT, PROGRESS. ITS DAYS ARE NUMBERED, IT'LL CHANGE OR IT'LL DIE.
WHAT IS THIS PLACE, EXACTLY?
IT'S A CLUB FOR... WELL, PEOPLE LIKE ME, I SUPPOSE.
IDI...!
?

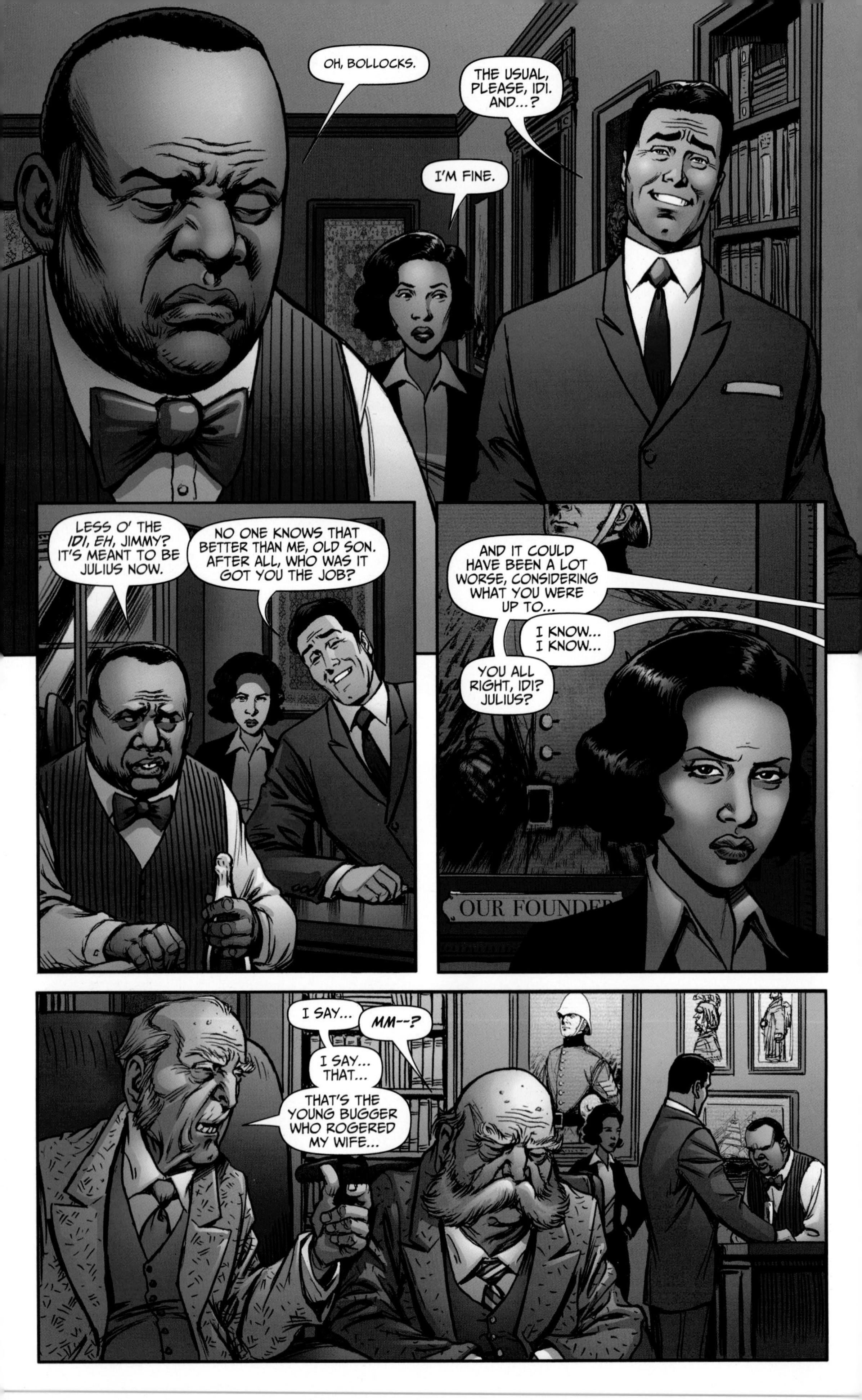
OH, BOLLOCKS.
THE USUAL, PLEASE, IDI. AND...?
I'M FINE.
LESS O' THE IDI, EH, JIMMY? IT'S MEANT TO BE JULIUS NOW.
NO ONE KNOWS THAT BETTER THAN ME, OLD SON. AFTER ALL, WHO WAS IT GOT YOU THE JOB?
AND IT COULD HAVE BEEN A LOT WORSE, CONSIDERING WHAT YOU WERE UP TO...
I KNOW... I KNOW...
YOU ALL RIGHT, IDI? JULIUS?
OUR FOUNDER
I SAY...
MM--?
I SAY... THAT...
THAT'S THE YOUNG BUGGER WHO ROGERED MY WIFE...

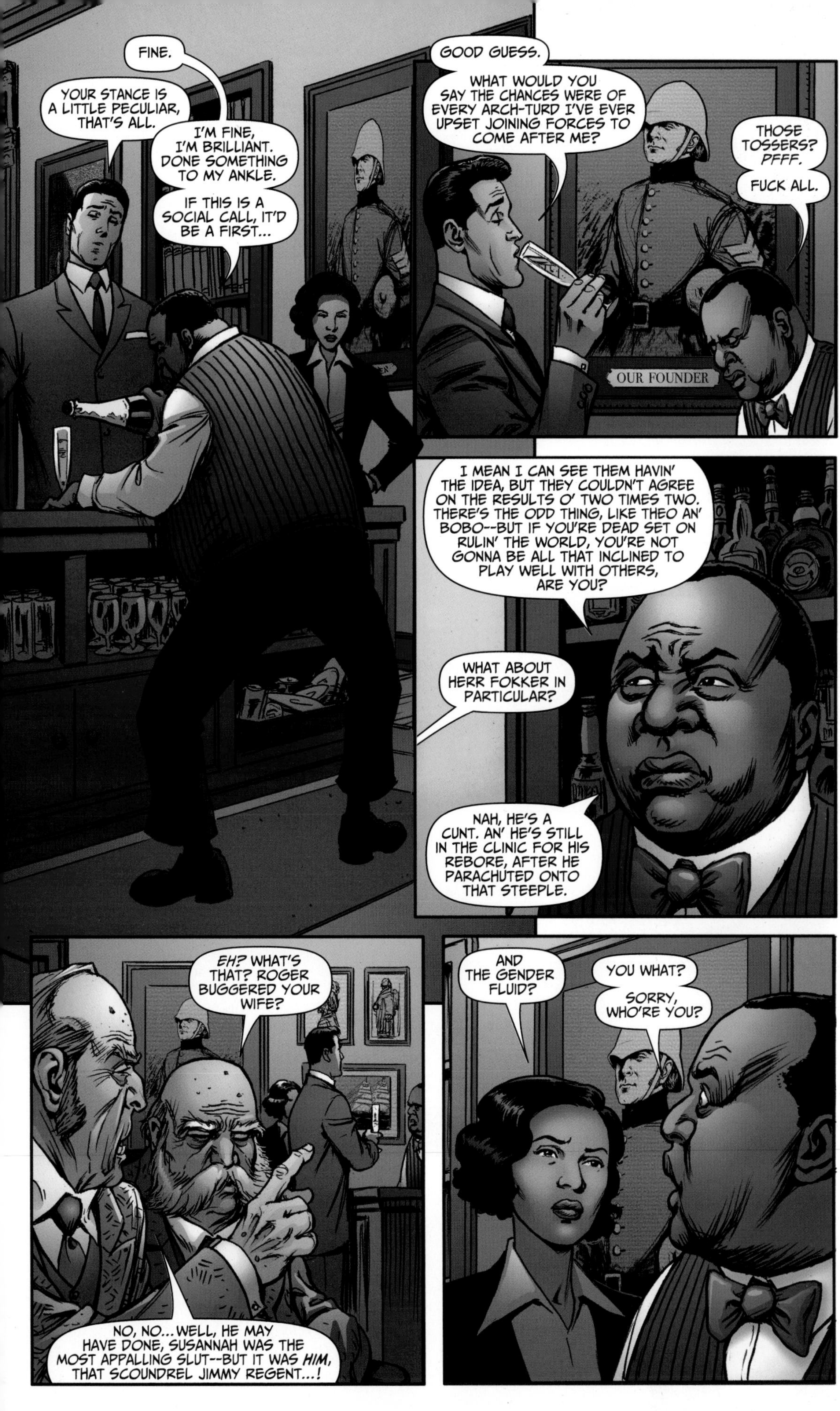
FINE.
YOUR STANCE IS A LITTLE PECULIAR, THAT'S ALL.
I'M FINE, I'M BRILLIANT. DONE SOMETHING TO MY ANKLE.
IF THIS IS A SOCIAL CALL, IT'D BE A FIRST...
GOOD GUESS.
WHAT WOULD YOU SAY THE CHANCES WERE OF EVERY ARCH-TURD I'VE EVER UPSET JOINING FORCES TO COME AFTER ME?
OUR FOUNDER
THOSE TOSSERS? *PFFF.*
FUCK ALL.
I MEAN I CAN SEE THEM HAVIN' THE IDEA, BUT THEY COULDN'T AGREE ON THE RESULTS O' TWO TIMES TWO. THERE'S THE ODD THING, LIKE THEO AN' BOBO--BUT IF YOU'RE DEAD SET ON RULIN' THE WORLD, YOU'RE NOT GONNA BE ALL THAT INCLINED TO PLAY WELL WITH OTHERS, ARE YOU?
WHAT ABOUT HERR FOKKER IN PARTICULAR?
NAH, HE'S A CUNT. AN' HE'S STILL IN THE CLINIC FOR HIS REBORE, AFTER HE PARACHUTED ONTO THAT STEEPLE.
EH? WHAT'S THAT? ROGER BUGGERED YOUR WIFE?
NO, NO... WELL, HE MAY HAVE DONE, SUSANNAH WAS THE MOST APPALLING SLUT--BUT IT WAS *HIM*, THAT SCOUNDREL JIMMY REGENT...!
AND THE GENDER FLUID?
YOU WHAT?
SORRY, WHO'RE YOU?

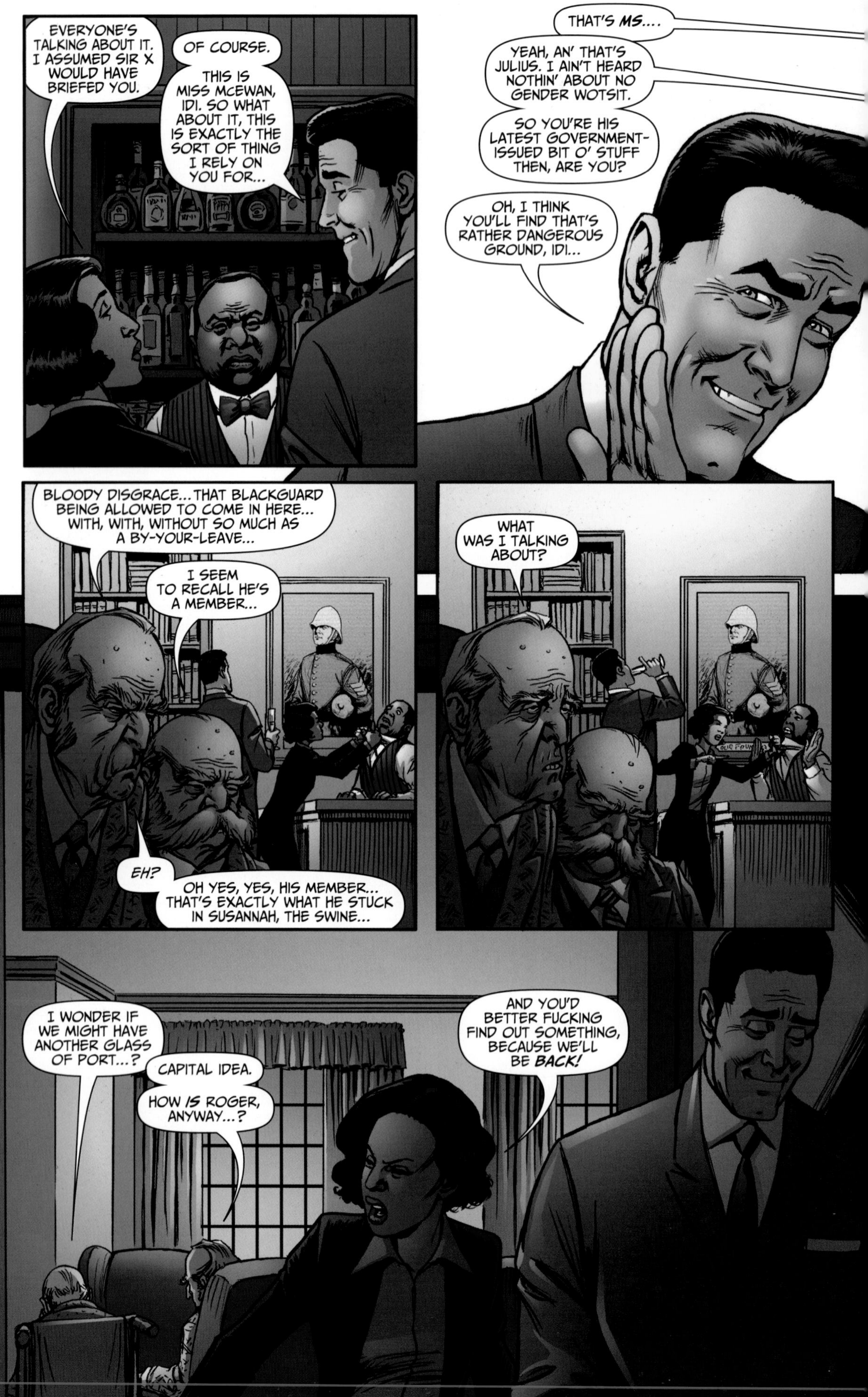
EVERYONE'S TALKING ABOUT IT. I ASSUMED SIR X WOULD HAVE BRIEFED YOU.
OF COURSE.
THIS IS MISS McEWAN, IDI. SO WHAT ABOUT IT, THIS IS EXACTLY THE SORT OF THING I RELY ON YOU FOR...
THAT'S *MS*....
YEAH, AN' THAT'S JULIUS. I AIN'T HEARD NOTHIN' ABOUT NO GENDER WOTSIT.
SO YOU'RE HIS LATEST GOVERNMENT-ISSUED BIT O' STUFF THEN, ARE YOU?
OH, I THINK YOU'LL FIND THAT'S RATHER DANGEROUS GROUND, IDI...
BLOODY DISGRACE... THAT BLACKGUARD BEING ALLOWED TO COME IN HERE... WITH, WITH, WITHOUT SO MUCH AS A BY-YOUR-LEAVE...
I SEEM TO RECALL HE'S A MEMBER...
EH?
OH YES, YES, HIS MEMBER... THAT'S EXACTLY WHAT HE STUCK IN SUSANNAH, THE SWINE...
WHAT WAS I TALKING ABOUT?
I WONDER IF WE MIGHT HAVE ANOTHER GLASS OF PORT...?
CAPITAL IDEA.
HOW *IS* ROGER, ANYWAY...?
AND YOU'D BETTER FUCKING FIND OUT SOMETHING, BECAUSE WE'LL BE *BACK!*

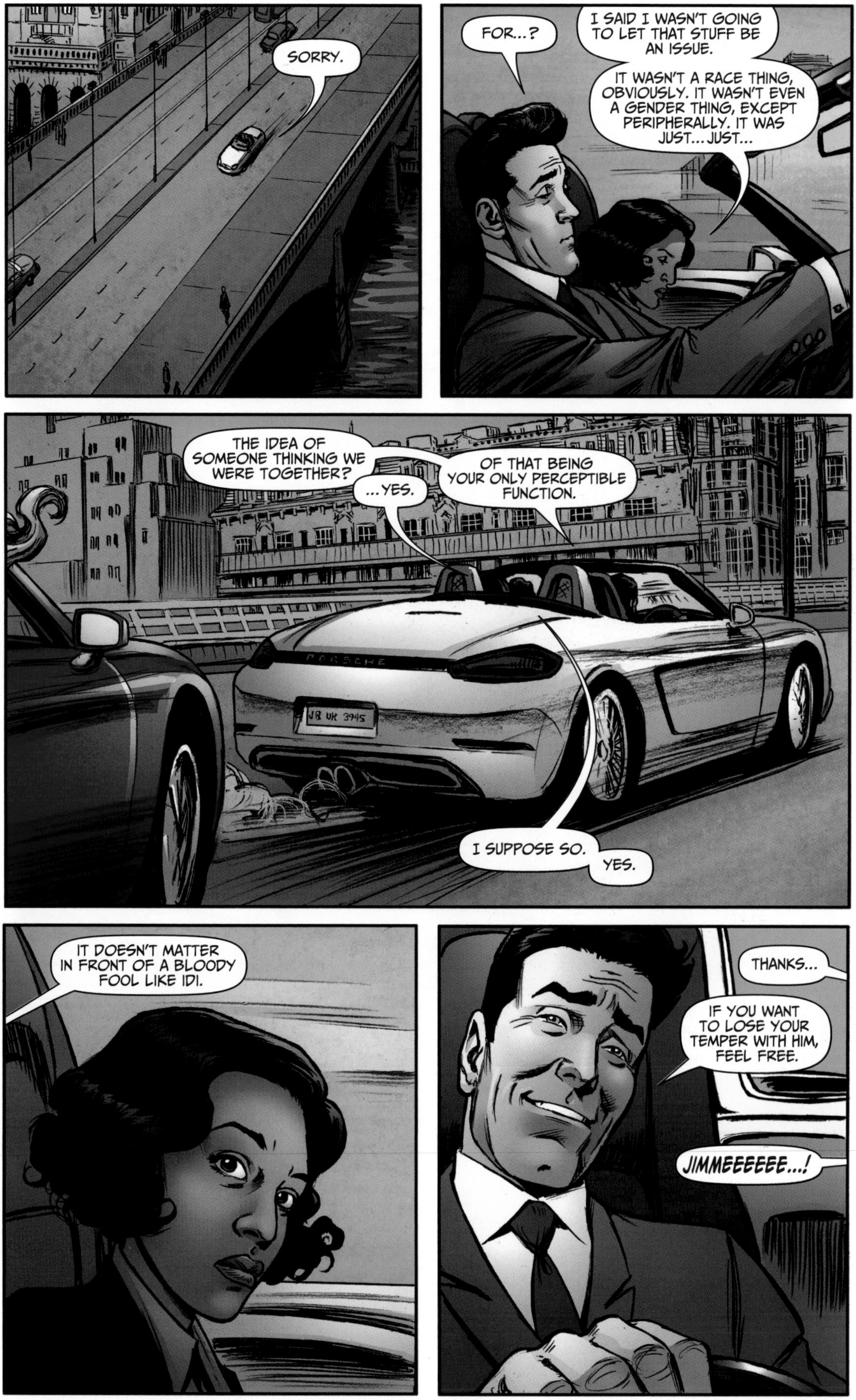
SORRY.
FOR...?
I SAID I WASN'T GOING TO LET THAT STUFF BE AN ISSUE.
IT WASN'T A RACE THING, OBVIOUSLY. IT WASN'T EVEN A GENDER THING, EXCEPT PERIPHERALLY. IT WAS JUST... JUST...
THE IDEA OF SOMEONE THINKING WE WERE TOGETHER?
...YES.
OF THAT BEING YOUR ONLY PERCEPTIBLE FUNCTION.
I SUPPOSE SO.
YES.
IT DOESN'T MATTER IN FRONT OF A BLOODY FOOL LIKE IDI.
THANKS...
IF YOU WANT TO LOSE YOUR TEMPER WITH HIM, FEEL FREE.
JIMMEEEEEE...!

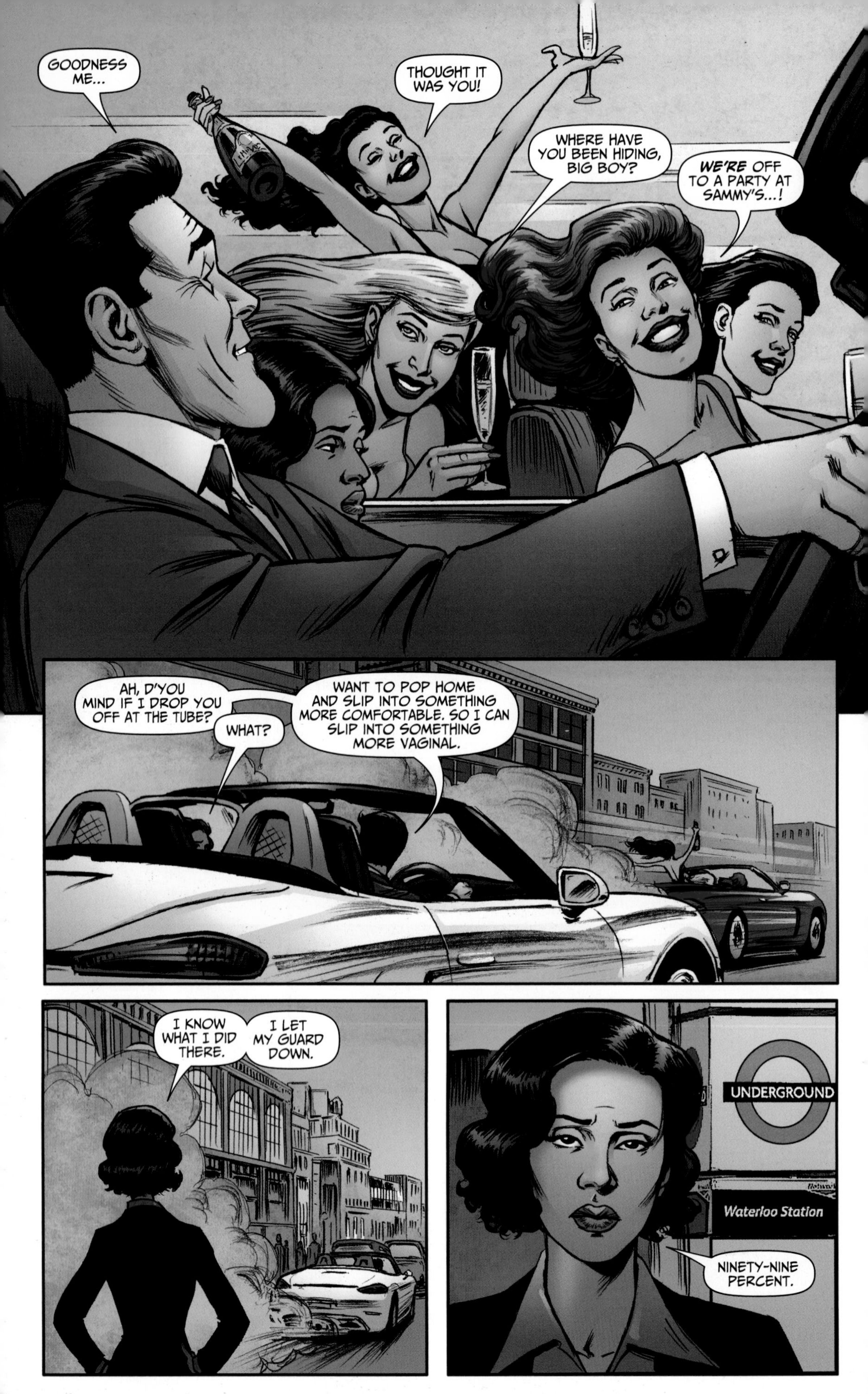
GOODNESS ME...
THOUGHT IT WAS YOU!
WHERE HAVE YOU BEEN HIDING, BIG BOY?
WE'RE OFF TO A PARTY AT SAMMY'S...!
AH, D'YOU MIND IF I DROP YOU OFF AT THE TUBE?
WHAT?
WANT TO POP HOME AND SLIP INTO SOMETHING MORE COMFORTABLE. SO I CAN SLIP INTO SOMETHING MORE VAGINAL.
I KNOW WHAT I DID THERE.
I LET MY GUARD DOWN.
UNDERGROUND
Waterloo Station
NINETY-NINE PERCENT.

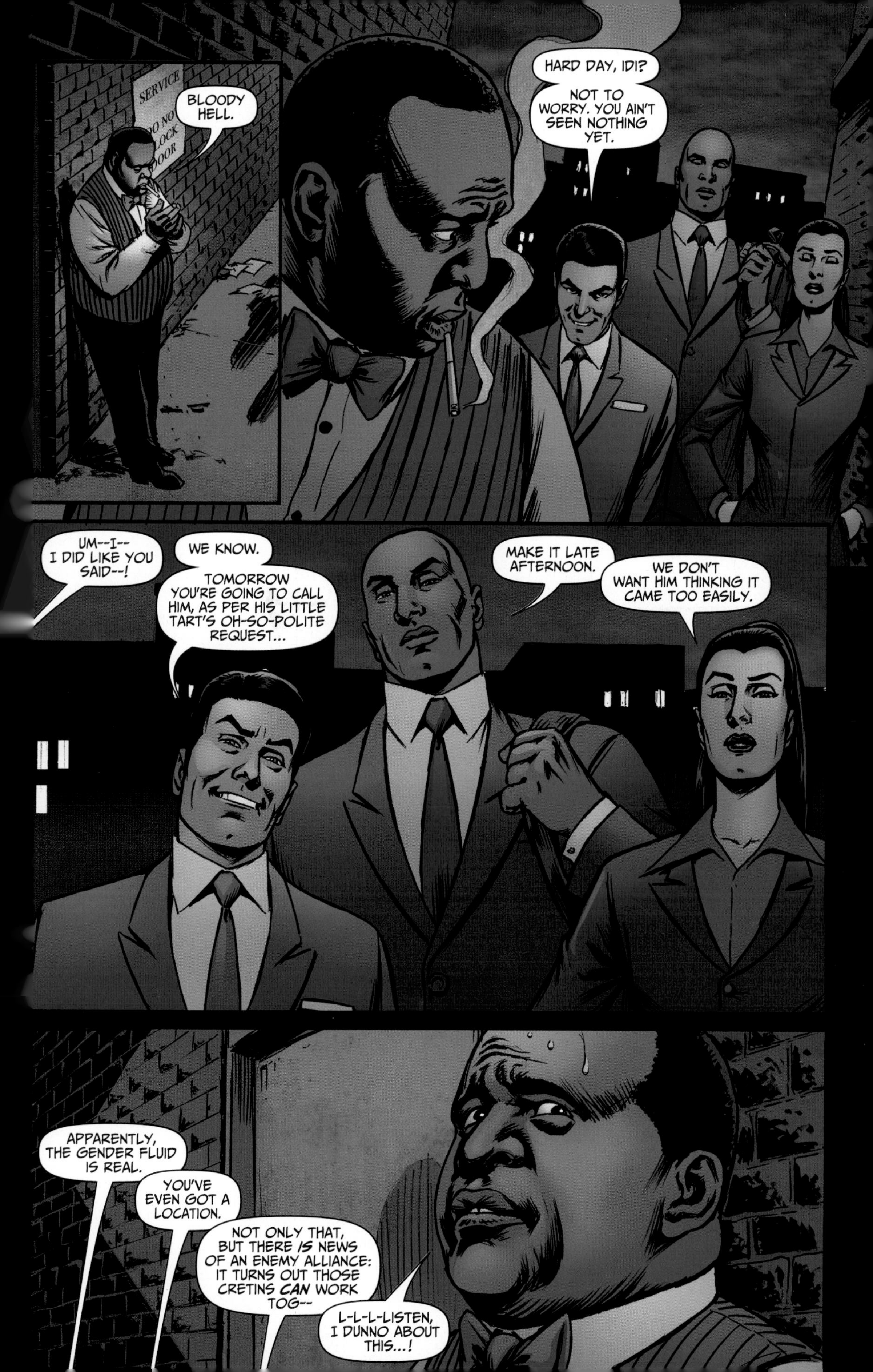
SERVICE
DO NOT
LOCK
DOOR
BLOODY HELL.
HARD DAY, IDI?
NOT TO WORRY. YOU AIN'T SEEN NOTHING YET.
UM--I-- I DID LIKE YOU SAID--!
WE KNOW.
TOMORROW YOU'RE GOING TO CALL HIM, AS PER HIS LITTLE TART'S OH-SO-POLITE REQUEST...
MAKE IT LATE AFTERNOON.
WE DON'T WANT HIM THINKING IT CAME TOO EASILY.
APPARENTLY, THE GENDER FLUID IS REAL.
YOU'VE EVEN GOT A LOCATION.
NOT ONLY THAT, BUT THERE *IS* NEWS OF AN ENEMY ALLIANCE: IT TURNS OUT THOSE CRETINS **CAN** WORK TOG--
L-L-L-LISTEN, I DUNNO ABOUT THIS...!

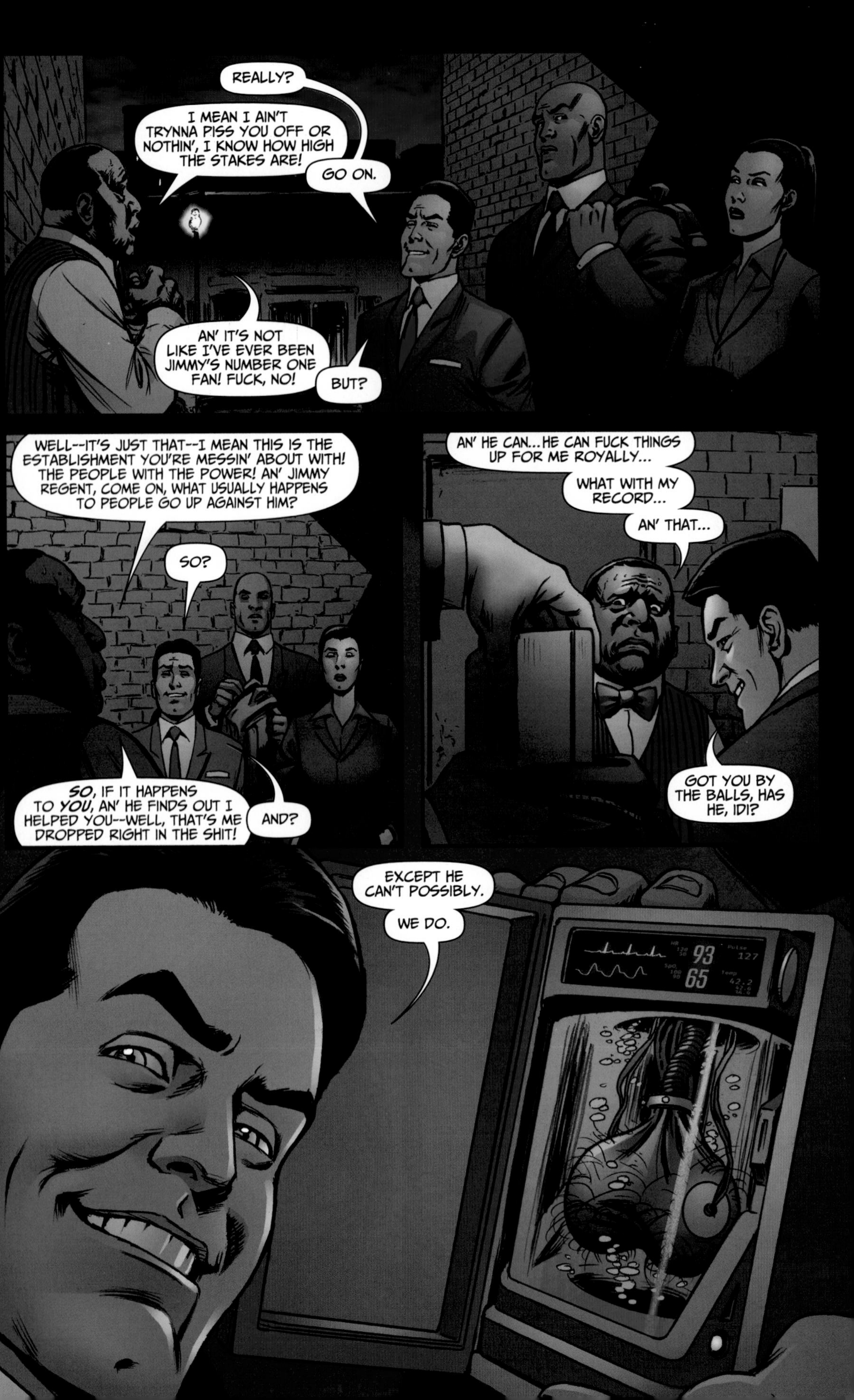
REALLY?
I MEAN I AIN'T TRYNNA PISS YOU OFF OR NOTHIN', I KNOW HOW HIGH THE STAKES ARE!
GO ON.
AN' IT'S NOT LIKE I'VE EVER BEEN JIMMY'S NUMBER ONE FAN! FUCK, NO!
BUT?
WELL--IT'S JUST THAT--I MEAN THIS IS THE ESTABLISHMENT YOU'RE MESSIN' ABOUT WITH! THE PEOPLE WITH THE POWER! AN' JIMMY REGENT, COME ON, WHAT USUALLY HAPPENS TO PEOPLE GO UP AGAINST HIM?
SO?
SO, IF IT HAPPENS TO YOU, AN' HE FINDS OUT I HELPED YOU--WELL, THAT'S ME DROPPED RIGHT IN THE SHIT!
AND?
AN' HE CAN...HE CAN FUCK THINGS UP FOR ME ROYALLY...
WHAT WITH MY RECORD...
AN' THAT...
GOT YOU BY THE BALLS, HAS HE, IDI?
EXCEPT HE CAN'T POSSIBLY.
WE DO.
93
65
127
42.2

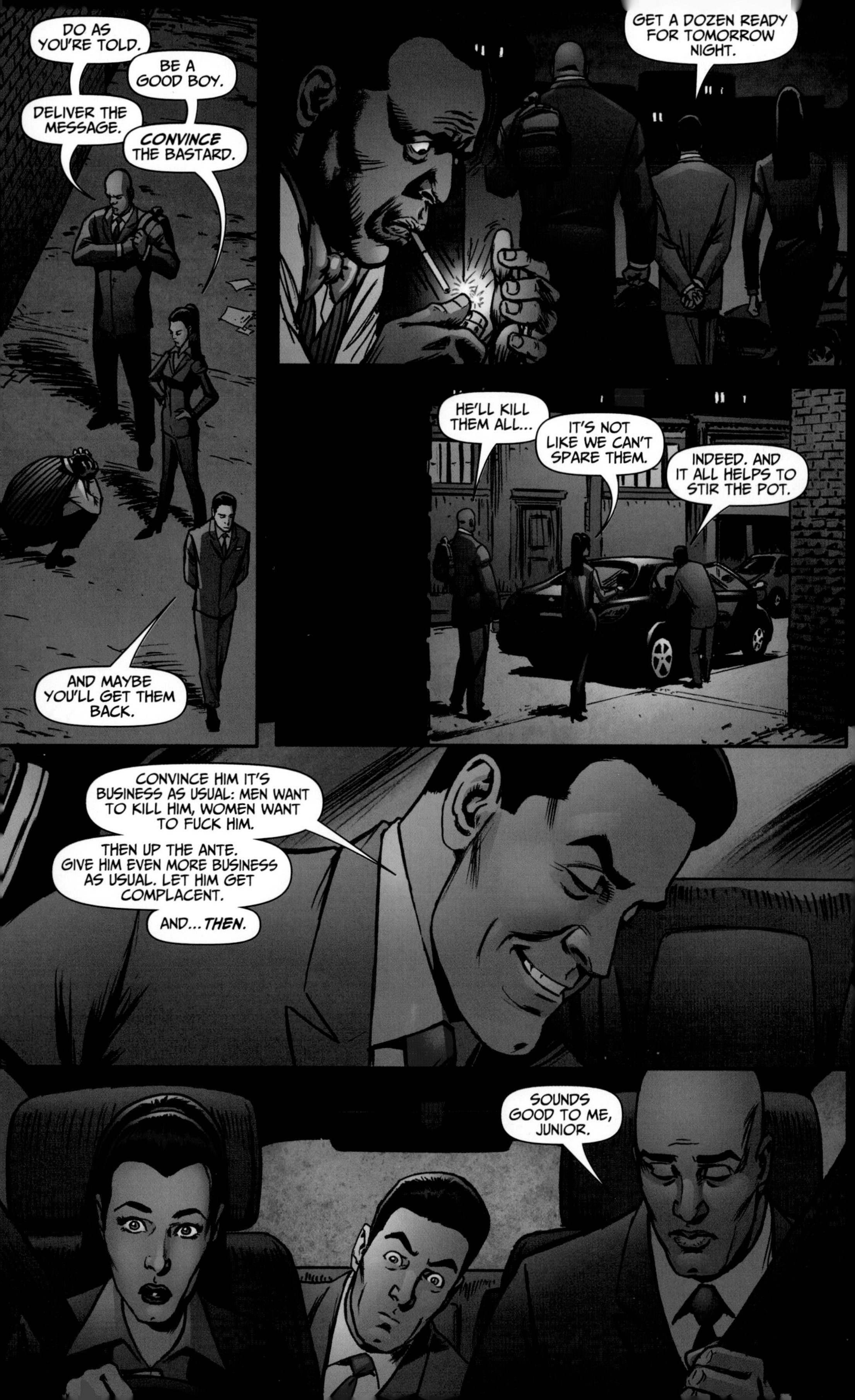
DO AS YOU'RE TOLD.
BE A GOOD BOY.
DELIVER THE MESSAGE.
CONVINCE THE BASTARD.
AND MAYBE YOU'LL GET THEM BACK.
GET A DOZEN READY FOR TOMORROW NIGHT.
HE'LL KILL THEM ALL...
IT'S NOT LIKE WE CAN'T SPARE THEM.
INDEED. AND IT ALL HELPS TO STIR THE POT.
CONVINCE HIM IT'S BUSINESS AS USUAL: MEN WANT TO KILL HIM, WOMEN WANT TO FUCK HIM.
THEN UP THE ANTE. GIVE HIM EVEN MORE BUSINESS AS USUAL. LET HIM GET COMPLACENT.
AND...THEN.
SOUNDS GOOD TO ME, JUNIOR.

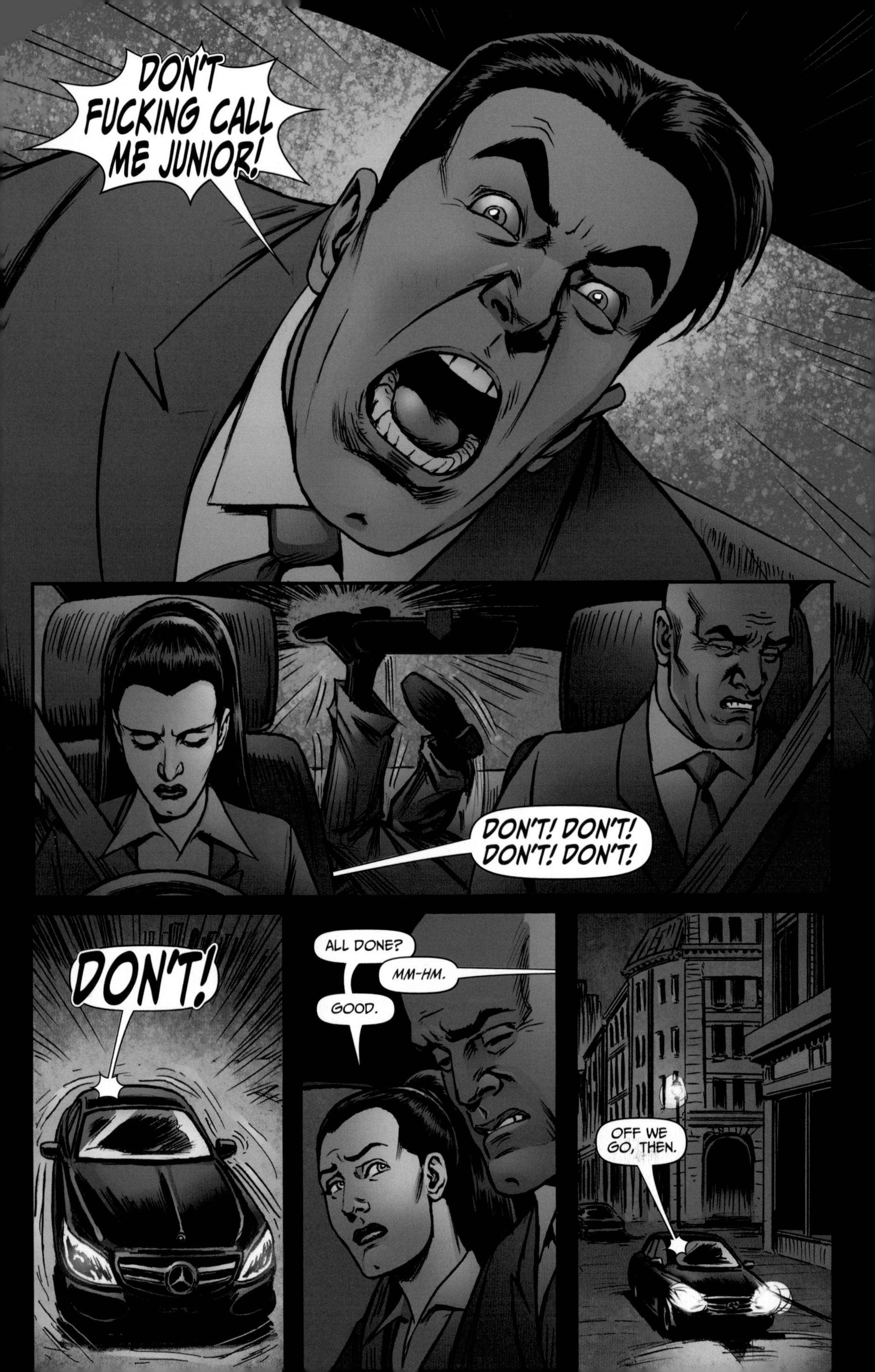
DON'T FUCKING CALL ME JUNIOR!
DON'T! DON'T! DON'T! DON'T!
DON'T!
ALL DONE?
MM-HM.
GOOD.
OFF WE GO, THEN.

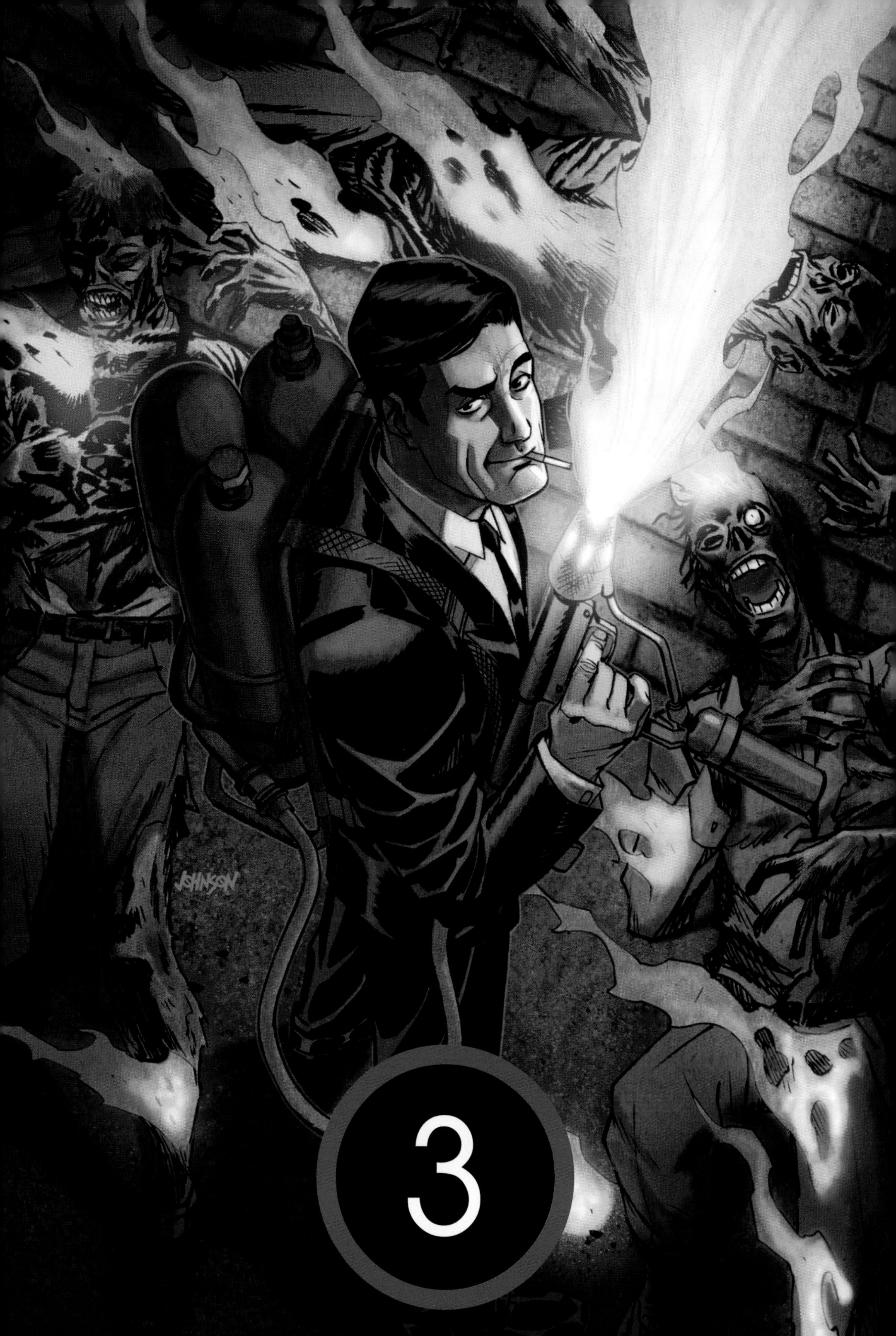
JOHNSON

3

SOME ANIMALS ARE MORE EQUAL THAN OTHERS

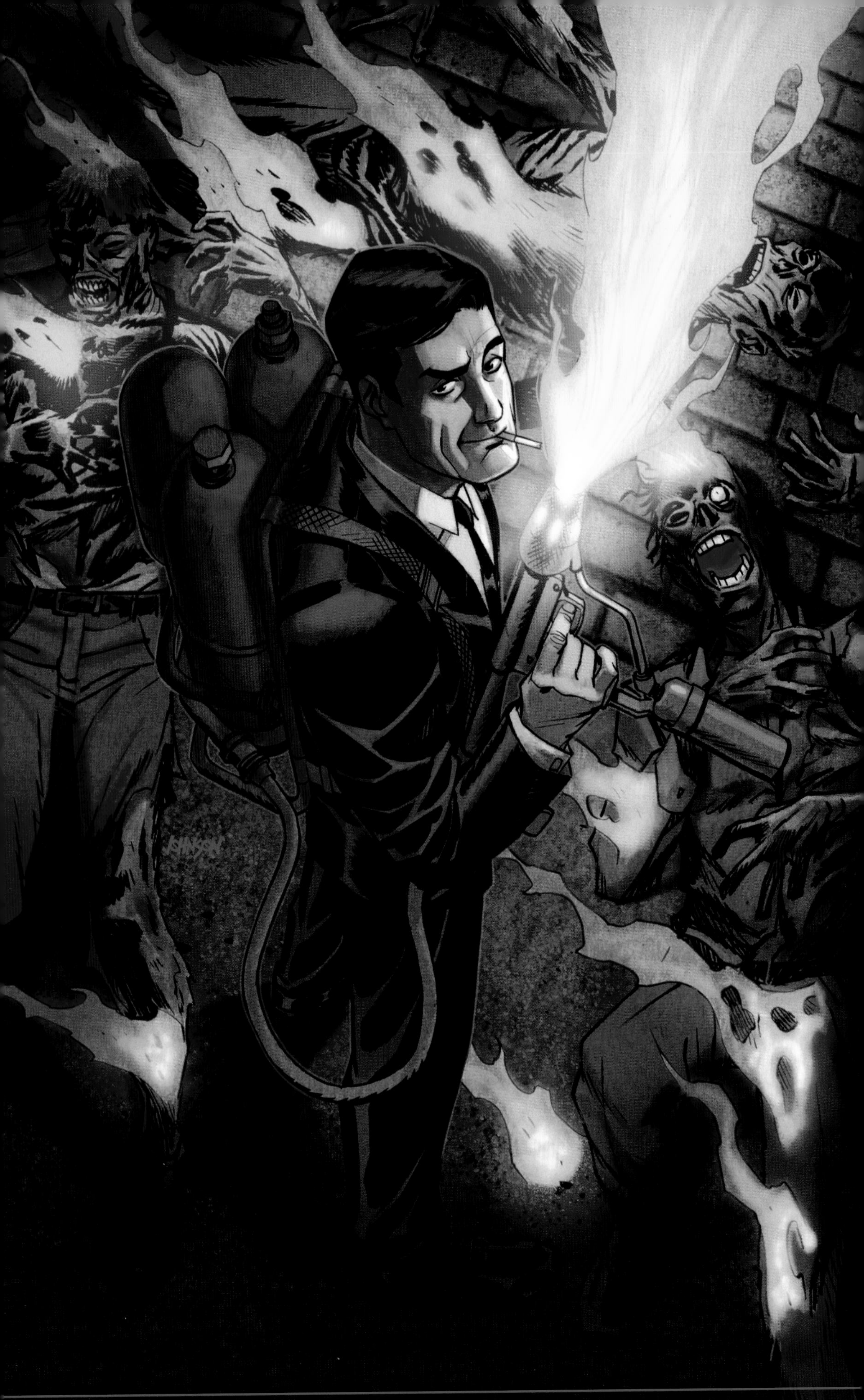
JOHNSON

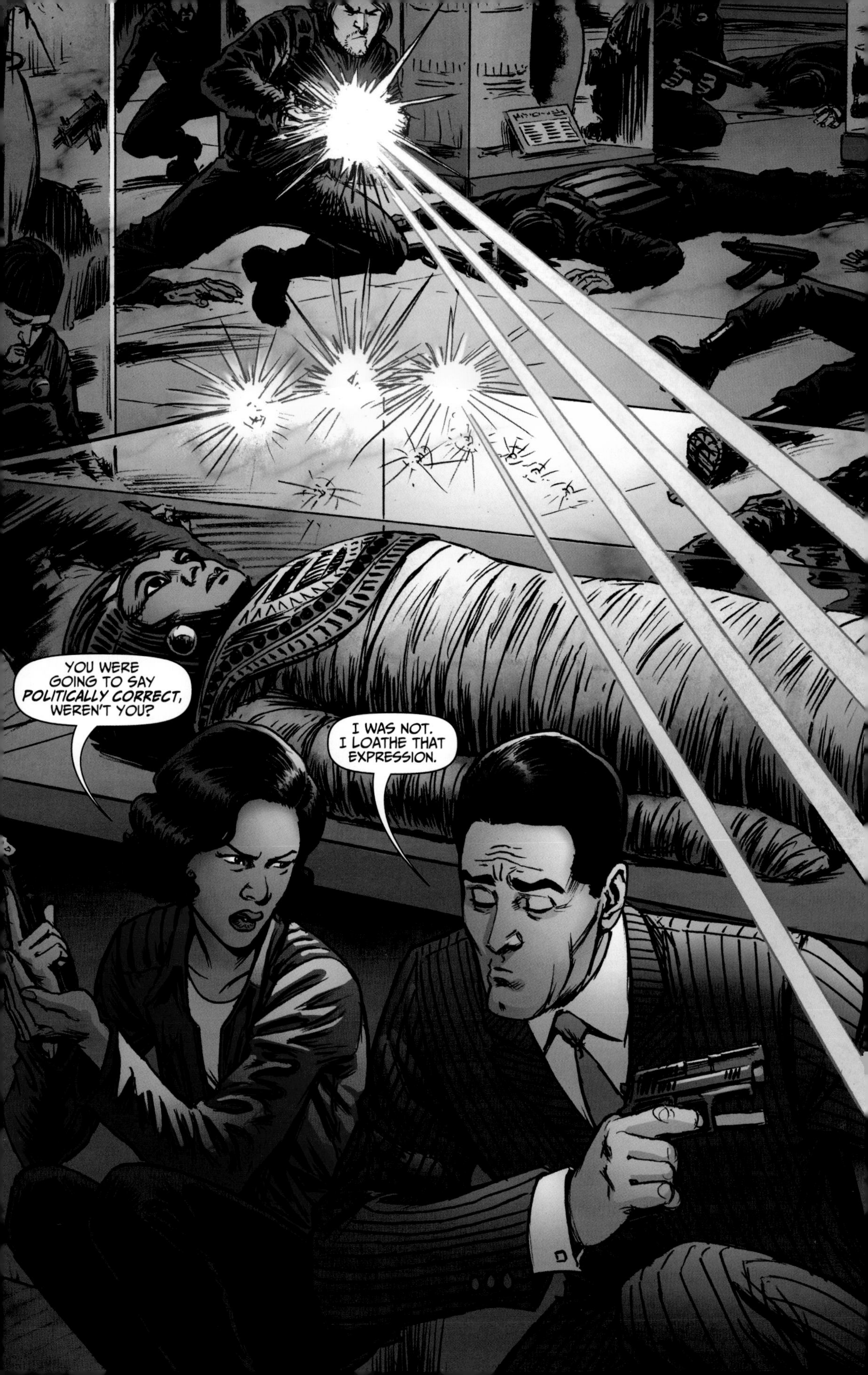
YOU WERE GOING TO SAY *POLITICALLY CORRECT*, WEREN'T YOU?
I WAS NOT. I LOATHE THAT EXPRESSION.

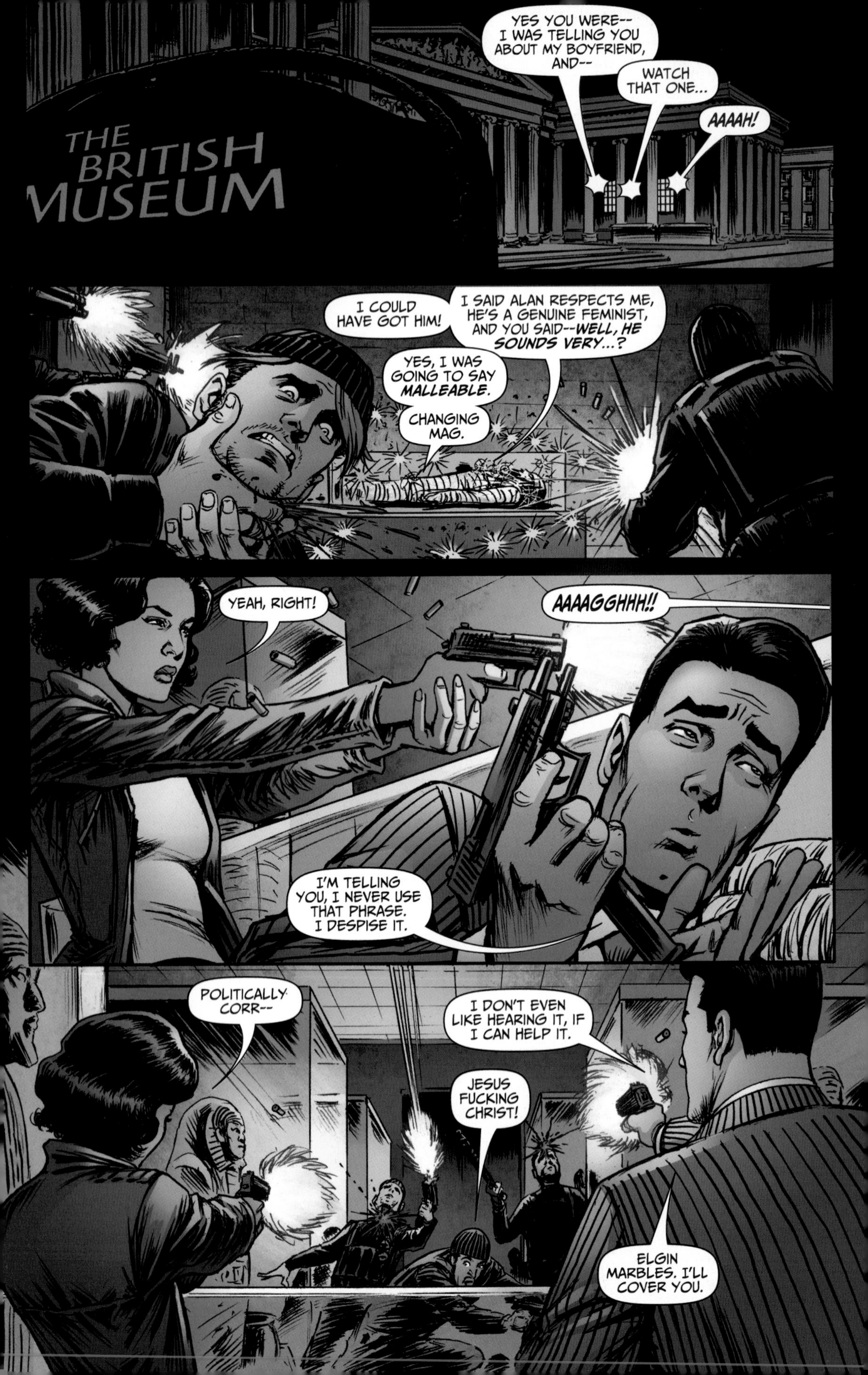
THE BRITISH MUSEUM
YES YOU WERE-- I WAS TELLING YOU ABOUT MY BOYFRIEND, AND--
WATCH THAT ONE...
AAAAH!
I COULD HAVE GOT HIM!
I SAID ALAN RESPECTS ME, HE'S A GENUINE FEMINIST, AND YOU SAID--WELL, HE SOUNDS VERY...?
YES, I WAS GOING TO SAY MALLEABLE.
CHANGING MAG.
YEAH, RIGHT!
AAAAGGHHH!!
I'M TELLING YOU, I NEVER USE THAT PHRASE. I DESPISE IT.
POLITICALLY CORR--
I DON'T EVEN LIKE HEARING IT, IF I CAN HELP IT.
JESUS FUCKING CHRIST!
ELGIN MARBLES. I'LL COVER YOU.

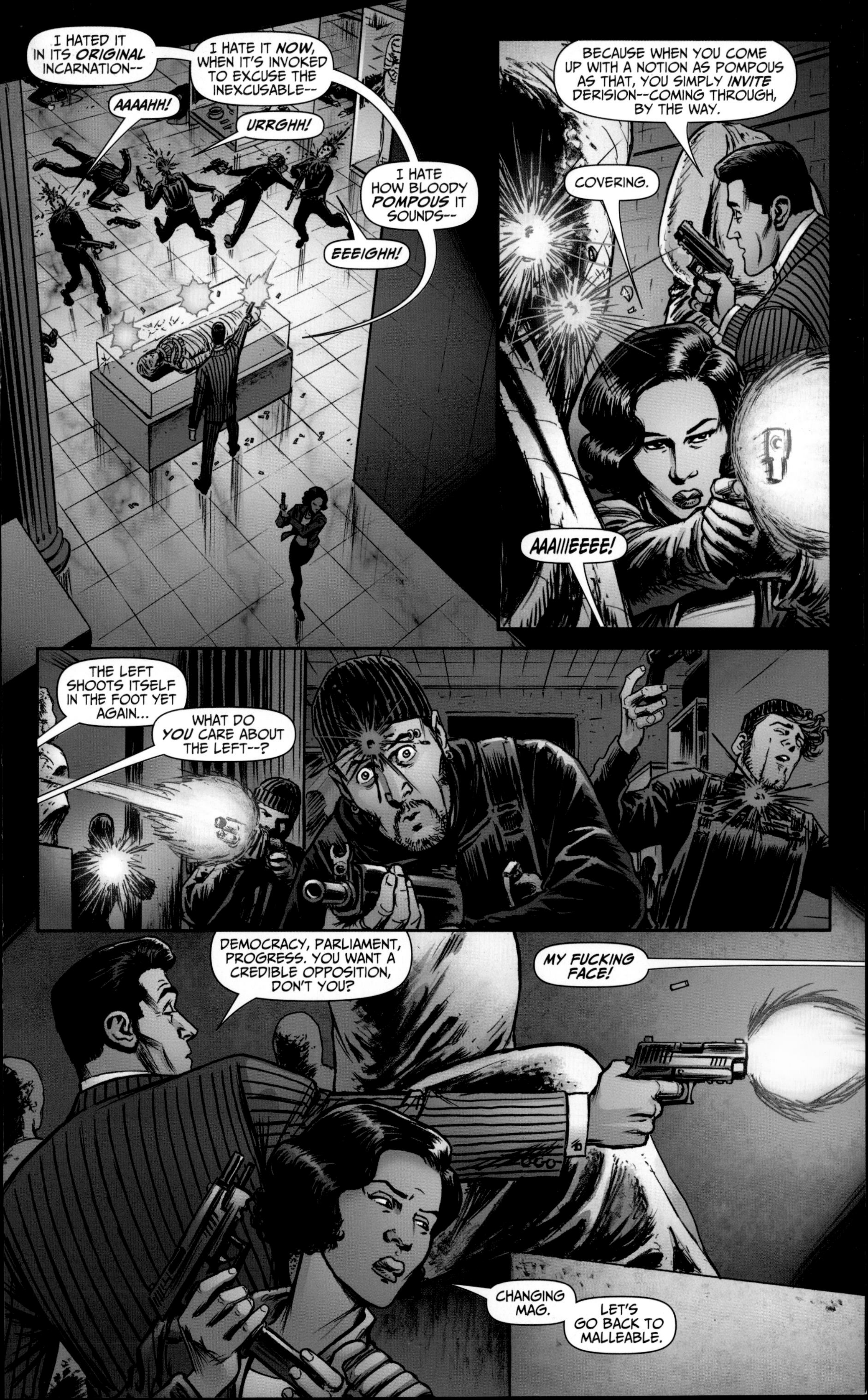
I HATED IT IN ITS ORIGINAL INCARNATION--
I HATE IT NOW, WHEN IT'S INVOKED TO EXCUSE THE INEXCUSABLE--
AAAAHH!
URRGHH!
I HATE HOW BLOODY POMPOUS IT SOUNDS--
EEEIGHH!
BECAUSE WHEN YOU COME UP WITH A NOTION AS POMPOUS AS THAT, YOU SIMPLY INVITE DERISION--COMING THROUGH, BY THE WAY.
COVERING.
AAAIIIEEEE!
THE LEFT SHOOTS ITSELF IN THE FOOT YET AGAIN...
WHAT DO YOU CARE ABOUT THE LEFT--?
DEMOCRACY, PARLIAMENT, PROGRESS. YOU WANT A CREDIBLE OPPOSITION, DON'T YOU?
MY FUCKING FACE!
CHANGING MAG.
LET'S GO BACK TO MALLEABLE.

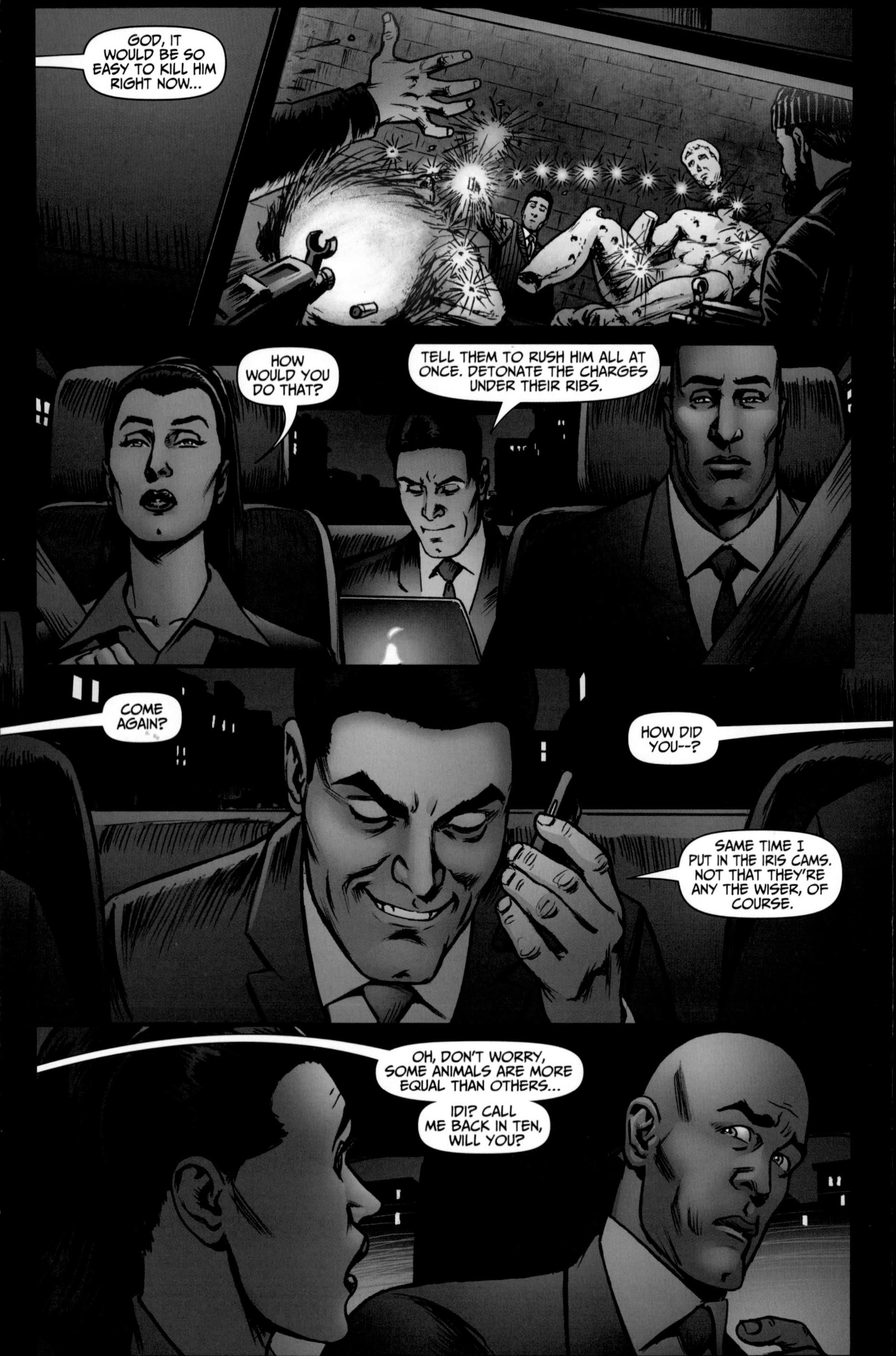
GOD, IT WOULD BE SO EASY TO KILL HIM RIGHT NOW...
HOW WOULD YOU DO THAT?
TELL THEM TO RUSH HIM ALL AT ONCE. DETONATE THE CHARGES UNDER THEIR RIBS.
COME AGAIN?
HOW DID YOU--?
SAME TIME I PUT IN THE IRIS CAMS. NOT THAT THEY'RE ANY THE WISER, OF COURSE.
OH, DON'T WORRY, SOME ANIMALS ARE MORE EQUAL THAN OTHERS...
IDI? CALL ME BACK IN TEN, WILL YOU?

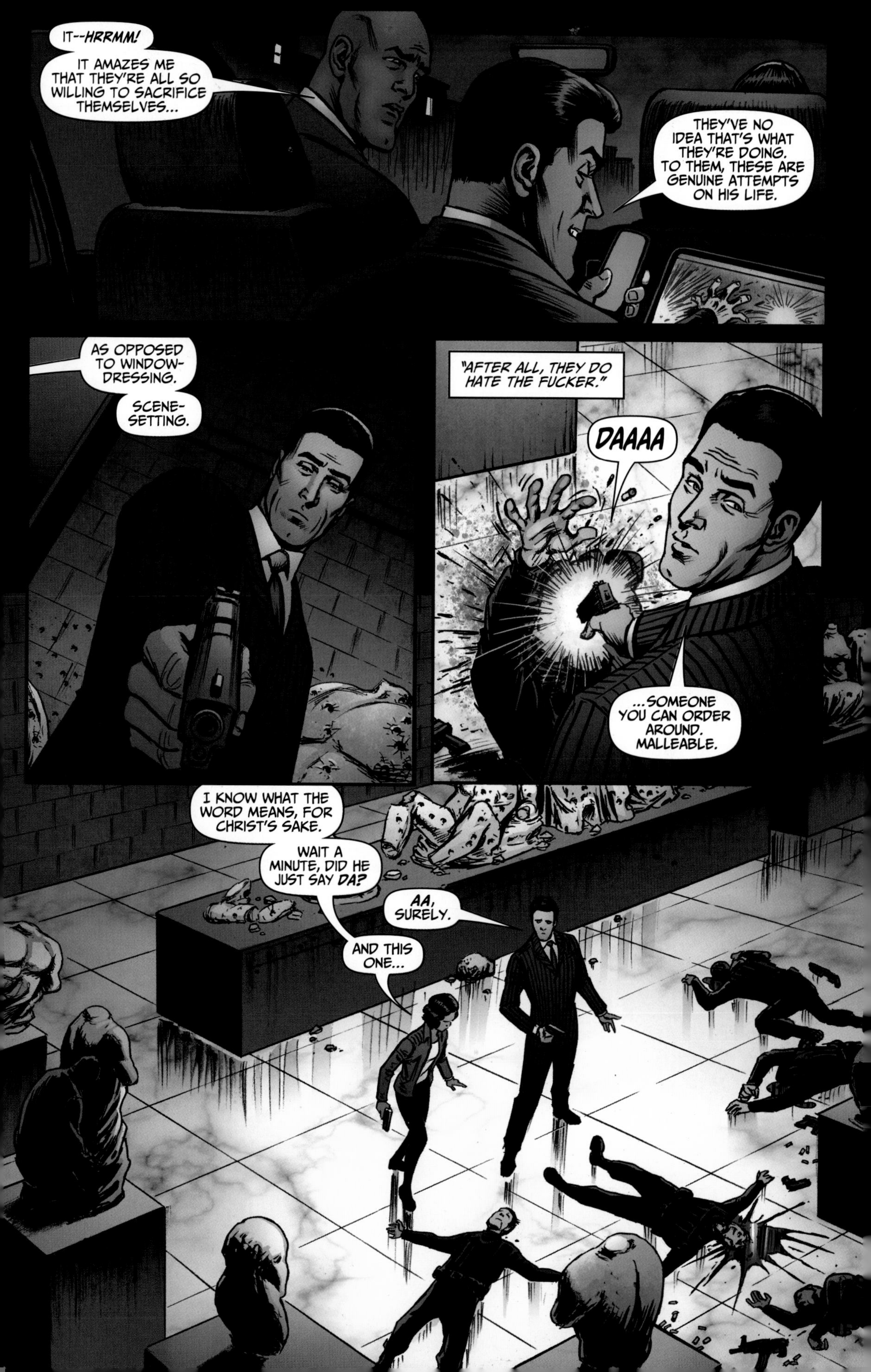

IT--HRRMM!
IT AMAZES ME THAT THEY'RE ALL SO WILLING TO SACRIFICE THEMSELVES...
THEY'VE NO IDEA THAT'S WHAT THEY'RE DOING. TO THEM, THESE ARE GENUINE ATTEMPTS ON HIS LIFE.
AS OPPOSED TO WINDOW-DRESSING.
SCENE-SETTING.
"AFTER ALL, THEY DO HATE THE FUCKER."
DAAAA
...SOMEONE YOU CAN ORDER AROUND. MALLEABLE.
I KNOW WHAT THE WORD MEANS, FOR CHRIST'S SAKE.
WAIT A MINUTE, DID HE JUST SAY DA?
AA, SURELY.
AND THIS ONE...

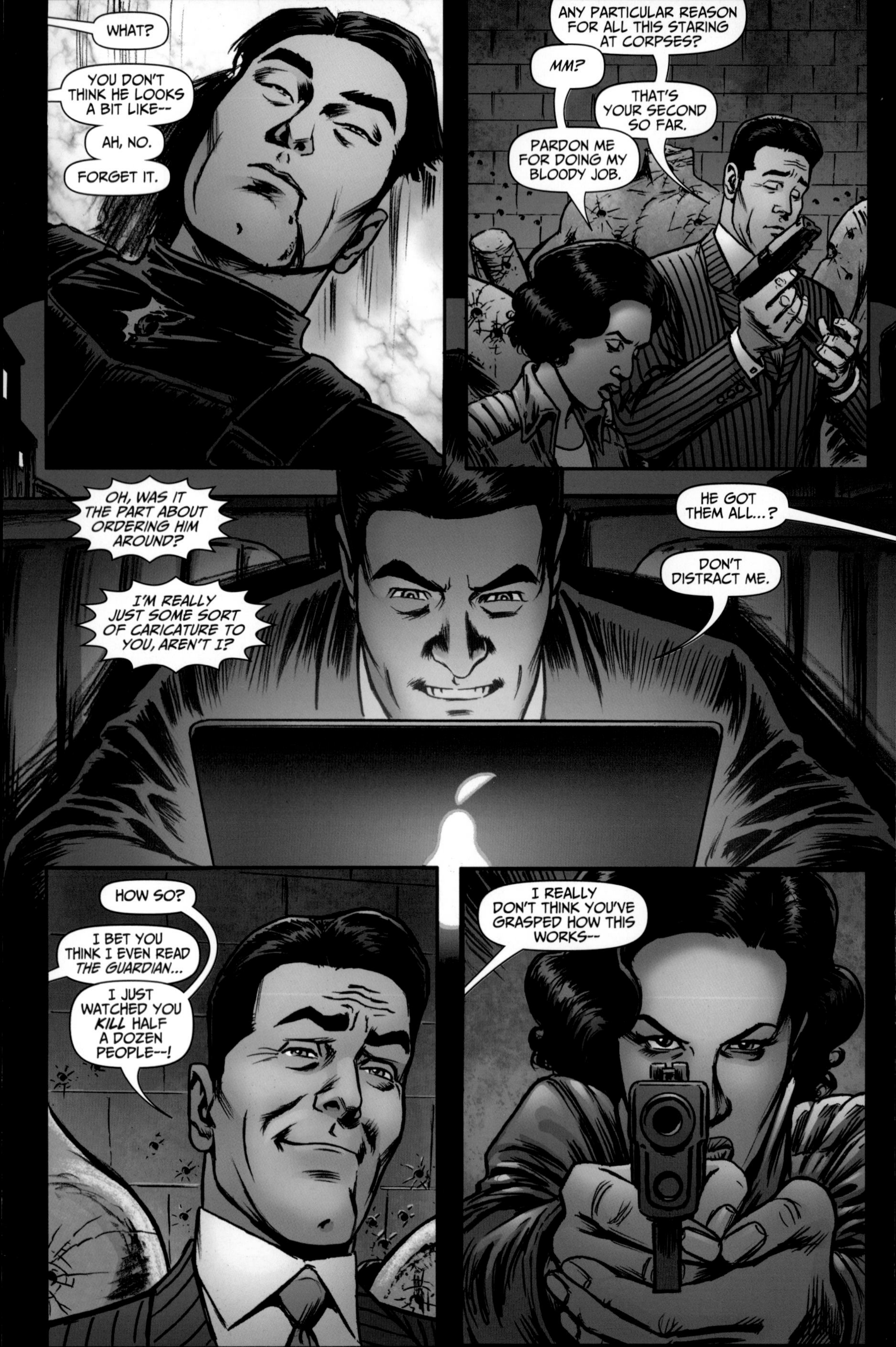
WHAT?
YOU DON'T THINK HE LOOKS A BIT LIKE--
AH, NO.
FORGET IT.
ANY PARTICULAR REASON FOR ALL THIS STARING AT CORPSES?
MM?
THAT'S YOUR SECOND SO FAR.
PARDON ME FOR DOING MY BLOODY JOB.
OH, WAS IT THE PART ABOUT ORDERING HIM AROUND?
I'M REALLY JUST SOME SORT OF CARICATURE TO YOU, AREN'T I?
HE GOT THEM ALL...?
DON'T DISTRACT ME.
HOW SO?
I BET YOU THINK I EVEN READ THE GUARDIAN...
I JUST WATCHED YOU KILL HALF A DOZEN PEOPLE--!
I REALLY DON'T THINK YOU'VE GRASPED HOW THIS WORKS--

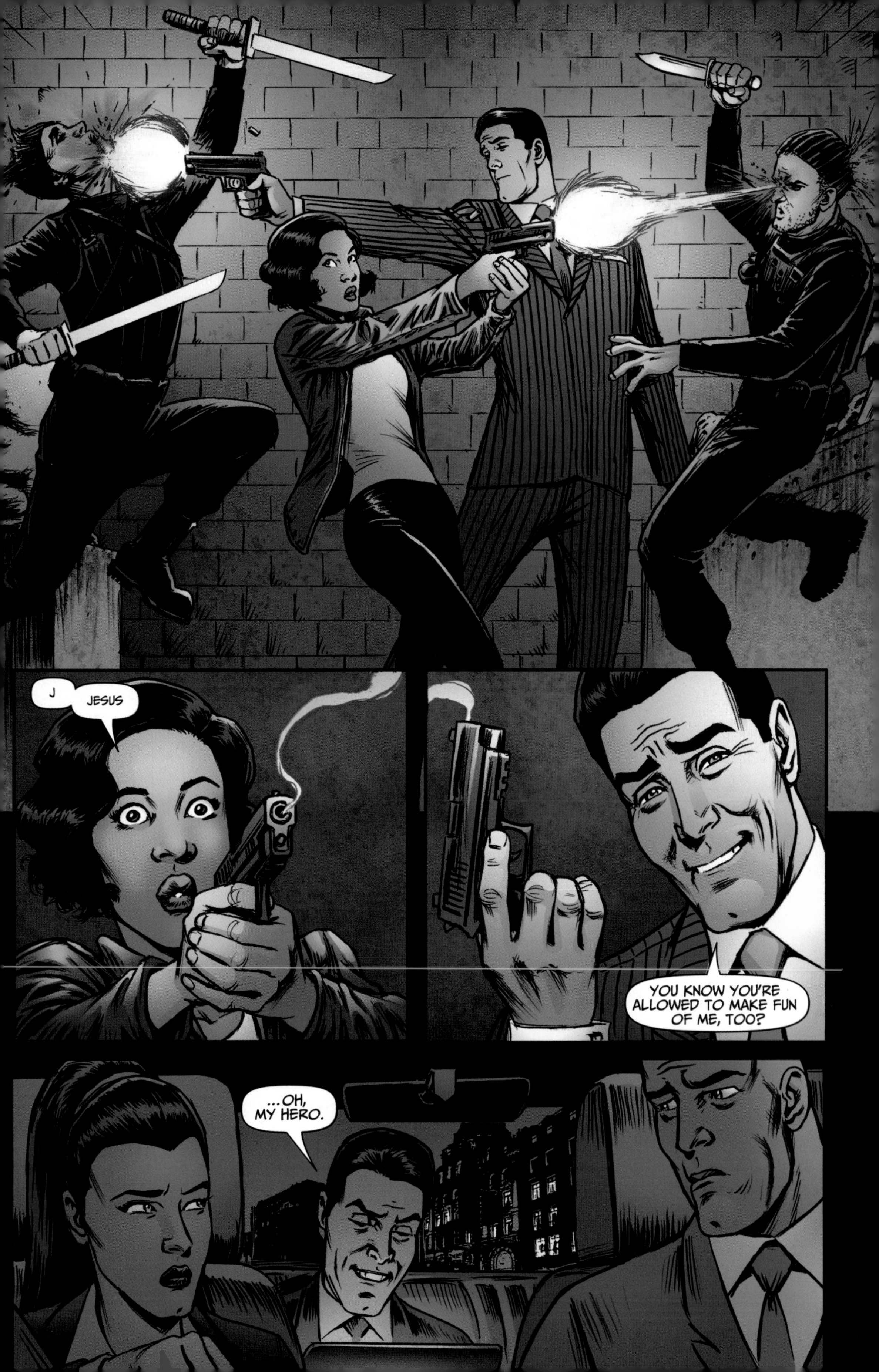

J
JESUS
YOU KNOW YOU'RE ALLOWED TO MAKE FUN OF ME, TOO?
...OH, MY HERO.

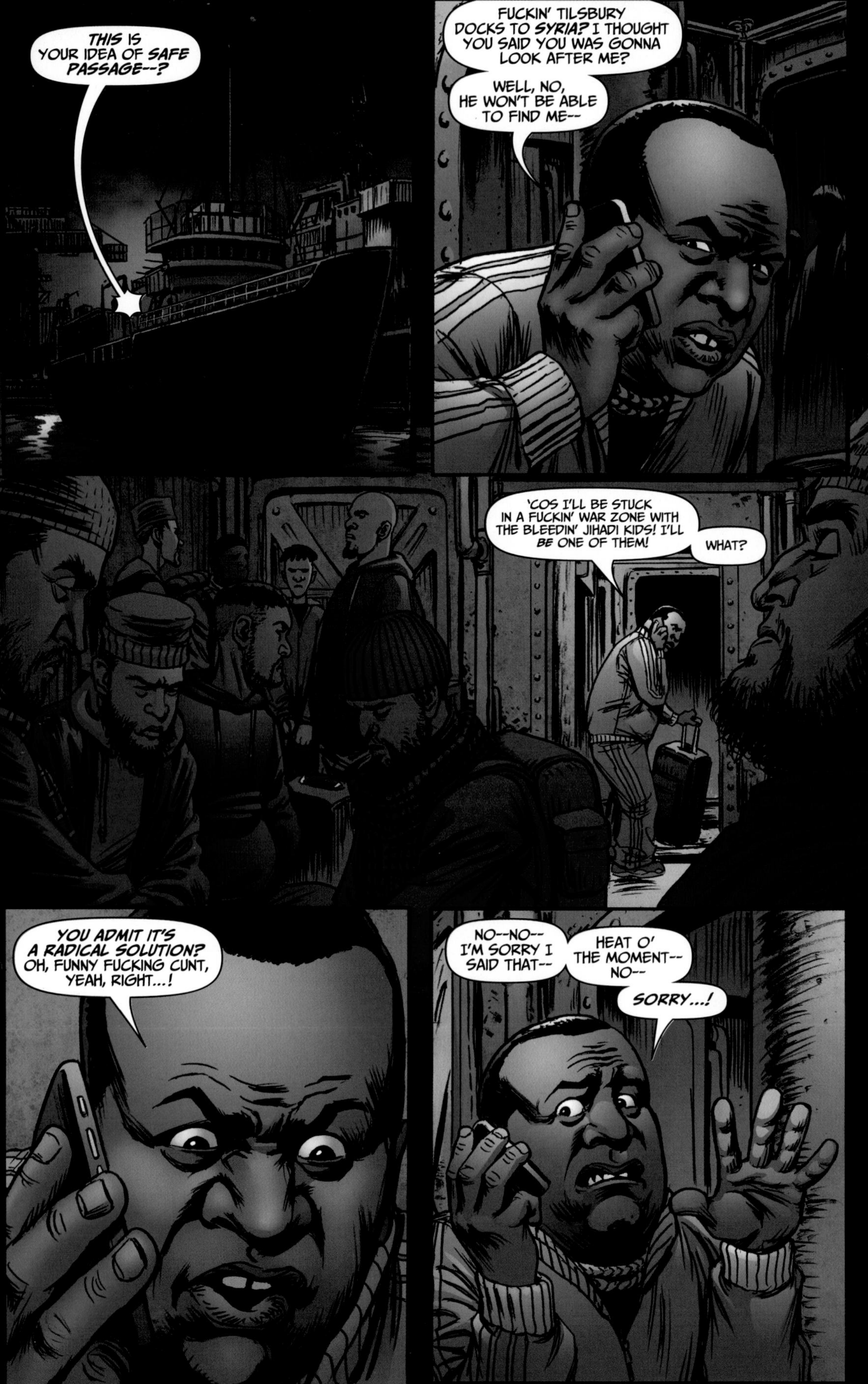
THIS IS YOUR IDEA OF SAFE PASSAGE--?
FUCKIN' TILSBURY DOCKS TO SYRIA? I THOUGHT YOU SAID YOU WAS GONNA LOOK AFTER ME?
WELL, NO, HE WON'T BE ABLE TO FIND ME--
'COS I'LL BE STUCK IN A FUCKIN' WAR ZONE WITH THE BLEEDIN' JIHADI KIDS! I'LL BE ONE OF THEM!
WHAT?
YOU ADMIT IT'S A RADICAL SOLUTION? OH, FUNNY FUCKING CUNT, YEAH, RIGHT...!
NO--NO-- I'M SORRY I SAID THAT--
HEAT O' THE MOMENT-- NO--
SORRY...!

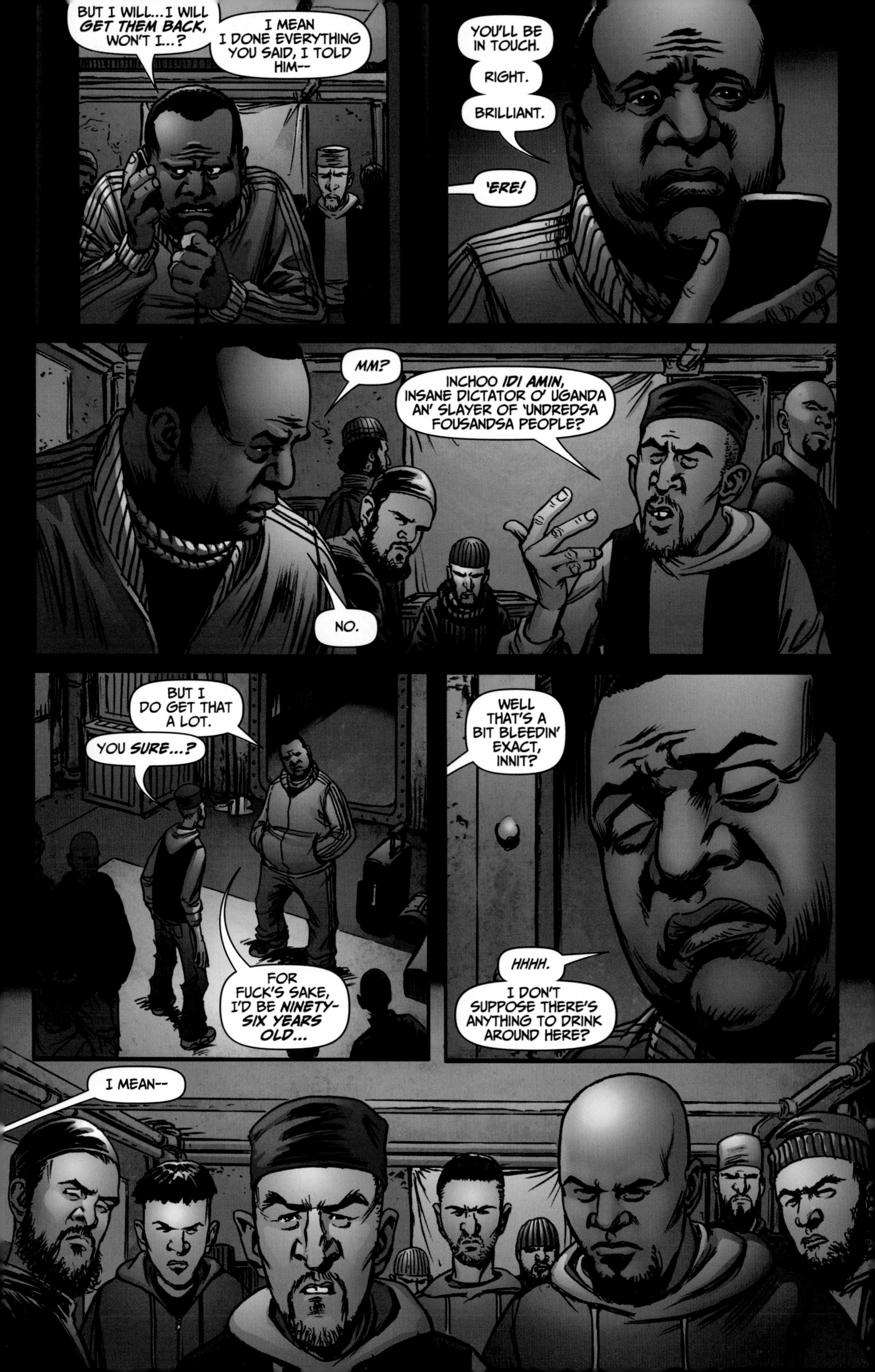
BUT I WILL... I WILL GET THEM BACK, WON'T I...?
I MEAN I DONE EVERYTHING YOU SAID, I TOLD HIM--
YOU'LL BE IN TOUCH.
RIGHT.
BRILLIANT.
'ERE!
MM?
INCHOO IDI AMIN, INSANE DICTATOR O' UGANDA AN' SLAYER OF 'UNDREDSA FOUSANDSA PEOPLE?
NO.
BUT I DO GET THAT A LOT.
YOU SURE...?
FOR FUCK'S SAKE, I'D BE NINETY-SIX YEARS OLD...
WELL THAT'S A BIT BLEEDIN' EXACT, INNIT?
HHHH.
I DON'T SUPPOSE THERE'S ANYTHING TO DRINK AROUND HERE?
I MEAN--

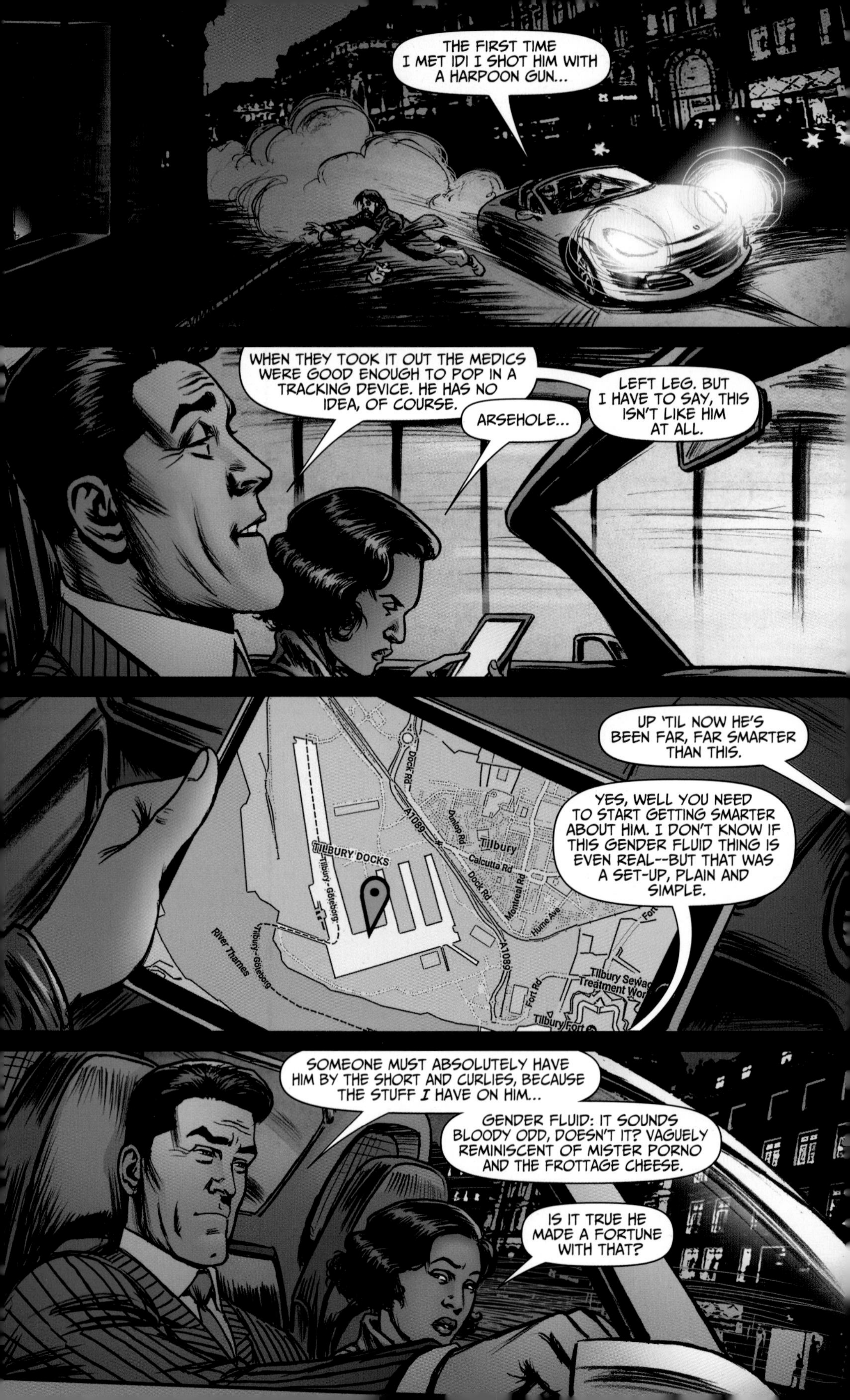
THE FIRST TIME I MET IDI I SHOT HIM WITH A HARPOON GUN...
WHEN THEY TOOK IT OUT THE MEDICS WERE GOOD ENOUGH TO POP IN A TRACKING DEVICE. HE HAS NO IDEA, OF COURSE.
ARSEHOLE...
LEFT LEG. BUT I HAVE TO SAY, THIS ISN'T LIKE HIM AT ALL.
UP 'TIL NOW HE'S BEEN FAR, FAR SMARTER THAN THIS.
YES, WELL YOU NEED TO START GETTING SMARTER ABOUT HIM. I DON'T KNOW IF THIS GENDER FLUID THING IS EVEN REAL--BUT THAT WAS A SET-UP, PLAIN AND SIMPLE.
Dock Rd
A1089
TILBURY DOCKS
Tilbury
Dunlop Rd
Calcutta Rd
Dock Rd
Montreal Rd
Hume Ave
Tilbury-Göteborg
River Thames
Fort Rd
Tilbury Fort
SOMEONE MUST ABSOLUTELY HAVE HIM BY THE SHORT AND CURLIES, BECAUSE THE STUFF *I* HAVE ON HIM...
GENDER FLUID: IT SOUNDS BLOODY ODD, DOESN'T IT? VAGUELY REMINISCENT OF MISTER PORNO AND THE FROTTAGE CHEESE.
IS IT TRUE HE MADE A FORTUNE WITH THAT?

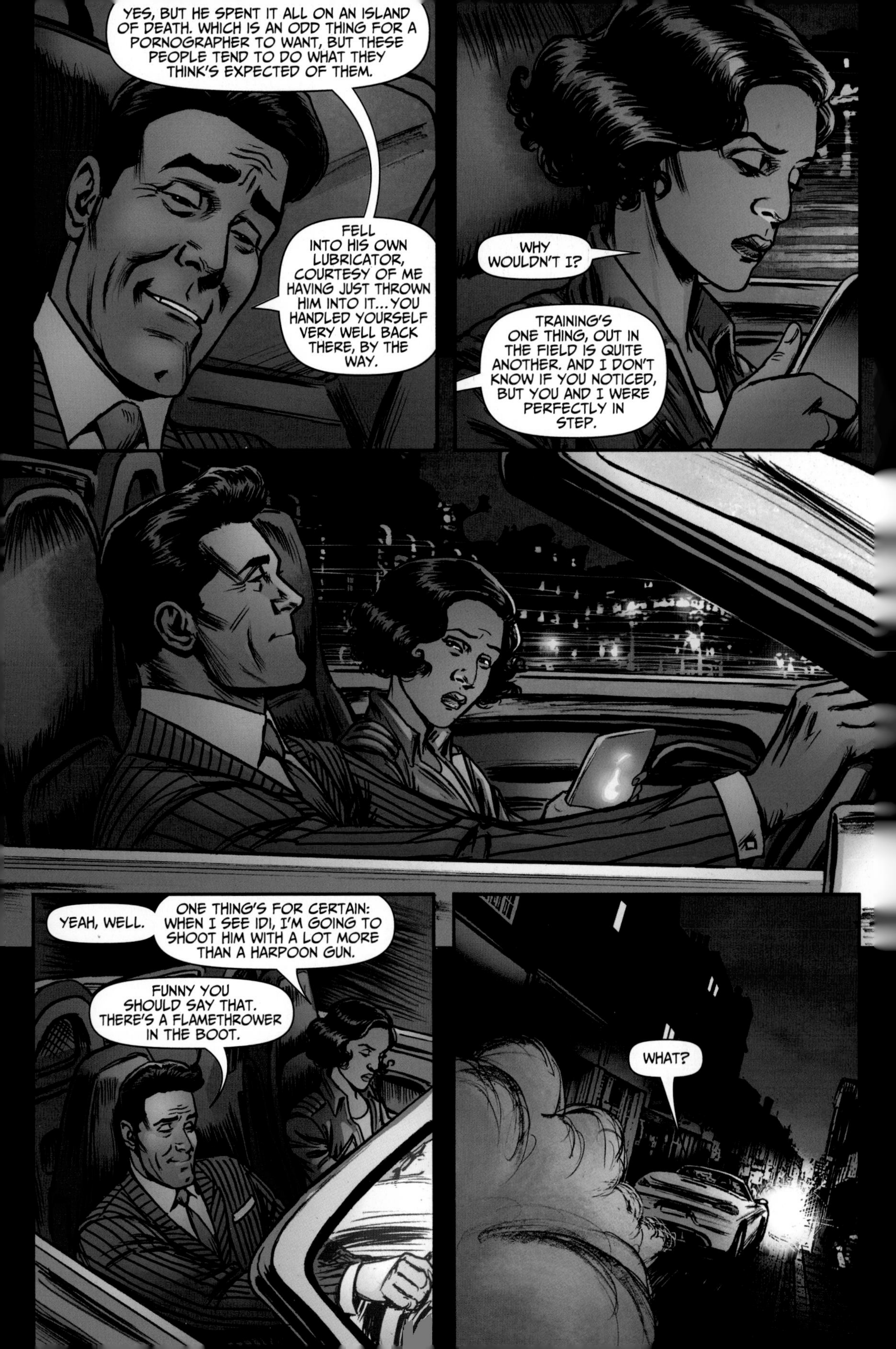
YES, BUT HE SPENT IT ALL ON AN ISLAND OF DEATH. WHICH IS AN ODD THING FOR A PORNOGRAPHER TO WANT, BUT THESE PEOPLE TEND TO DO WHAT THEY THINK'S EXPECTED OF THEM.
FELL INTO HIS OWN LUBRICATOR, COURTESY OF ME HAVING JUST THROWN HIM INTO IT...YOU HANDLED YOURSELF VERY WELL BACK THERE, BY THE WAY.
WHY WOULDN'T I?
TRAINING'S ONE THING, OUT IN THE FIELD IS QUITE ANOTHER. AND I DON'T KNOW IF YOU NOTICED, BUT YOU AND I WERE PERFECTLY IN STEP.
YEAH, WELL.
ONE THING'S FOR CERTAIN: WHEN I SEE IDI, I'M GOING TO SHOOT HIM WITH A LOT MORE THAN A HARPOON GUN.
FUNNY YOU SHOULD SAY THAT. THERE'S A FLAMETHROWER IN THE BOOT.
WHAT?

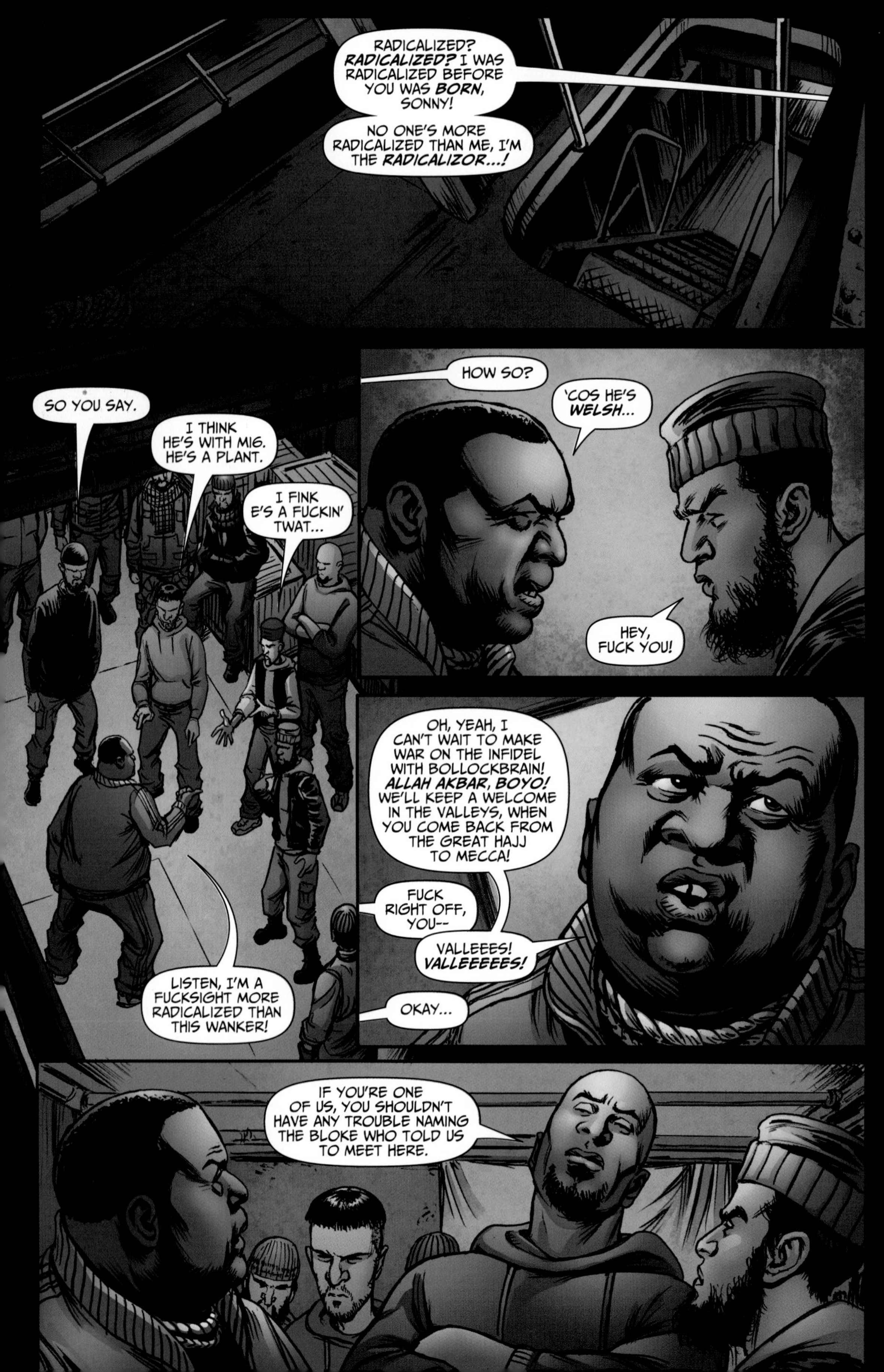
RADICALIZED? RADICALIZED? I WAS RADICALIZED BEFORE YOU WAS BORN, SONNY!
NO ONE'S MORE RADICALIZED THAN ME, I'M THE RADICALIZOR...!
SO YOU SAY.
I THINK HE'S WITH MI6. HE'S A PLANT.
I FINK E'S A FUCKIN' TWAT...
LISTEN, I'M A FUCKSIGHT MORE RADICALIZED THAN THIS WANKER!
HOW SO?
'COS HE'S WELSH...
HEY, FUCK YOU!
OH, YEAH, I CAN'T WAIT TO MAKE WAR ON THE INFIDEL WITH BOLLOCKBRAIN! ALLAH AKBAR, BOYO! WE'LL KEEP A WELCOME IN THE VALLEYS, WHEN YOU COME BACK FROM THE GREAT HAJJ TO MECCA!
FUCK RIGHT OFF, YOU--
VALLEEES! VALLEEEEEES!
OKAY...
IF YOU'RE ONE OF US, YOU SHOULDN'T HAVE ANY TROUBLE NAMING THE BLOKE WHO TOLD US TO MEET HERE.

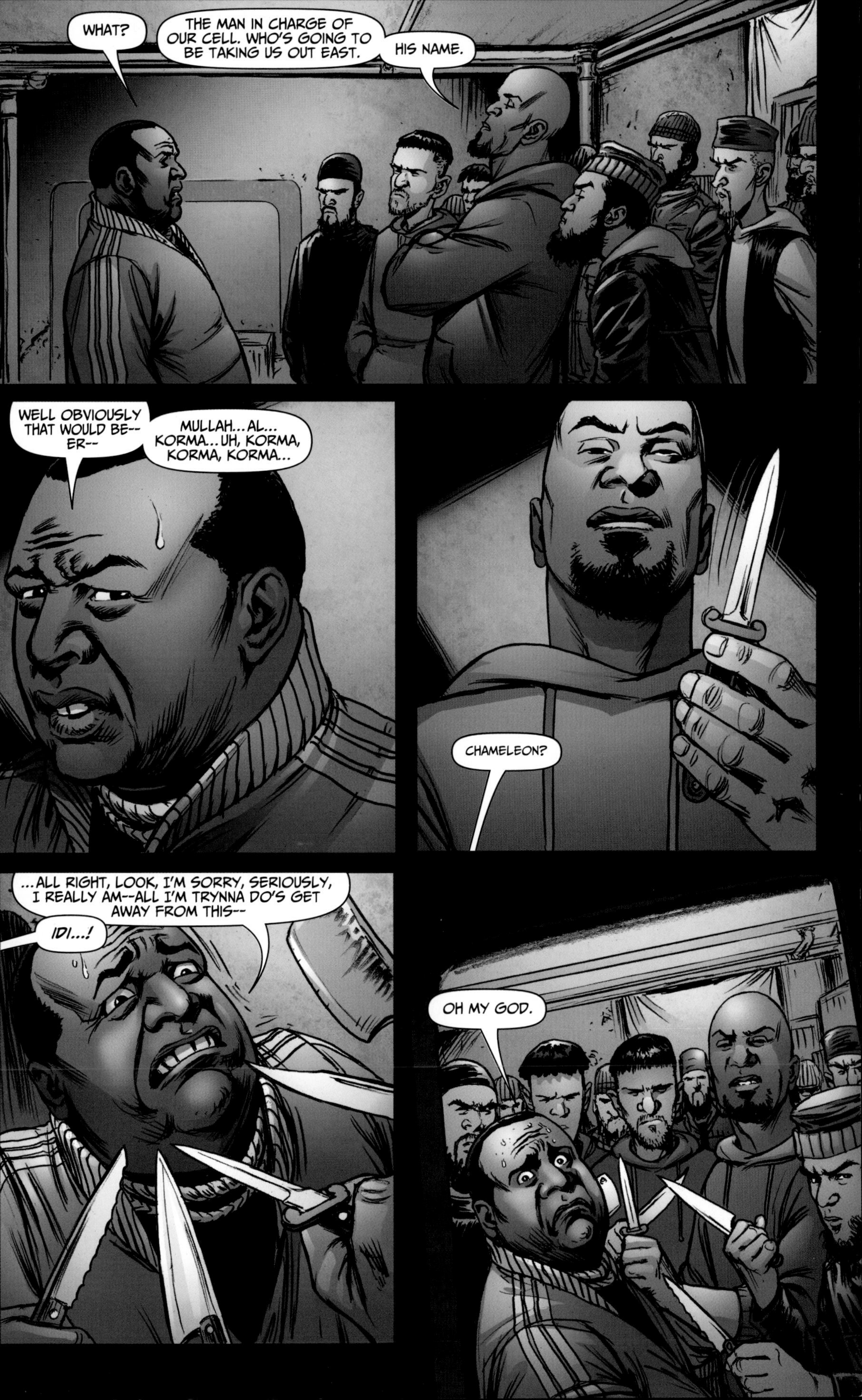
WHAT?
THE MAN IN CHARGE OF OUR CELL. WHO'S GOING TO BE TAKING US OUT EAST.
HIS NAME.
WELL OBVIOUSLY THAT WOULD BE-- ER--
MULLAH...AL... KORMA...UH, KORMA, KORMA, KORMA...
CHAMELEON?
...ALL RIGHT, LOOK, I'M SORRY, SERIOUSLY, I REALLY AM--ALL I'M TRYNNA DO'S GET AWAY FROM THIS--
IDI...!
OH MY GOD.

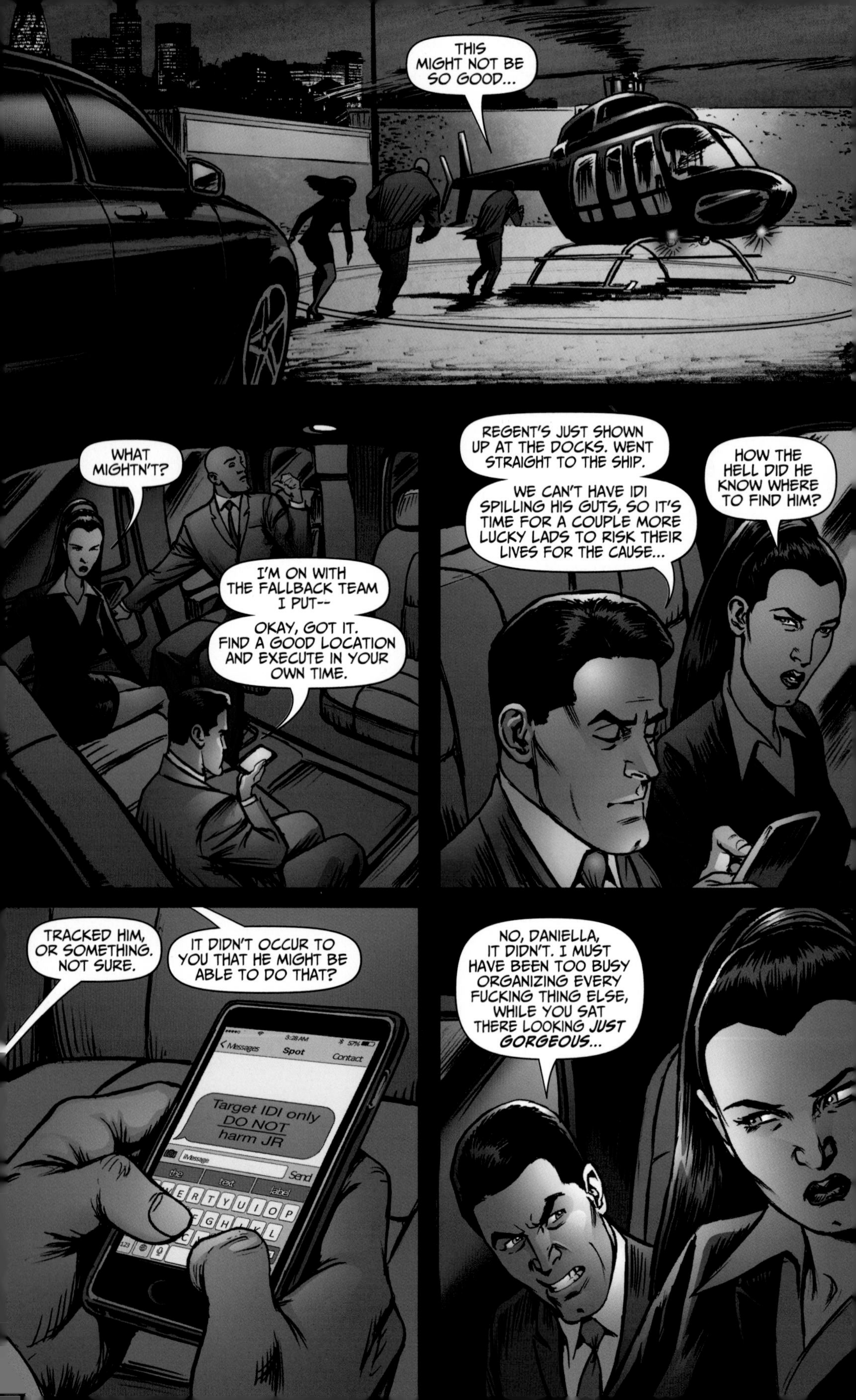
THIS MIGHT NOT BE SO GOOD...
WHAT MIGHTN'T?
I'M ON WITH THE FALLBACK TEAM I PUT--
OKAY, GOT IT. FIND A GOOD LOCATION AND EXECUTE IN YOUR OWN TIME.
REGENT'S JUST SHOWN UP AT THE DOCKS. WENT STRAIGHT TO THE SHIP.
WE CAN'T HAVE IDI SPILLING HIS GUTS, SO IT'S TIME FOR A COUPLE MORE LUCKY LADS TO RISK THEIR LIVES FOR THE CAUSE...
HOW THE HELL DID HE KNOW WHERE TO FIND HIM?
TRACKED HIM, OR SOMETHING. NOT SURE.
IT DIDN'T OCCUR TO YOU THAT HE MIGHT BE ABLE TO DO THAT?
Messages
Spot
Contact
Target IDI only
DO NOT
harm JR
Send
NO, DANIELLA, IT DIDN'T. I MUST HAVE BEEN TOO BUSY ORGANIZING EVERY FUCKING THING ELSE, WHILE YOU SAT THERE LOOKING JUST GORGEOUS...

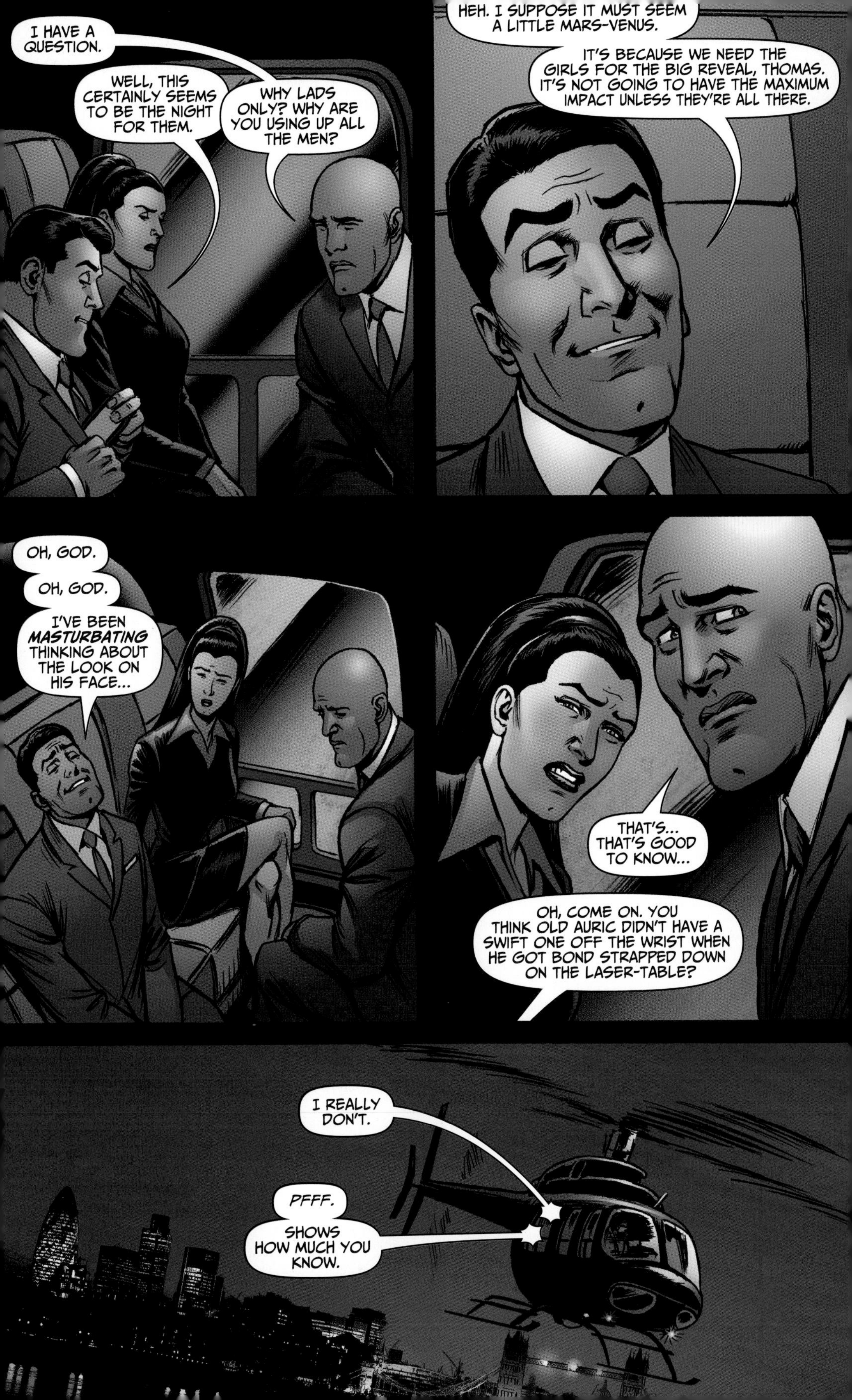
I HAVE A QUESTION.
WELL, THIS CERTAINLY SEEMS TO BE THE NIGHT FOR THEM.
WHY LADS ONLY? WHY ARE YOU USING UP ALL THE MEN?
HEH. I SUPPOSE IT MUST SEEM A LITTLE MARS-VENUS.
IT'S BECAUSE WE NEED THE GIRLS FOR THE BIG REVEAL, THOMAS. IT'S NOT GOING TO HAVE THE MAXIMUM IMPACT UNLESS THEY'RE ALL THERE.
OH, GOD.
OH, GOD.
I'VE BEEN *MASTURBATING* THINKING ABOUT THE LOOK ON HIS FACE...
THAT'S... THAT'S GOOD TO KNOW...
OH, COME ON. YOU THINK OLD AURIC DIDN'T HAVE A SWIFT ONE OFF THE WRIST WHEN HE GOT BOND STRAPPED DOWN ON THE LASER-TABLE?
I REALLY DON'T.
PFFF.
SHOWS HOW MUCH YOU KNOW.

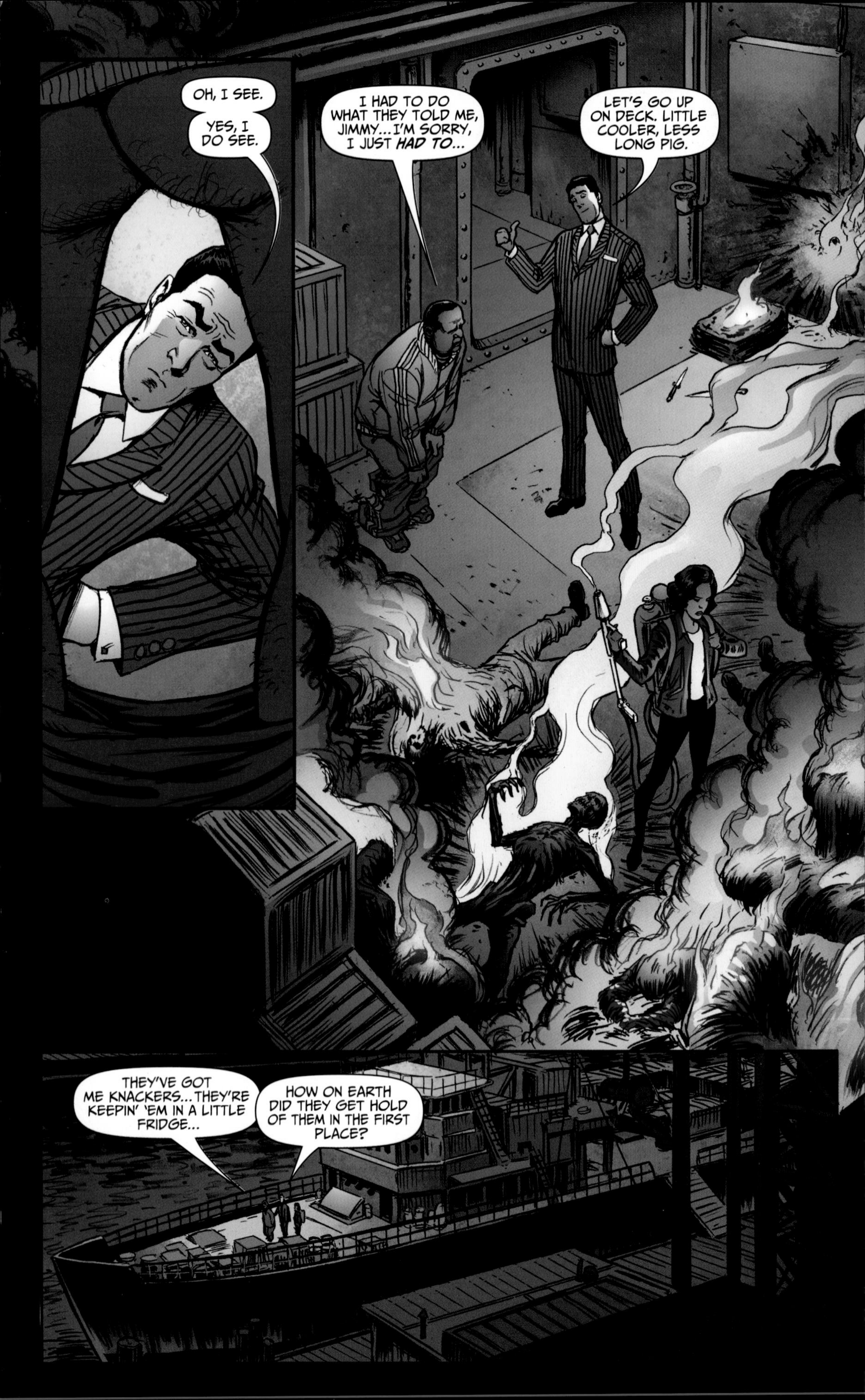
OH, I SEE.
YES, I DO SEE.
I HAD TO DO WHAT THEY TOLD ME, JIMMY... I'M SORRY, I JUST HAD TO...
LET'S GO UP ON DECK. LITTLE COOLER, LESS LONG PIG.
THEY'VE GOT ME KNACKERS... THEY'RE KEEPIN' 'EM IN A LITTLE FRIDGE...
HOW ON EARTH DID THEY GET HOLD OF THEM IN THE FIRST PLACE?

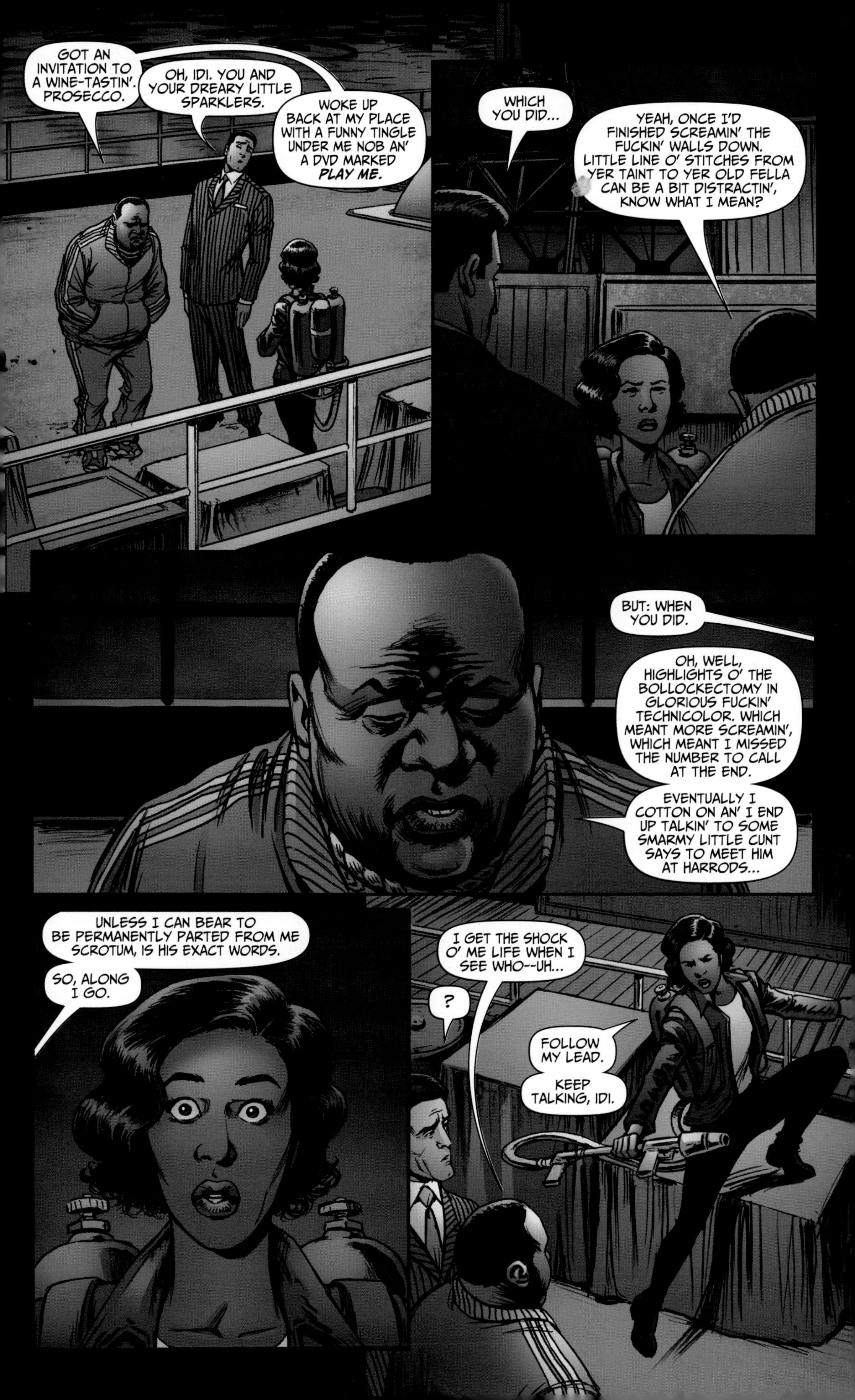

GOT AN INVITATION TO A WINE-TASTIN'. PROSECCO.
OH, IDI. YOU AND YOUR DREARY LITTLE SPARKLERS.
WOKE UP BACK AT MY PLACE WITH A FUNNY TINGLE UNDER ME NOB AN' A DVD MARKED ***PLAY ME.***
WHICH YOU DID...
YEAH, ONCE I'D FINISHED SCREAMIN' THE FUCKIN' WALLS DOWN. LITTLE LINE O' STITCHES FROM YER TAINT TO YER OLD FELLA CAN BE A BIT DISTRACTIN', KNOW WHAT I MEAN?
BUT: WHEN YOU DID.
OH, WELL, HIGHLIGHTS O' THE BOLLOCKECTOMY IN GLORIOUS FUCKIN' TECHNICOLOR. WHICH MEANT MORE SCREAMIN', WHICH MEANT I MISSED THE NUMBER TO CALL AT THE END.
EVENTUALLY I COTTON ON AN' I END UP TALKIN' TO SOME SMARMY LITTLE CUNT SAYS TO MEET HIM AT HARRODS...
UNLESS I CAN BEAR TO BE PERMANENTLY PARTED FROM ME SCROTUM, IS HIS EXACT WORDS.
SO, ALONG I GO.
I GET THE SHOCK O' ME LIFE WHEN I SEE WHO--UH...
?
FOLLOW MY LEAD.
KEEP TALKING, IDI.

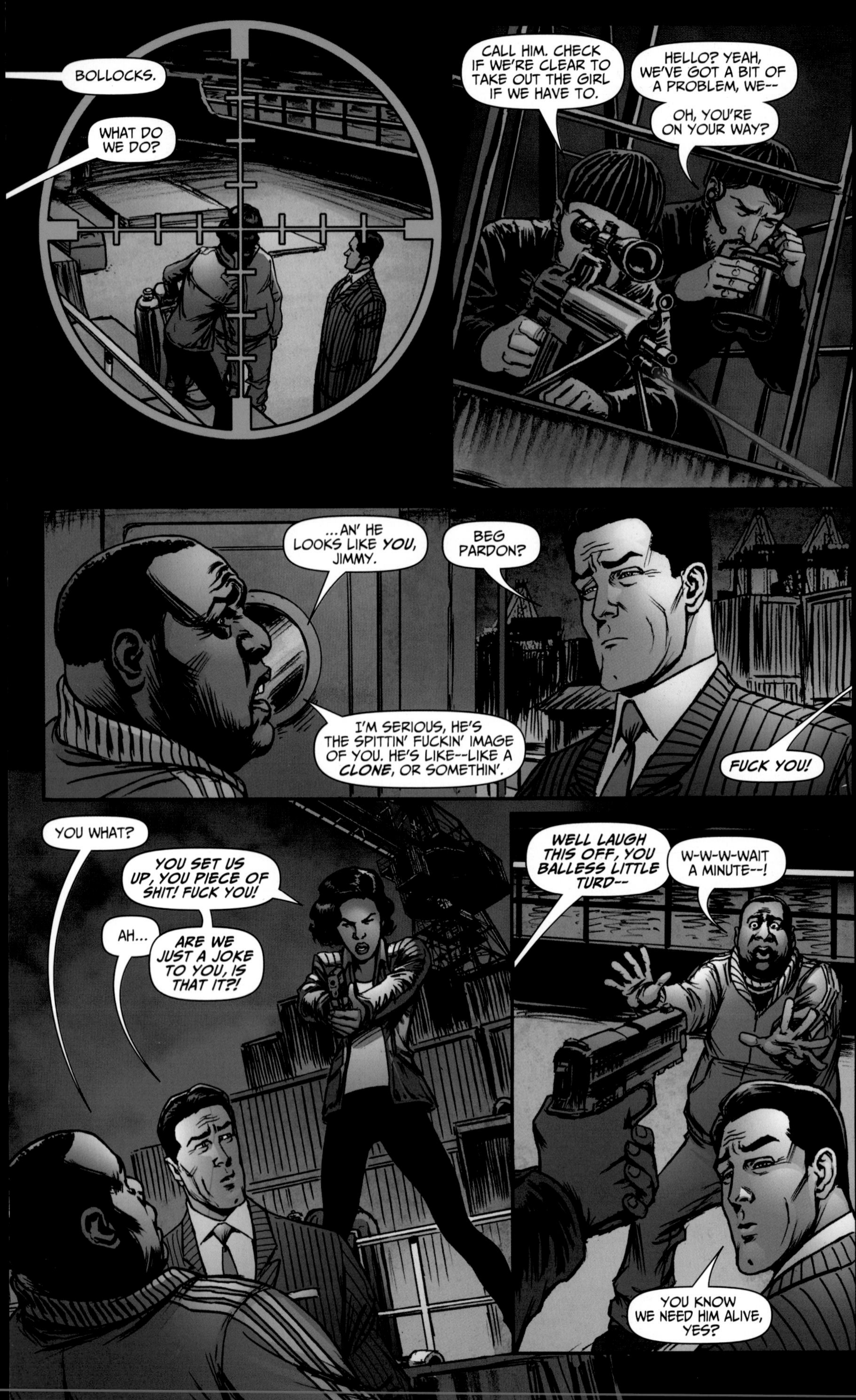
BOLLOCKS.
WHAT DO WE DO?
CALL HIM. CHECK IF WE'RE CLEAR TO TAKE OUT THE GIRL IF WE HAVE TO.
HELLO? YEAH, WE'VE GOT A BIT OF A PROBLEM, WE--
OH, YOU'RE ON YOUR WAY?
...AN' HE LOOKS LIKE YOU, JIMMY.
BEG PARDON?
I'M SERIOUS, HE'S THE SPITTIN' FUCKIN' IMAGE OF YOU. HE'S LIKE--LIKE A CLONE, OR SOMETHIN'.
FUCK YOU!
YOU WHAT?
YOU SET US UP, YOU PIECE OF SHIT! FUCK YOU!
AH...
ARE WE JUST A JOKE TO YOU, IS THAT IT?!
WELL LAUGH THIS OFF, YOU BALLESS LITTLE TURD--
W-W-W-WAIT A MINUTE--!
YOU KNOW WE NEED HIM ALIVE, YES?

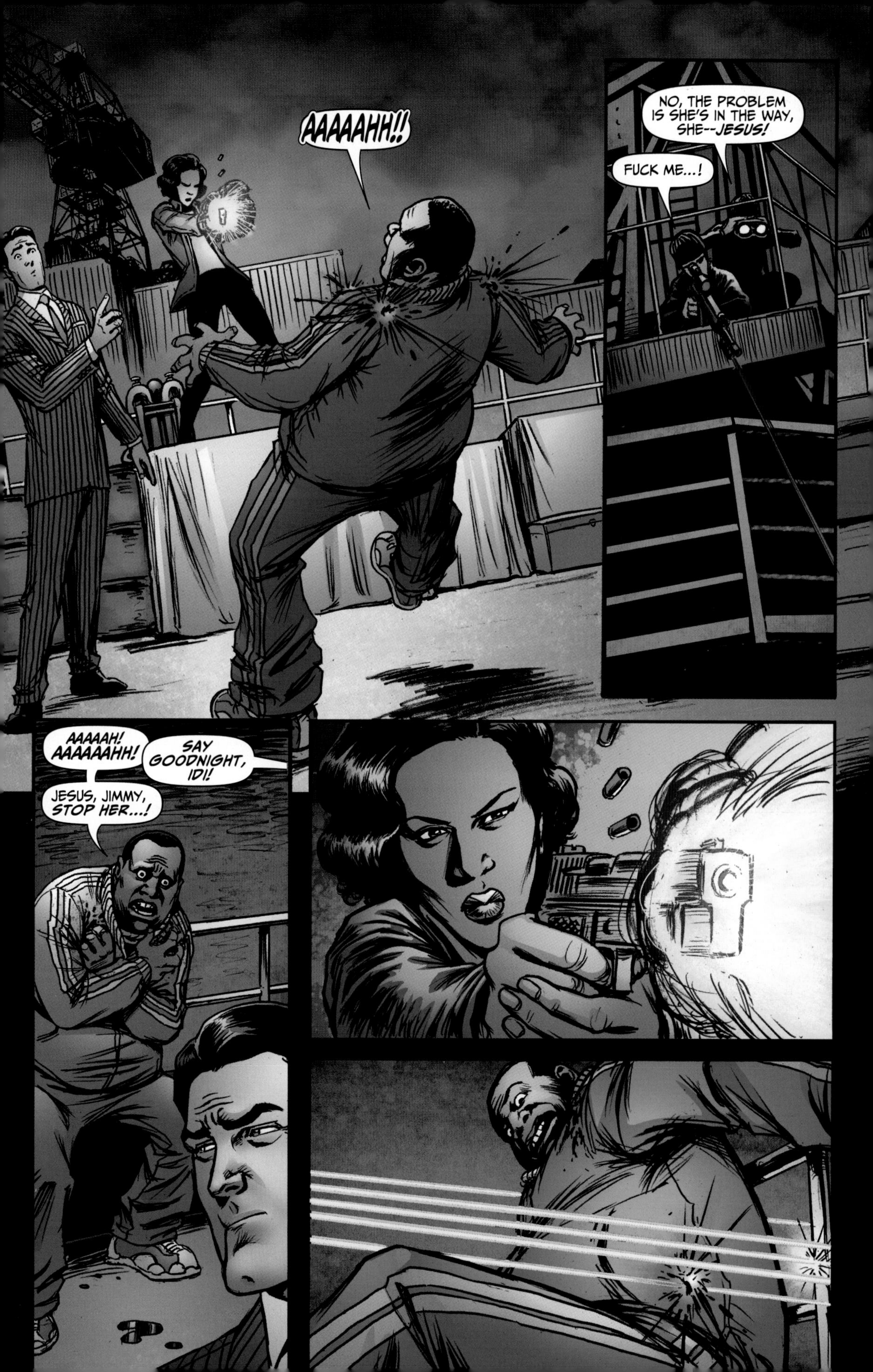

AAAAAHH!!
NO, THE PROBLEM IS SHE'S IN THE WAY, SHE--JESUS!
FUCK ME...!
AAAAAH! AAAAAAHH!
SAY GOODNIGHT, IDI!
JESUS, JIMMY, STOP HER...!

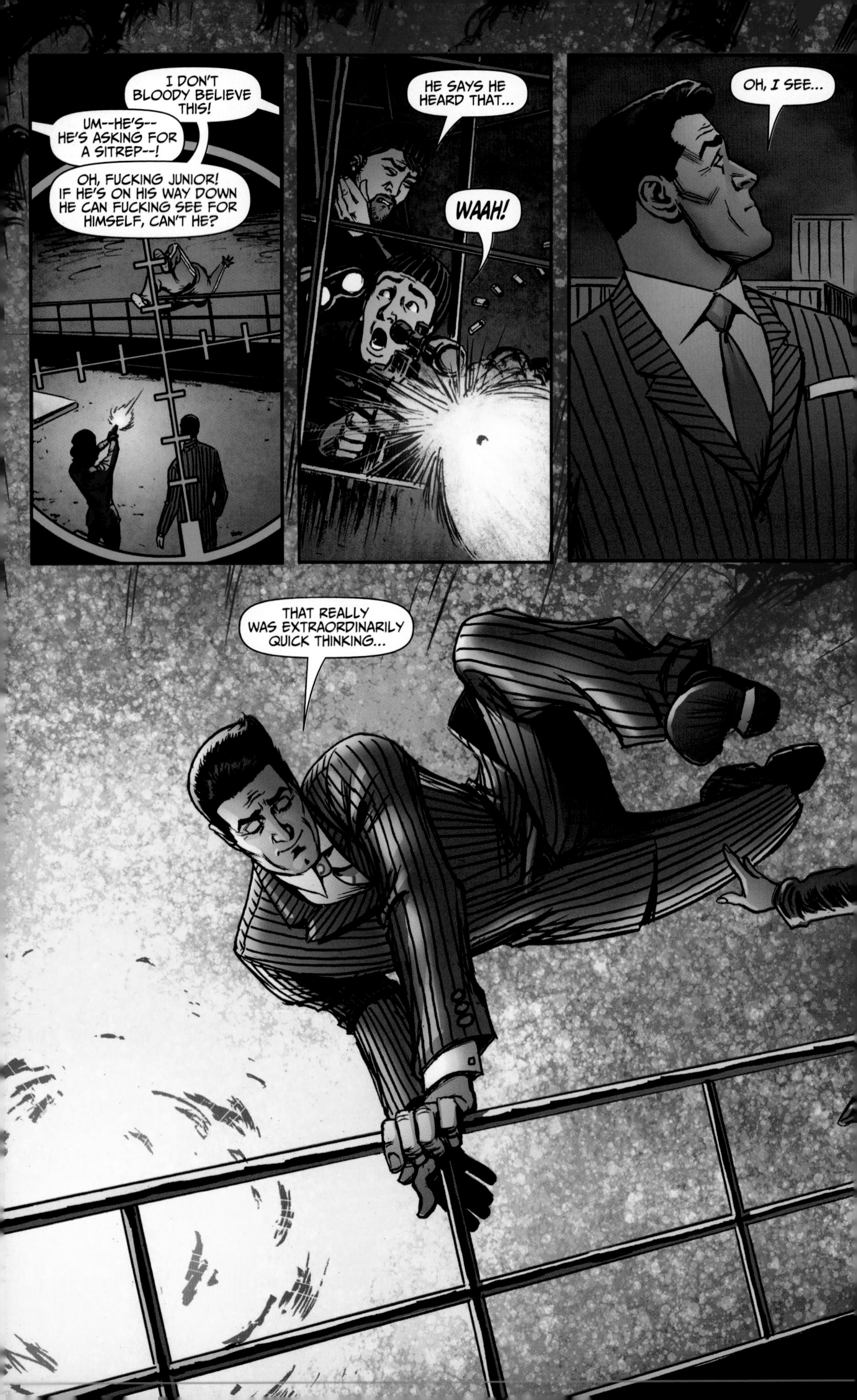
I DON'T BLOODY BELIEVE THIS!
UM--HE'S-- HE'S ASKING FOR A SITREP--!
OH, FUCKING JUNIOR! IF HE'S ON HIS WAY DOWN HE CAN FUCKING SEE FOR HIMSELF, CAN'T HE?
HE SAYS HE HEARD THAT...
WAAH!
OH, I SEE...
THAT REALLY WAS EXTRAORDINARILY QUICK THINKING...

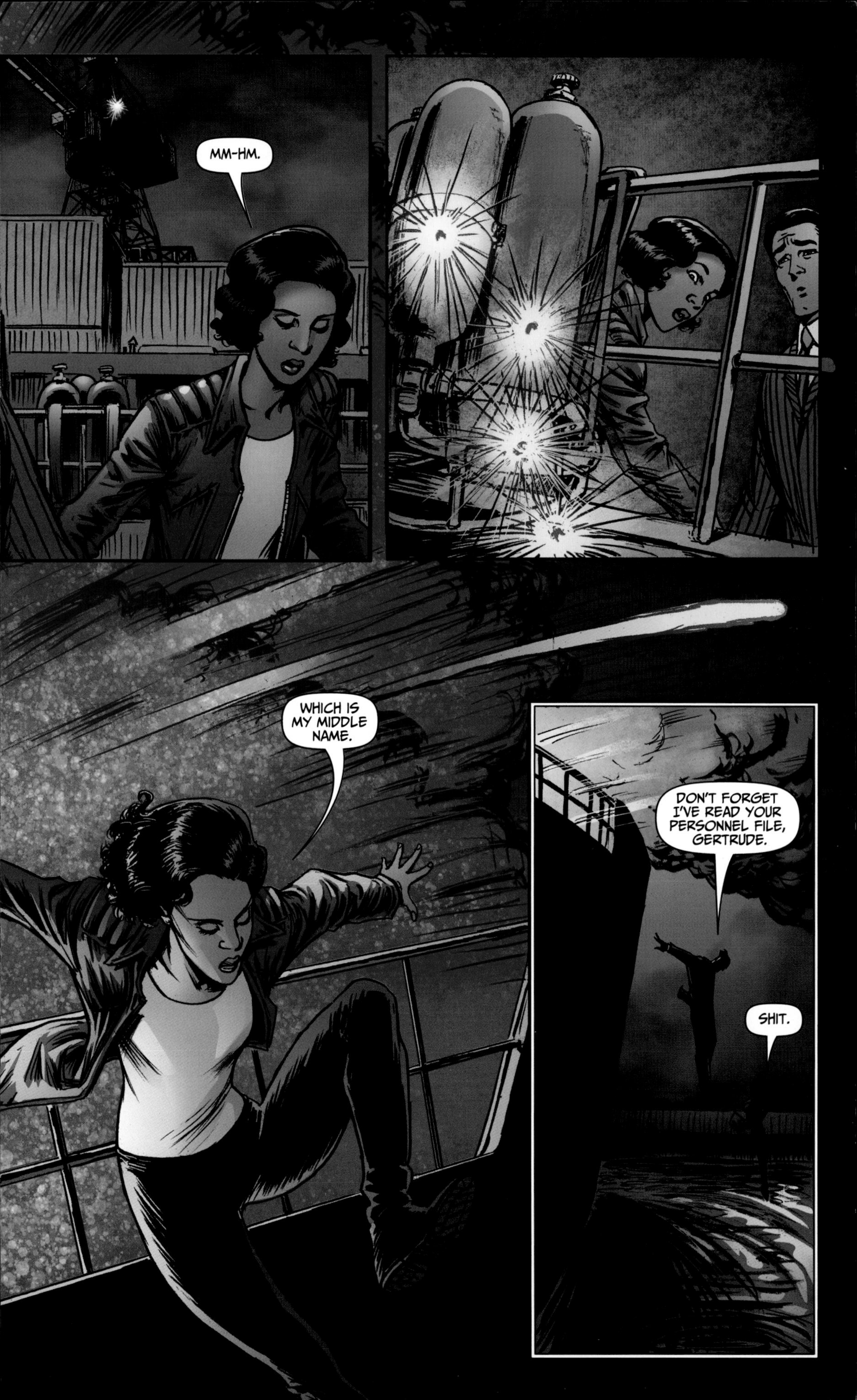
MM-HM.
WHICH IS MY MIDDLE NAME.
DON'T FORGET I'VE READ YOUR PERSONNEL FILE, GERTRUDE.
SHIT.

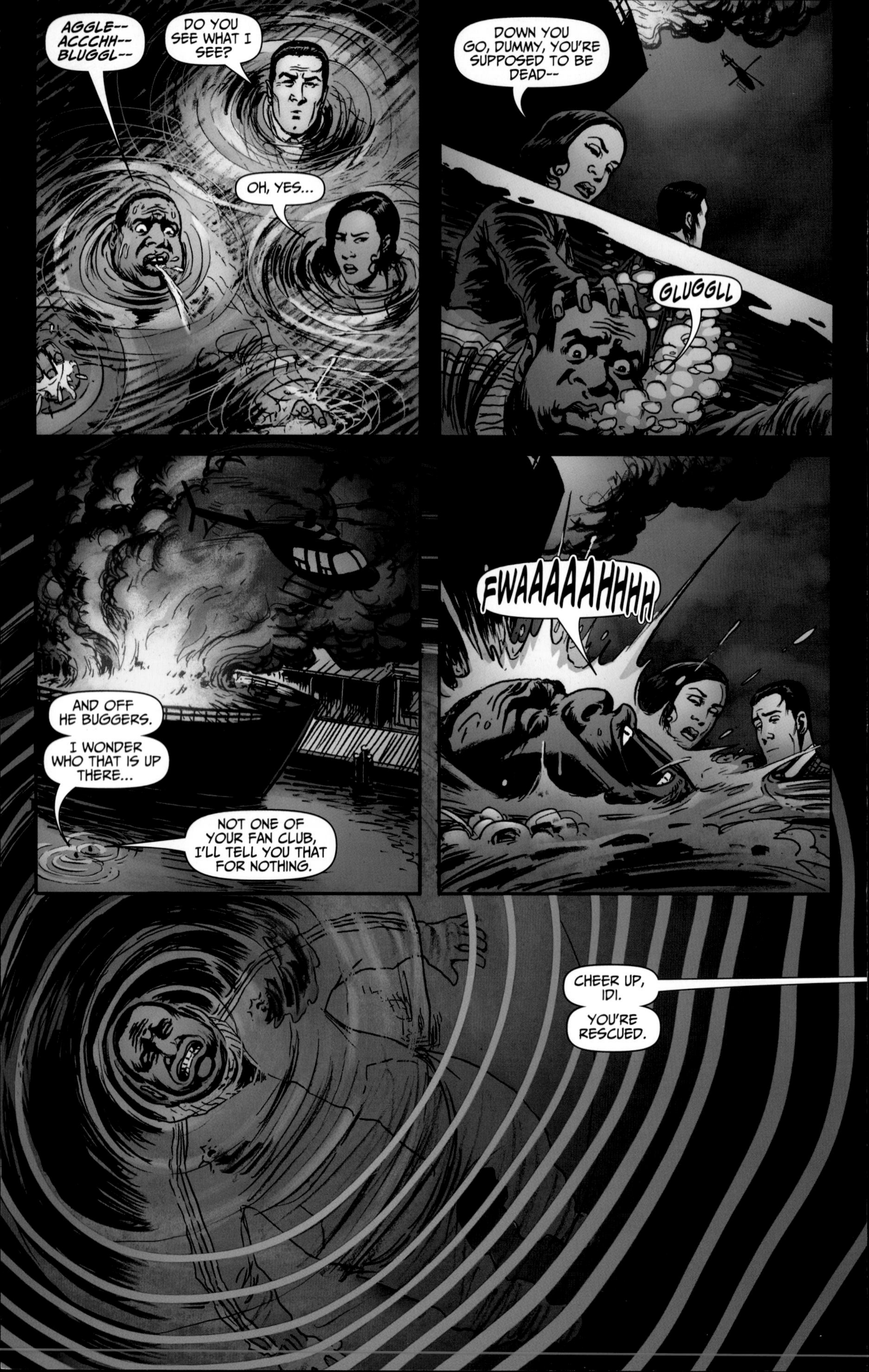
AGGLE--ACCCHH--BLUGGL--
DO YOU SEE WHAT I SEE?
OH, YES...
DOWN YOU GO, DUMMY, YOU'RE SUPPOSED TO BE DEAD--
GLUGGLL
AND OFF HE BUGGERS.
I WONDER WHO THAT IS UP THERE...
NOT ONE OF YOUR FAN CLUB, I'LL TELL YOU THAT FOR NOTHING.
FWAAAAAHHHH
CHEER UP, IDI.
YOU'RE RESCUED.

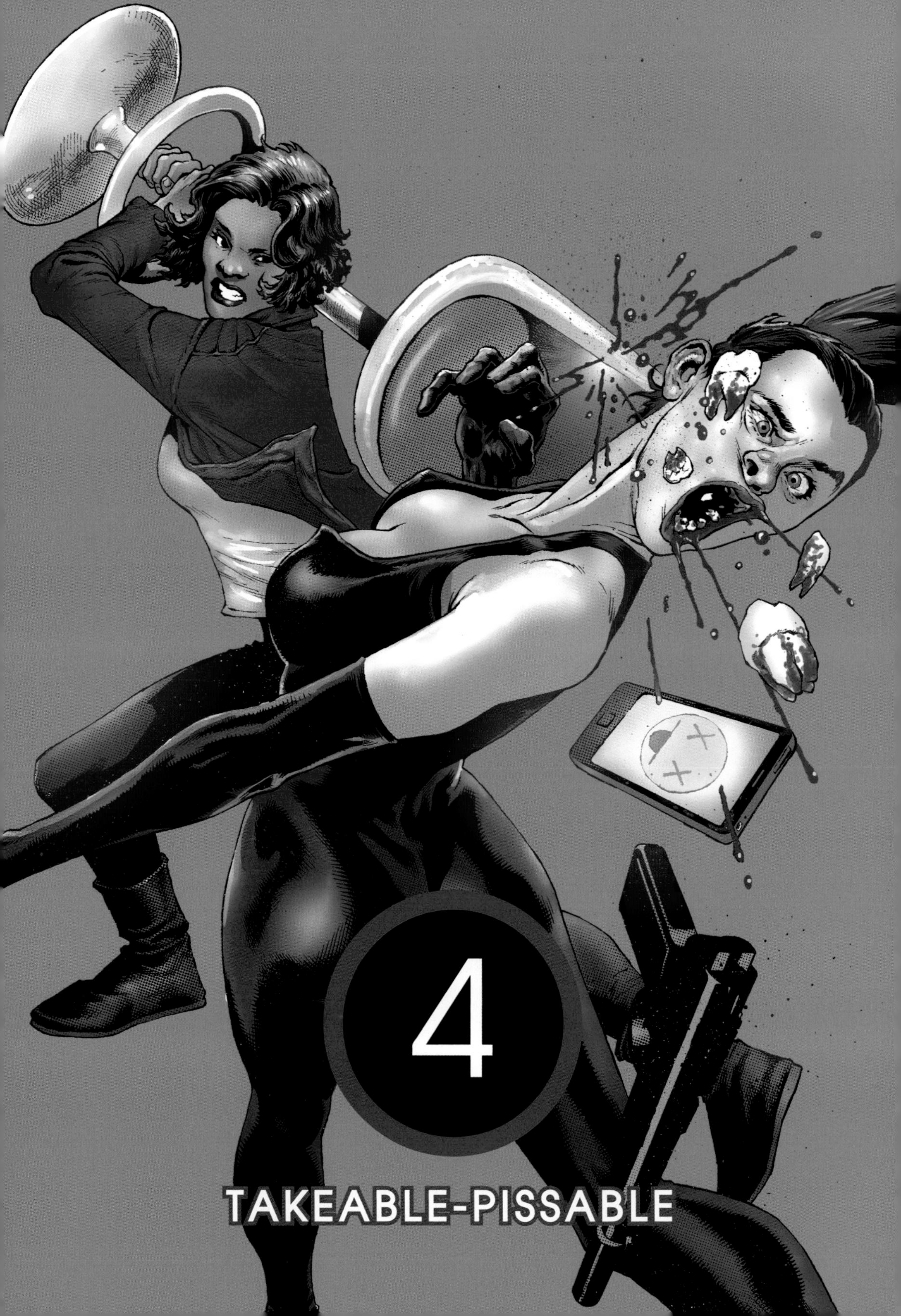

4

TAKEABLE-PISSABLE

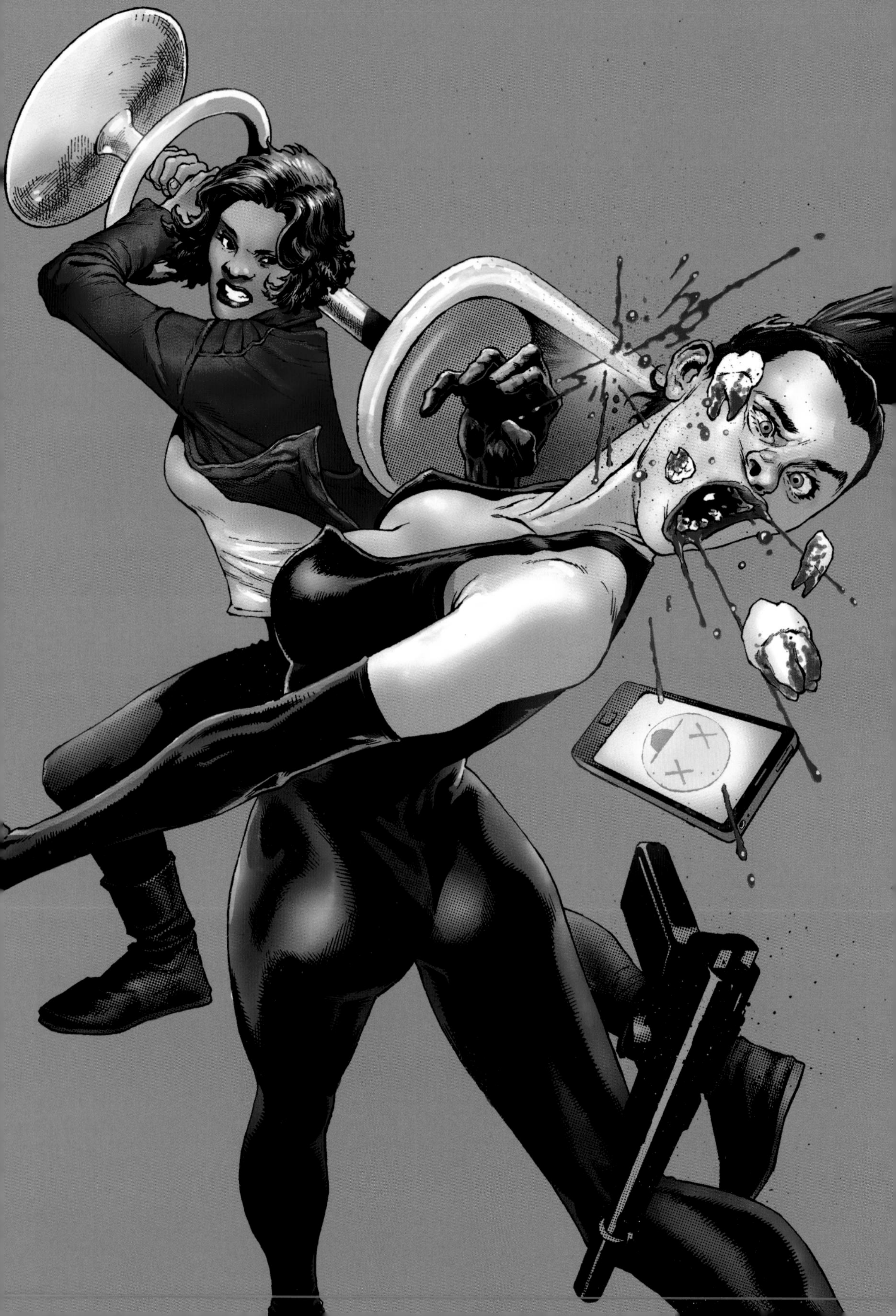

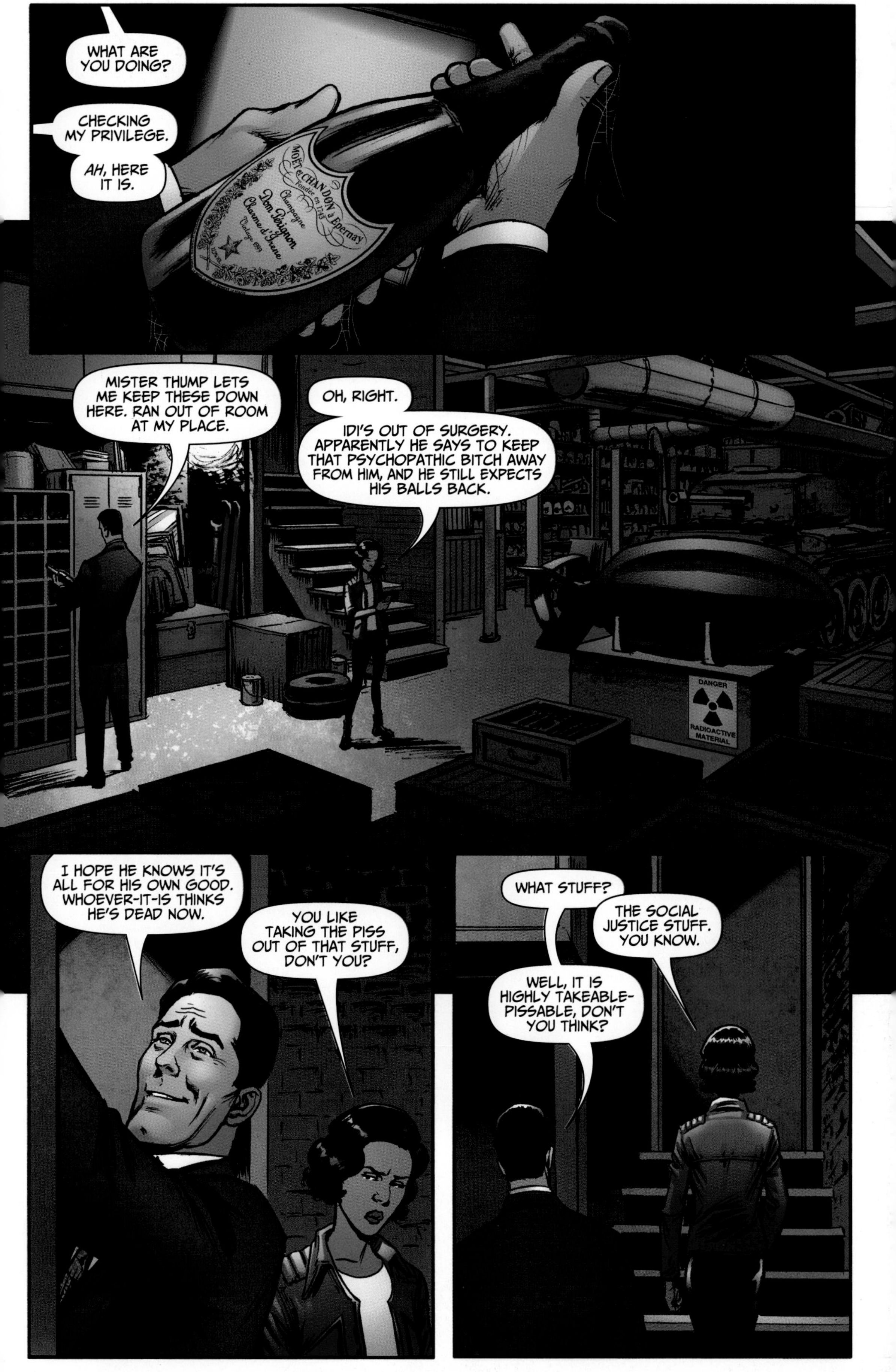
WHAT ARE YOU DOING?
CHECKING MY PRIVILEGE.
AH, HERE IT IS.
MISTER THUMP LETS ME KEEP THESE DOWN HERE. RAN OUT OF ROOM AT MY PLACE.
OH, RIGHT.
IDI'S OUT OF SURGERY. APPARENTLY HE SAYS TO KEEP THAT PSYCHOPATHIC BITCH AWAY FROM HIM, AND HE STILL EXPECTS HIS BALLS BACK.
DANGER RADIOACTIVE MATERIAL
I HOPE HE KNOWS IT'S ALL FOR HIS OWN GOOD. WHOEVER-IT-IS THINKS HE'S DEAD NOW.
YOU LIKE TAKING THE PISS OUT OF THAT STUFF, DON'T YOU?
WHAT STUFF?
THE SOCIAL JUSTICE STUFF. YOU KNOW.
WELL, IT IS HIGHLY TAKEABLE-PISSABLE, DON'T YOU THINK?

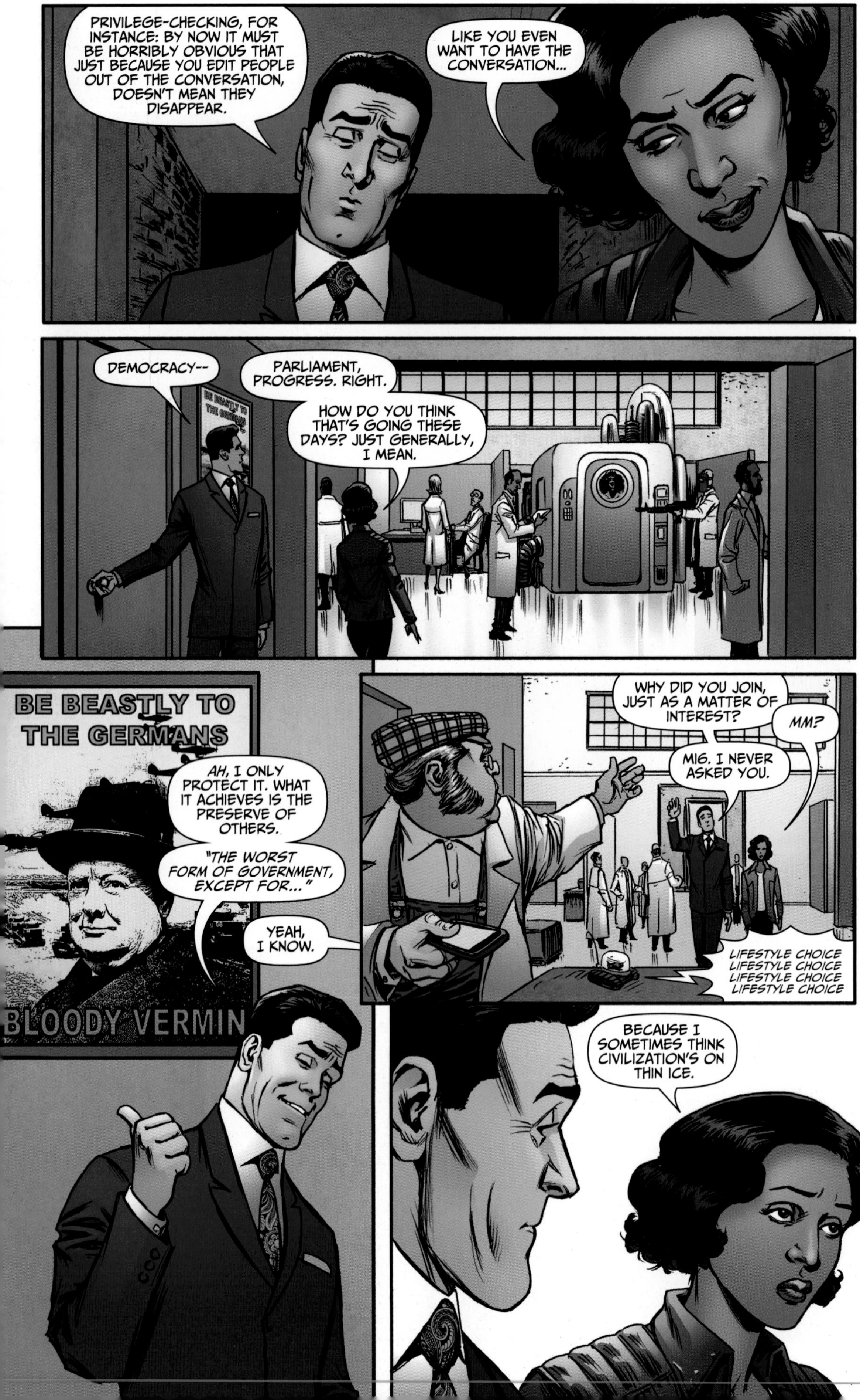
PRIVILEGE-CHECKING, FOR INSTANCE: BY NOW IT MUST BE HORRIBLY OBVIOUS THAT JUST BECAUSE YOU EDIT PEOPLE OUT OF THE CONVERSATION, DOESN'T MEAN THEY DISAPPEAR.
LIKE YOU EVEN WANT TO HAVE THE CONVERSATION...
DEMOCRACY--
PARLIAMENT, PROGRESS. RIGHT.
HOW DO YOU THINK THAT'S GOING THESE DAYS? JUST GENERALLY, I MEAN.
BE BEASTLY TO THE GERMANS
AH, I ONLY PROTECT IT. WHAT IT ACHIEVES IS THE PRESERVE OF OTHERS.
"THE WORST FORM OF GOVERNMENT, EXCEPT FOR..."
YEAH, I KNOW.
BLOODY VERMIN
WHY DID YOU JOIN, JUST AS A MATTER OF INTEREST?
MM?
MI6. I NEVER ASKED YOU.
LIFESTYLE CHOICE
LIFESTYLE CHOICE
LIFESTYLE CHOICE
LIFESTYLE CHOICE
BECAUSE I SOMETIMES THINK CIVILIZATION'S ON THIN ICE.

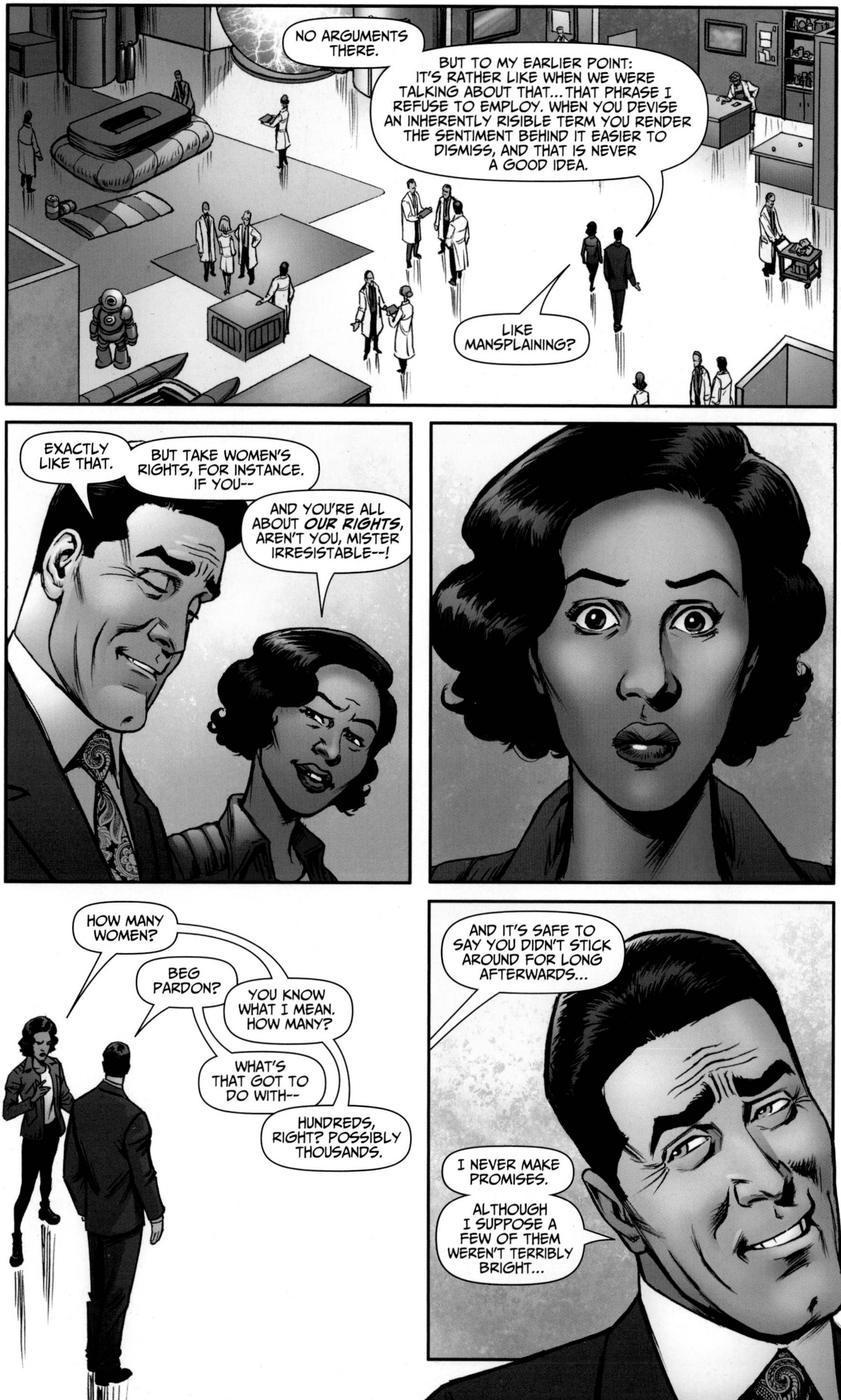
NO ARGUMENTS THERE.
BUT TO MY EARLIER POINT: IT'S RATHER LIKE WHEN WE WERE TALKING ABOUT THAT... THAT PHRASE I REFUSE TO EMPLOY. WHEN YOU DEVISE AN INHERENTLY RISIBLE TERM YOU RENDER THE SENTIMENT BEHIND IT EASIER TO DISMISS, AND THAT IS NEVER A GOOD IDEA.
LIKE MANSPLAINING?
EXACTLY LIKE THAT.
BUT TAKE WOMEN'S RIGHTS, FOR INSTANCE. IF YOU--
AND YOU'RE ALL ABOUT ***OUR RIGHTS***, AREN'T YOU, MISTER IRRESISTABLE--!
HOW MANY WOMEN?
BEG PARDON?
YOU KNOW WHAT I MEAN. HOW MANY?
WHAT'S THAT GOT TO DO WITH--
HUNDREDS, RIGHT? POSSIBLY THOUSANDS.
AND IT'S SAFE TO SAY YOU DIDN'T STICK AROUND FOR LONG AFTERWARDS...
I NEVER MAKE PROMISES.
ALTHOUGH I SUPPOSE A FEW OF THEM WEREN'T TERRIBLY BRIGHT...

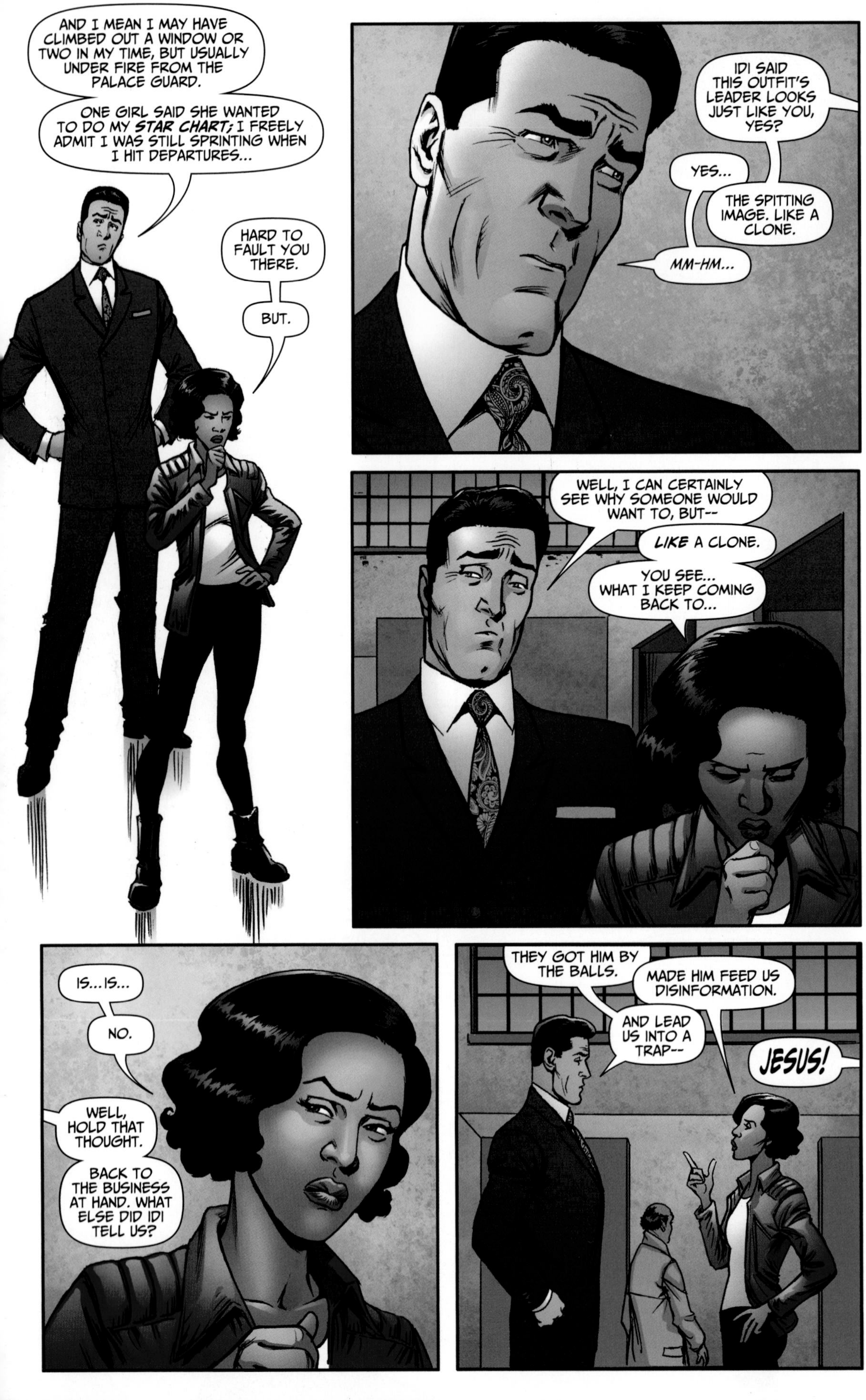
AND I MEAN I MAY HAVE CLIMBED OUT A WINDOW OR TWO IN MY TIME, BUT USUALLY UNDER FIRE FROM THE PALACE GUARD.
ONE GIRL SAID SHE WANTED TO DO MY STAR CHART; I FREELY ADMIT I WAS STILL SPRINTING WHEN I HIT DEPARTURES...
HARD TO FAULT YOU THERE.
BUT.
IDI SAID THIS OUTFIT'S LEADER LOOKS JUST LIKE YOU, YES?
YES...
THE SPITTING IMAGE. LIKE A CLONE.
MM-HM...
WELL, I CAN CERTAINLY SEE WHY SOMEONE WOULD WANT TO, BUT--
LIKE A CLONE.
YOU SEE... WHAT I KEEP COMING BACK TO...
IS... IS...
NO.
WELL, HOLD THAT THOUGHT.
BACK TO THE BUSINESS AT HAND. WHAT ELSE DID IDI TELL US?
THEY GOT HIM BY THE BALLS.
MADE HIM FEED US DISINFORMATION.
AND LEAD US INTO A TRAP--
JESUS!

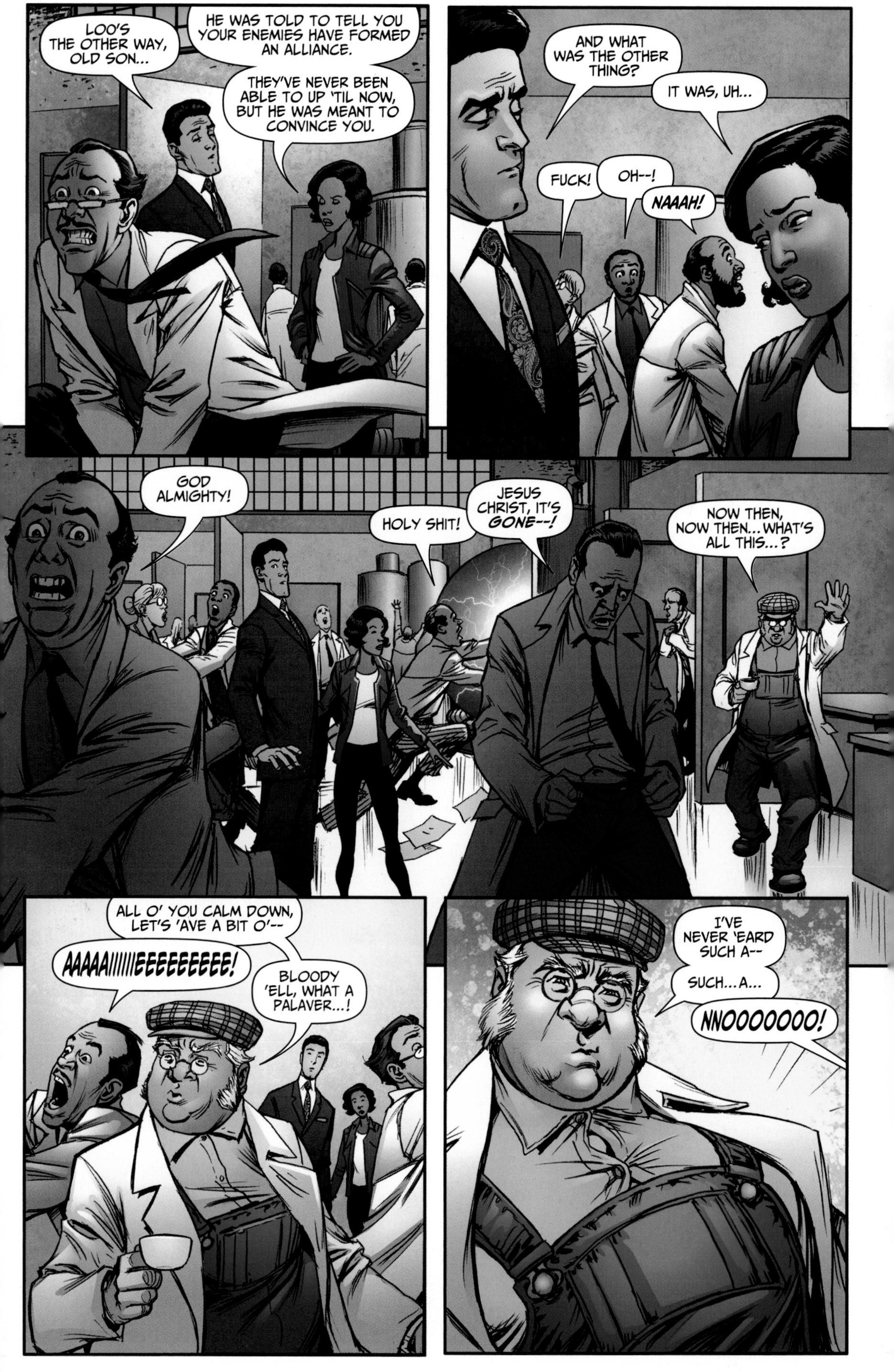
LOO'S THE OTHER WAY, OLD SON...
HE WAS TOLD TO TELL YOU YOUR ENEMIES HAVE FORMED AN ALLIANCE.
THEY'VE NEVER BEEN ABLE TO UP 'TIL NOW, BUT HE WAS MEANT TO CONVINCE YOU.
AND WHAT WAS THE OTHER THING?
IT WAS, UH...
FUCK!
OH--!
NAAAH!
GOD ALMIGHTY!
HOLY SHIT!
JESUS CHRIST, IT'S GONE--!
NOW THEN, NOW THEN... WHAT'S ALL THIS...?
ALL O' YOU CALM DOWN, LET'S 'AVE A BIT O'--
AAAAAIIIIIIEEEEEEEEEE!
BLOODY 'ELL, WHAT A PALAVER...!
I'VE NEVER 'EARD SUCH A--
SUCH... A...
NNOOOOOOO!

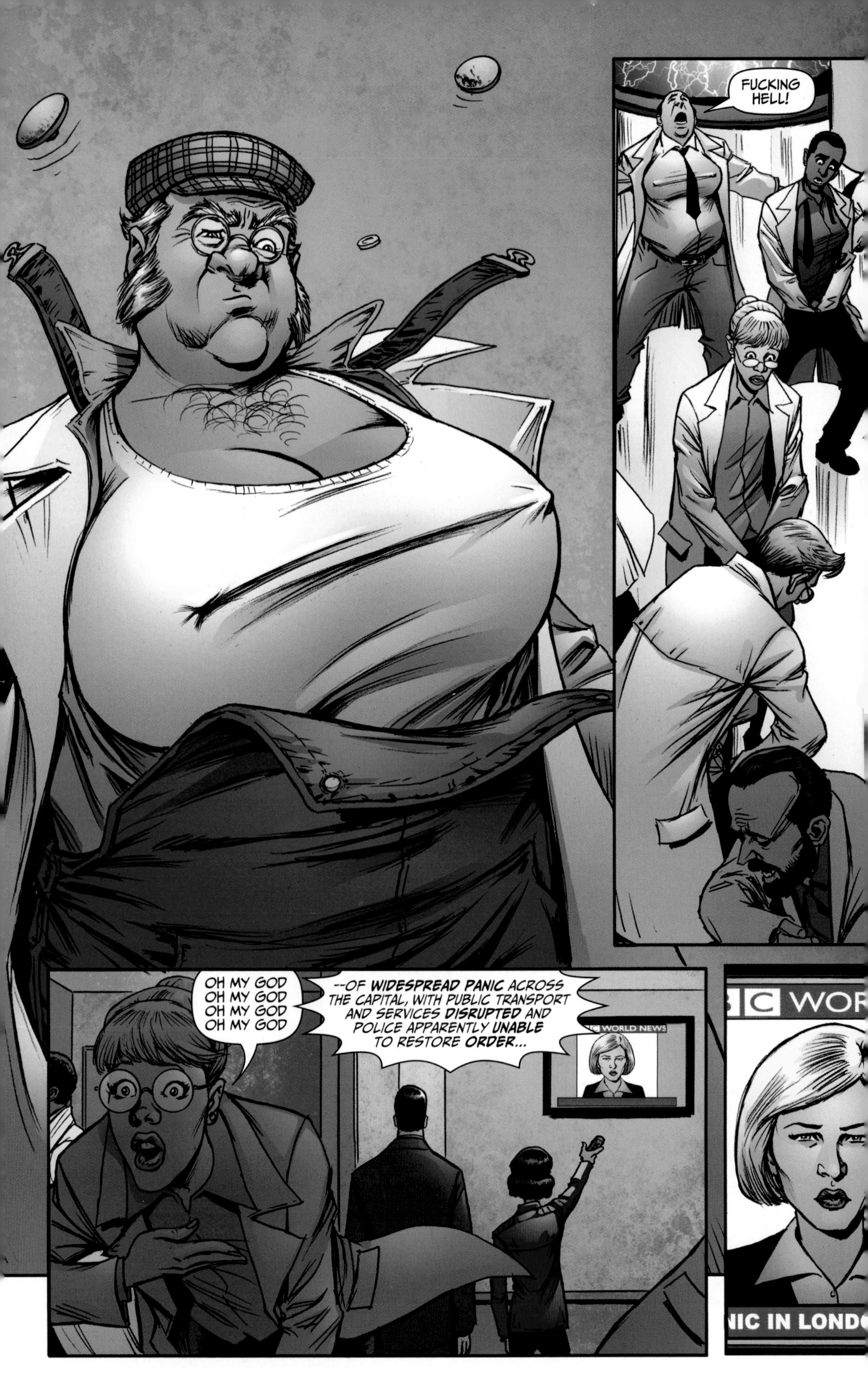
FUCKING HELL!
OH MY GOD OH MY GOD OH MY GOD OH MY GOD
--OF WIDESPREAD PANIC ACROSS THE CAPITAL, WITH PUBLIC TRANSPORT AND SERVICES DISRUPTED AND POLICE APPARENTLY UNABLE TO RESTORE ORDER...
BC WORLD NEWS
BC WOR
NIC IN LONDO

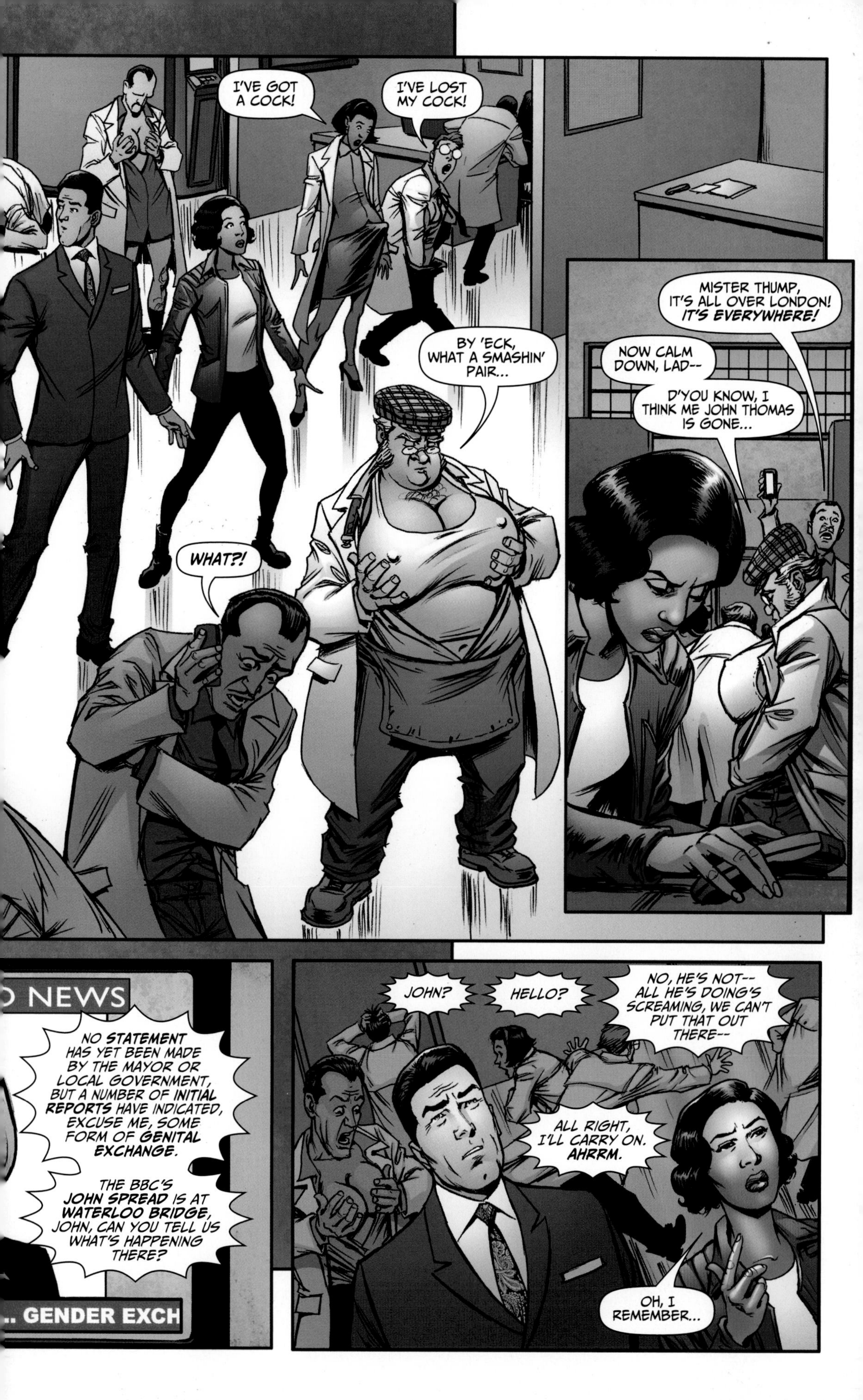
I'VE GOT A COCK!
I'VE LOST MY COCK!
BY 'ECK, WHAT A SMASHIN' PAIR...
WHAT?!
MISTER THUMP, IT'S ALL OVER LONDON! *IT'S EVERYWHERE!*
NOW CALM DOWN, LAD--
D'YOU KNOW, I THINK ME JOHN THOMAS IS GONE...
O NEWS
NO **STATEMENT** HAS YET BEEN MADE BY THE MAYOR OR LOCAL GOVERNMENT, BUT A NUMBER OF **INITIAL REPORTS** HAVE INDICATED, EXCUSE ME, SOME FORM OF **GENITAL EXCHANGE**.
THE BBC'S **JOHN SPREAD** IS AT **WATERLOO BRIDGE**, JOHN, CAN YOU TELL US WHAT'S HAPPENING THERE?
.. GENDER EXCH
JOHN?
HELLO?
NO, HE'S NOT-- ALL HE'S DOING'S SCREAMING, WE CAN'T PUT THAT OUT THERE--
ALL RIGHT, I'LL CARRY ON. **AHRRM.**
OH, I REMEMBER...

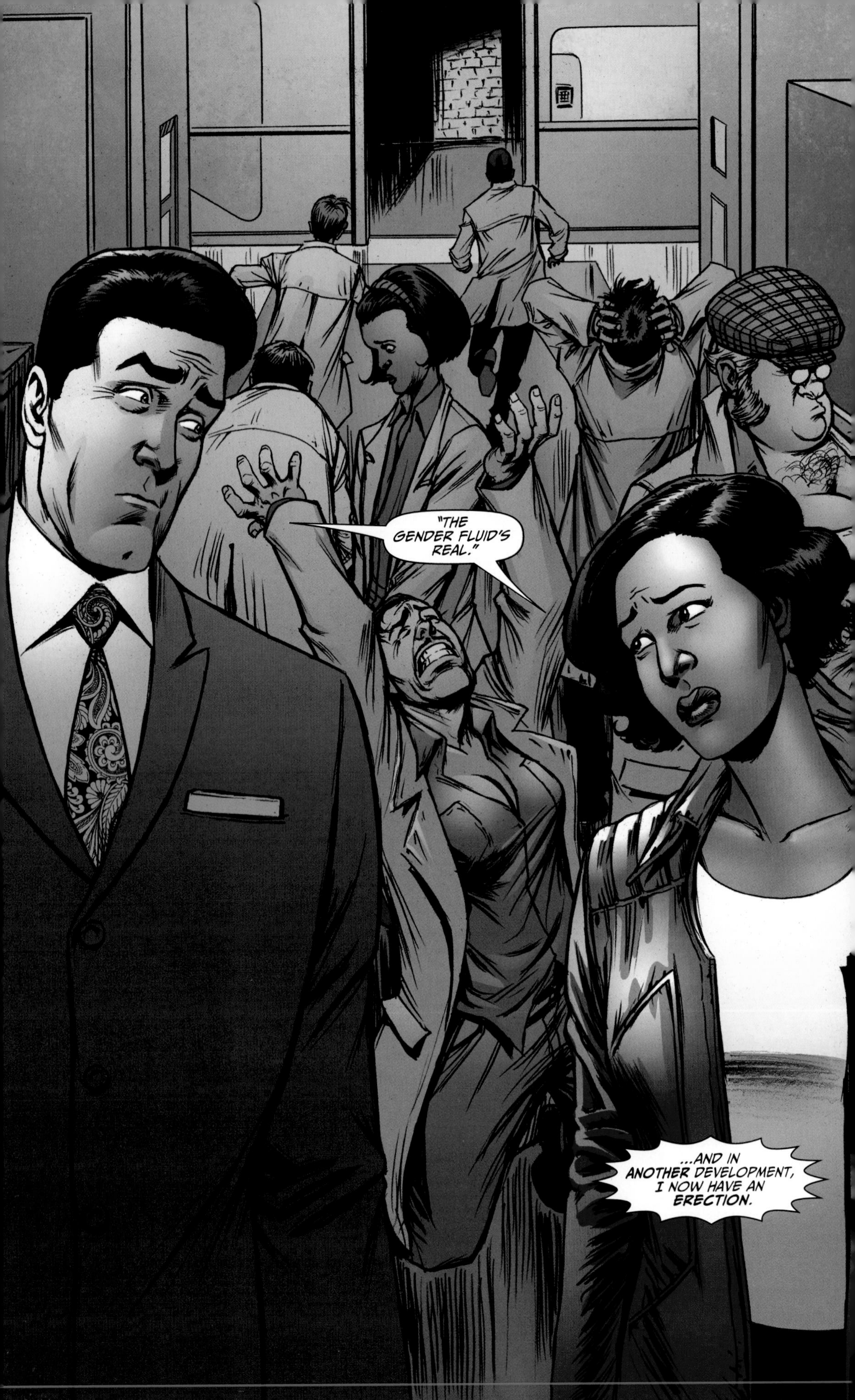
"THE GENDER FLUID'S REAL."
...AND IN ANOTHER DEVELOPMENT, I NOW HAVE AN ERECTION.

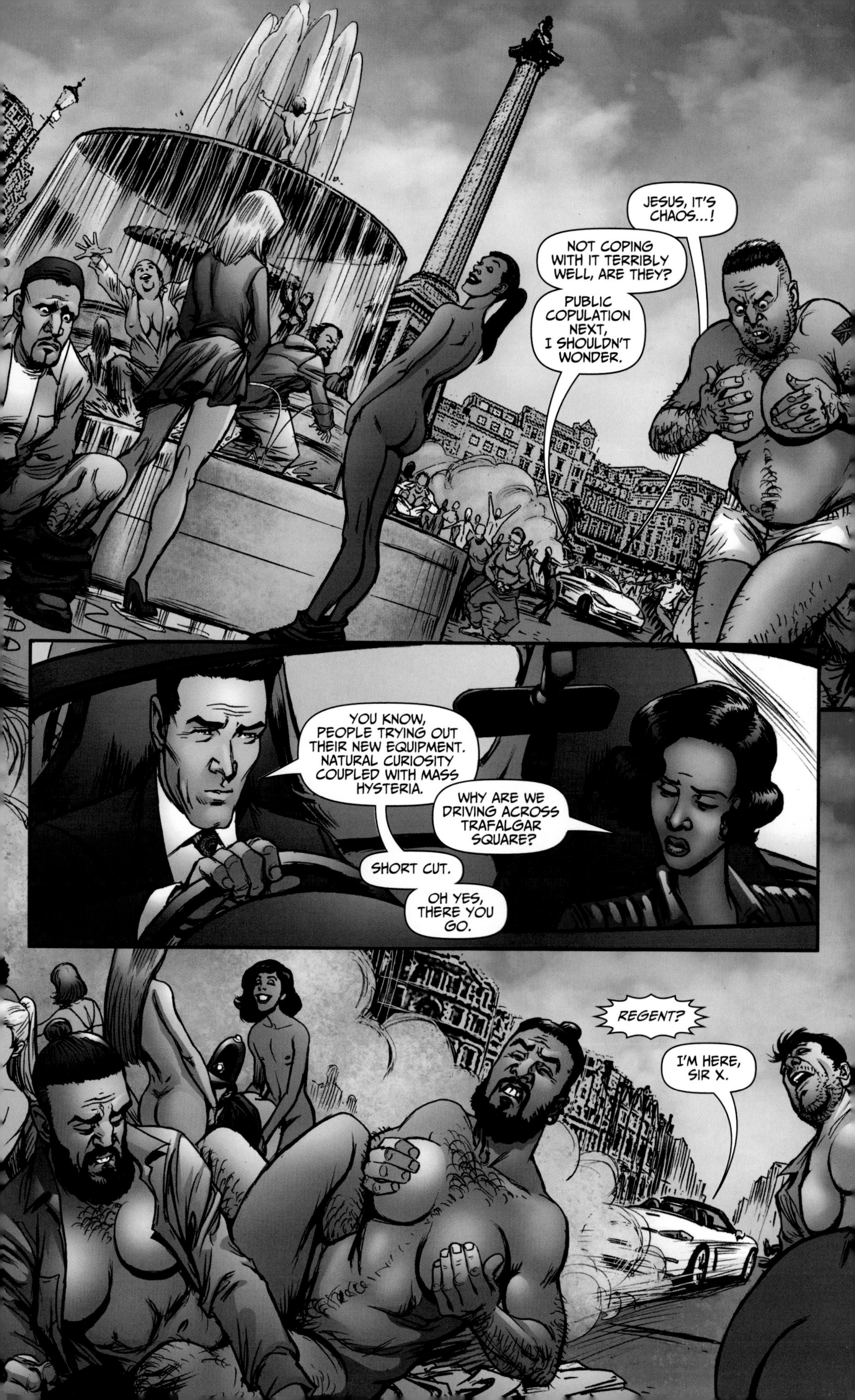
JESUS, IT'S CHAOS...!
NOT COPING WITH IT TERRIBLY WELL, ARE THEY?
PUBLIC COPULATION NEXT, I SHOULDN'T WONDER.
YOU KNOW, PEOPLE TRYING OUT THEIR NEW EQUIPMENT. NATURAL CURIOSITY COUPLED WITH MASS HYSTERIA.
WHY ARE WE DRIVING ACROSS TRAFALGAR SQUARE?
SHORT CUT.
OH YES, THERE YOU GO.
REGENT?
I'M HERE, SIR X.

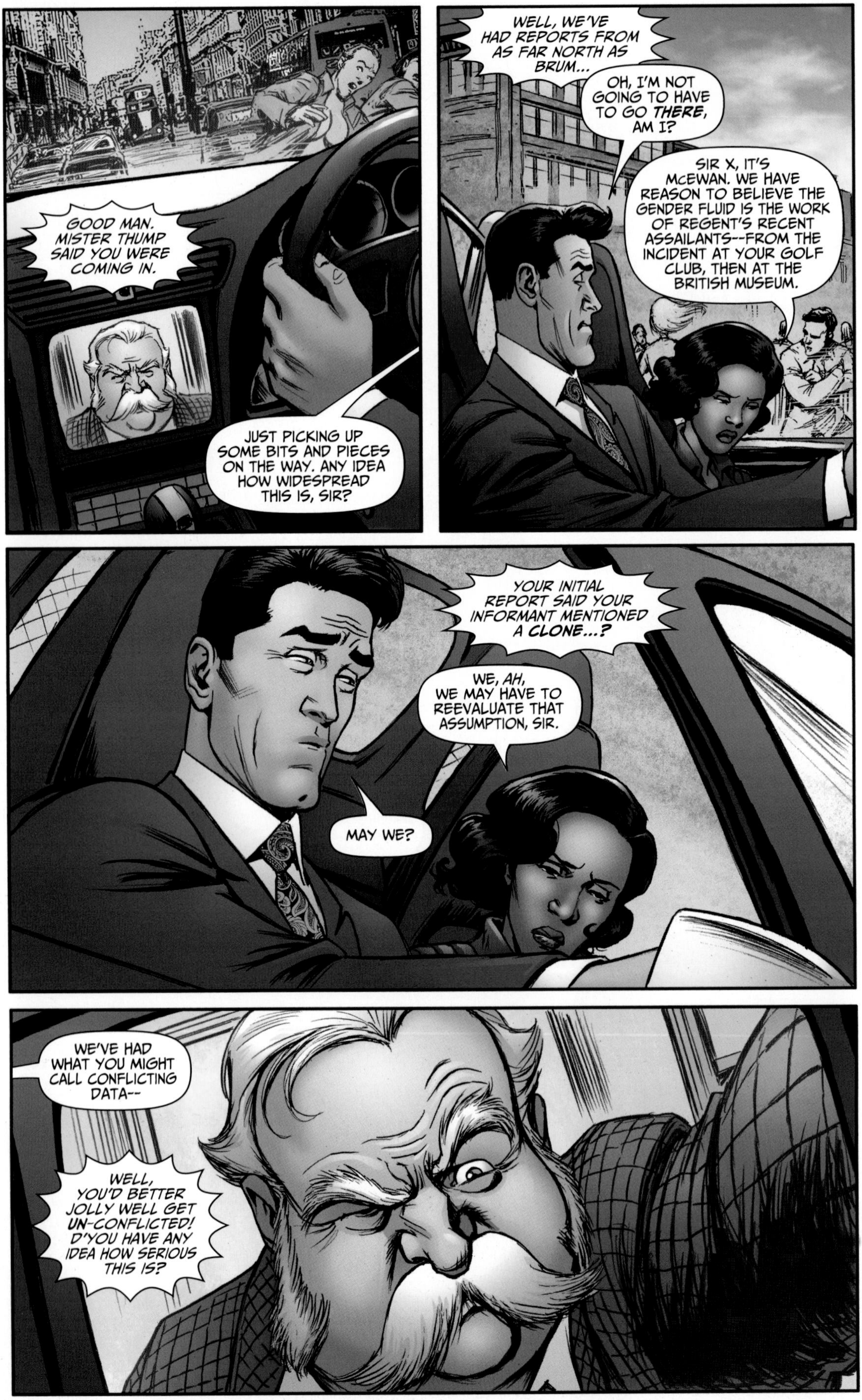
GOOD MAN. MISTER THUMP SAID YOU WERE COMING IN.
JUST PICKING UP SOME BITS AND PIECES ON THE WAY. ANY IDEA HOW WIDESPREAD THIS IS, SIR?
WELL, WE'VE HAD REPORTS FROM AS FAR NORTH AS BRUM...
OH, I'M NOT GOING TO HAVE TO GO THERE, AM I?
SIR X, IT'S McEWAN. WE HAVE REASON TO BELIEVE THE GENDER FLUID IS THE WORK OF REGENT'S RECENT ASSAILANTS--FROM THE INCIDENT AT YOUR GOLF CLUB, THEN AT THE BRITISH MUSEUM.
YOUR INITIAL REPORT SAID YOUR INFORMANT MENTIONED A CLONE...?
WE, AH, WE MAY HAVE TO REEVALUATE THAT ASSUMPTION, SIR.
MAY WE?
WE'VE HAD WHAT YOU MIGHT CALL CONFLICTING DATA--
WELL, YOU'D BETTER JOLLY WELL GET UN-CONFLICTED! D'YOU HAVE ANY IDEA HOW SERIOUS THIS IS?

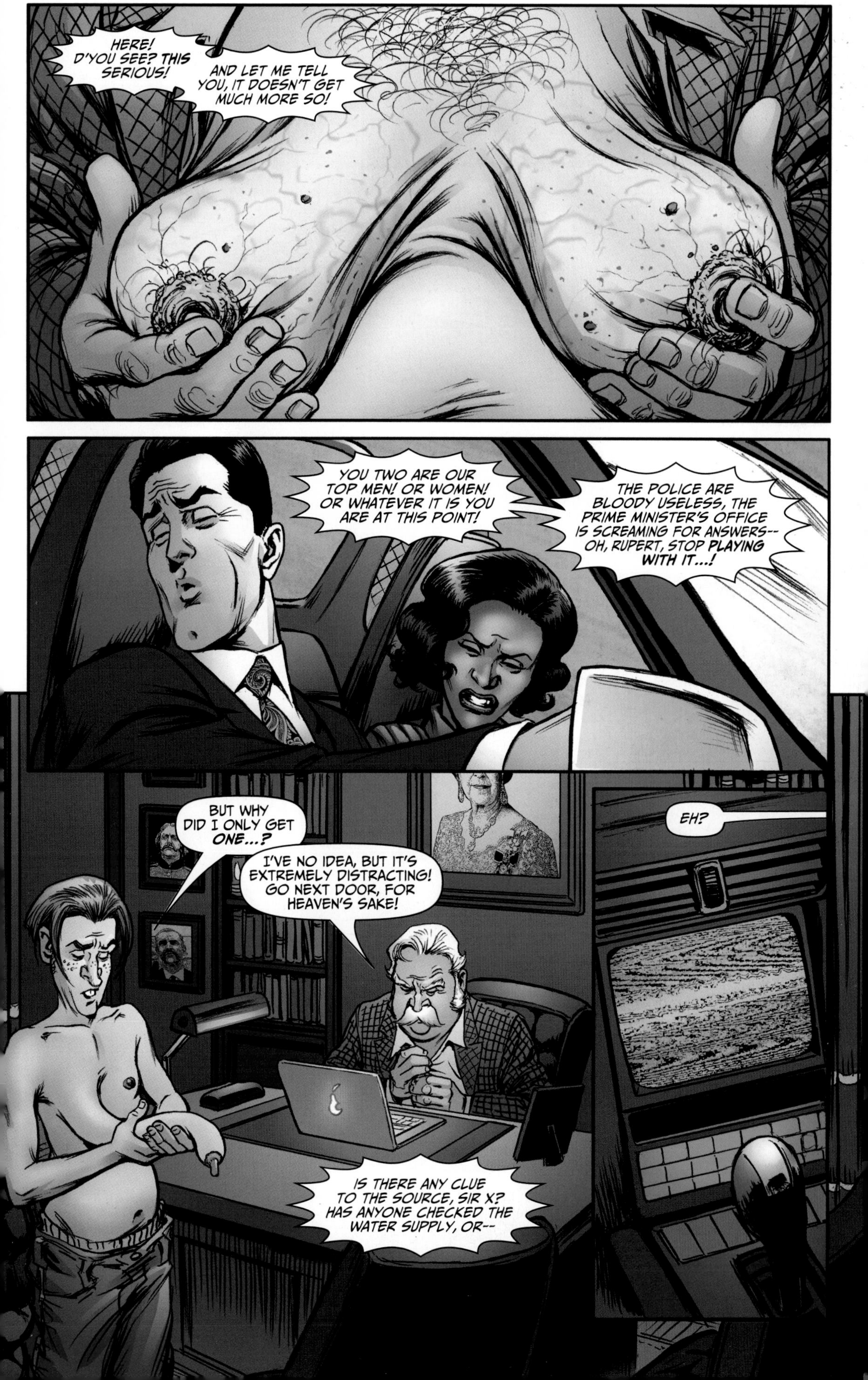
HERE! D'YOU SEE? THIS SERIOUS!
AND LET ME TELL YOU, IT DOESN'T GET MUCH MORE SO!
YOU TWO ARE OUR TOP MEN! OR WOMEN! OR WHATEVER IT IS YOU ARE AT THIS POINT!
THE POLICE ARE BLOODY USELESS, THE PRIME MINISTER'S OFFICE IS SCREAMING FOR ANSWERS-- OH, RUPERT, STOP PLAYING WITH IT...!
BUT WHY DID I ONLY GET ONE...?
I'VE NO IDEA, BUT IT'S EXTREMELY DISTRACTING! GO NEXT DOOR, FOR HEAVEN'S SAKE!
EH?
IS THERE ANY CLUE TO THE SOURCE, SIR X? HAS ANYONE CHECKED THE WATER SUPPLY, OR--

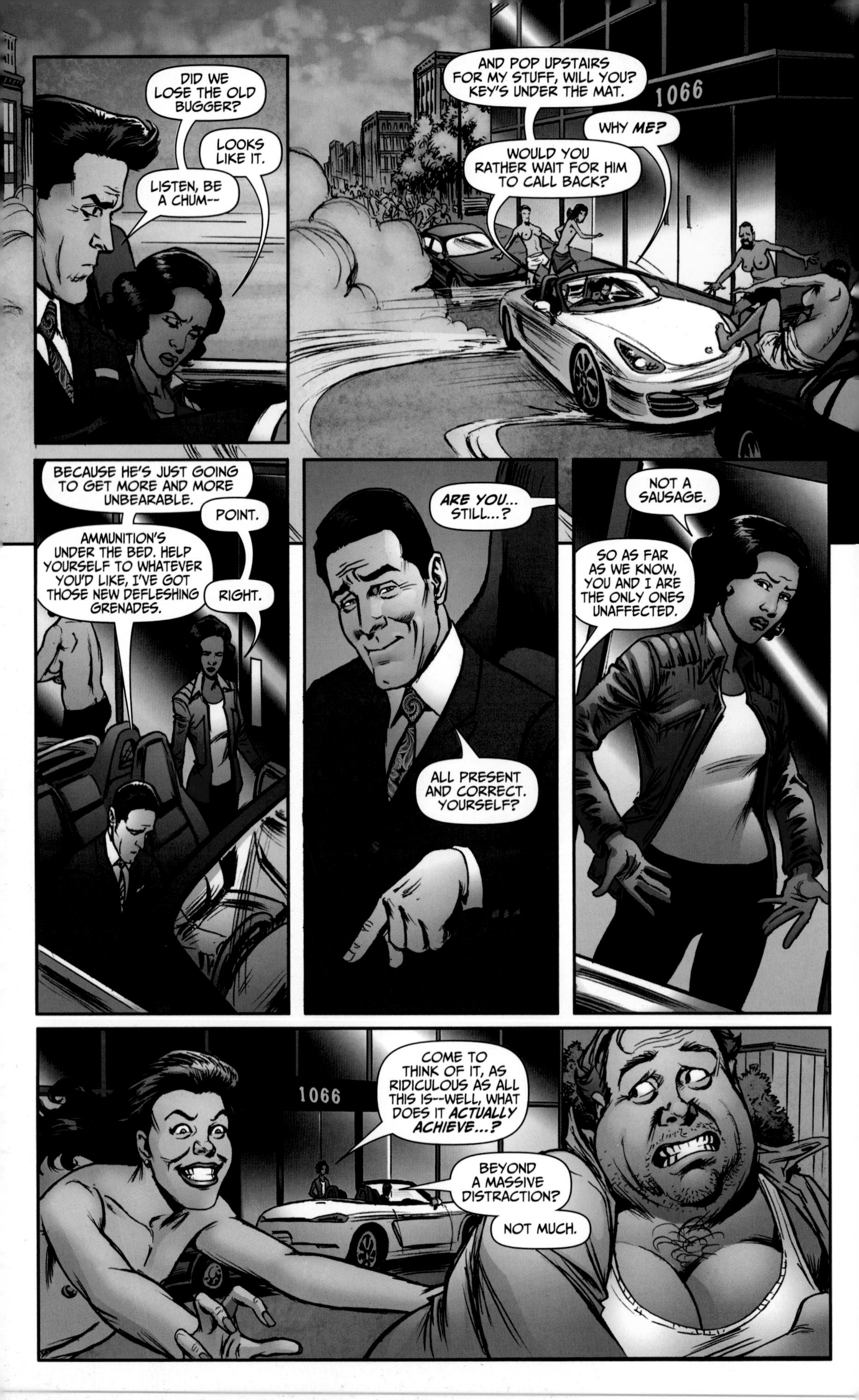

DID WE LOSE THE OLD BUGGER?
LOOKS LIKE IT.
LISTEN, BE A CHUM--
AND POP UPSTAIRS FOR MY STUFF, WILL YOU? KEY'S UNDER THE MAT.
1066
WHY *ME?*
WOULD YOU RATHER WAIT FOR HIM TO CALL BACK?
BECAUSE HE'S JUST GOING TO GET MORE AND MORE UNBEARABLE.
POINT.
AMMUNITION'S UNDER THE BED. HELP YOURSELF TO WHATEVER YOU'D LIKE, I'VE GOT THOSE NEW DEFLESHING GRENADES.
RIGHT.
ARE YOU... STILL...?
ALL PRESENT AND CORRECT. YOURSELF?
NOT A SAUSAGE.
SO AS FAR AS WE KNOW, YOU AND I ARE THE ONLY ONES UNAFFECTED.
1066
COME TO THINK OF IT, AS RIDICULOUS AS ALL THIS IS--WELL, WHAT DOES IT *ACTUALLY ACHIEVE...?*
BEYOND A MASSIVE DISTRACTION?
NOT MUCH.

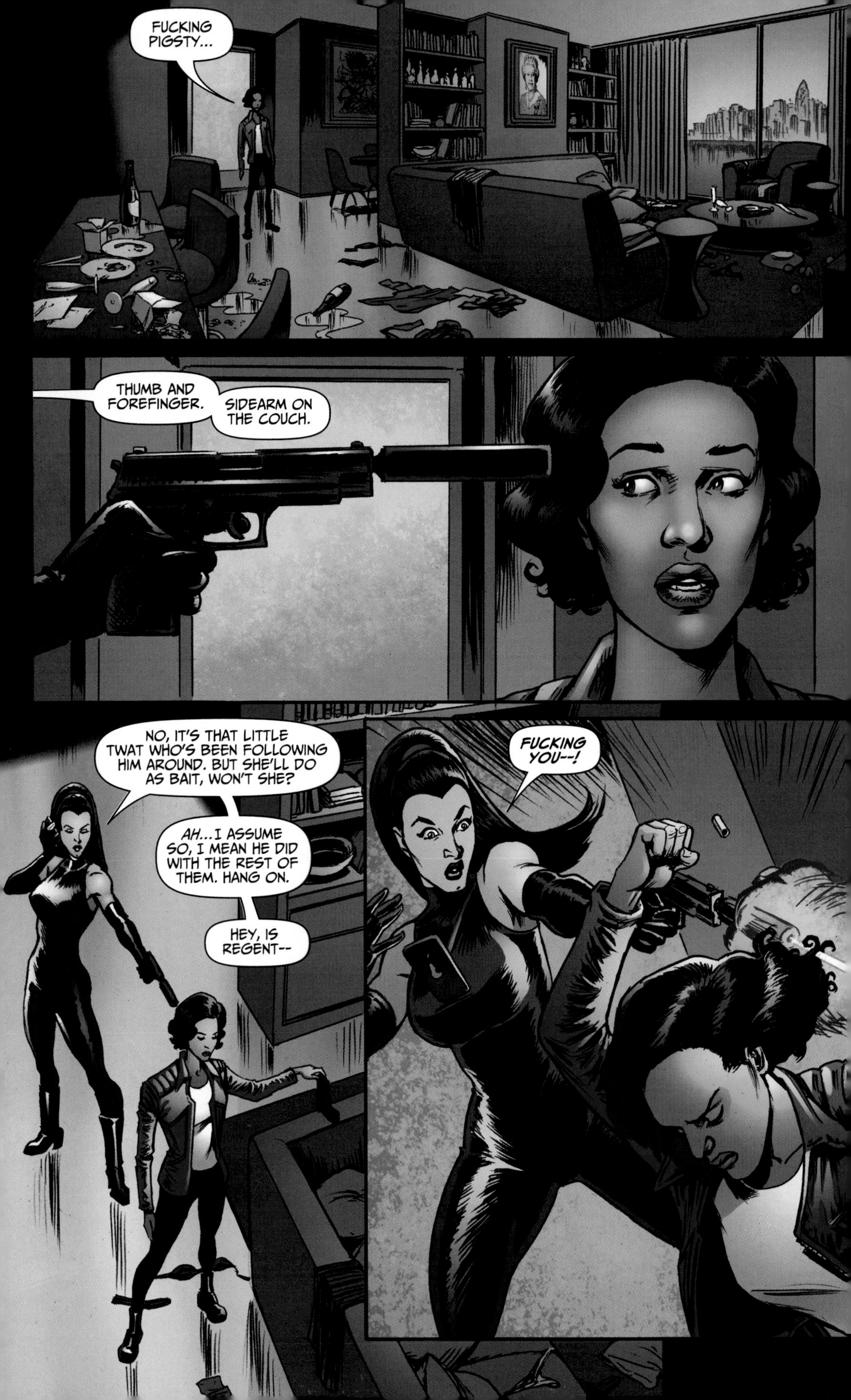
FUCKING PIGSTY...
THUMB AND FOREFINGER.
SIDEARM ON THE COUCH.
NO, IT'S THAT LITTLE TWAT WHO'S BEEN FOLLOWING HIM AROUND. BUT SHE'LL DO AS BAIT, WON'T SHE?
AH...I ASSUME SO, I MEAN HE DID WITH THE REST OF THEM. HANG ON.
HEY, IS REGENT--
FUCKING YOU--!

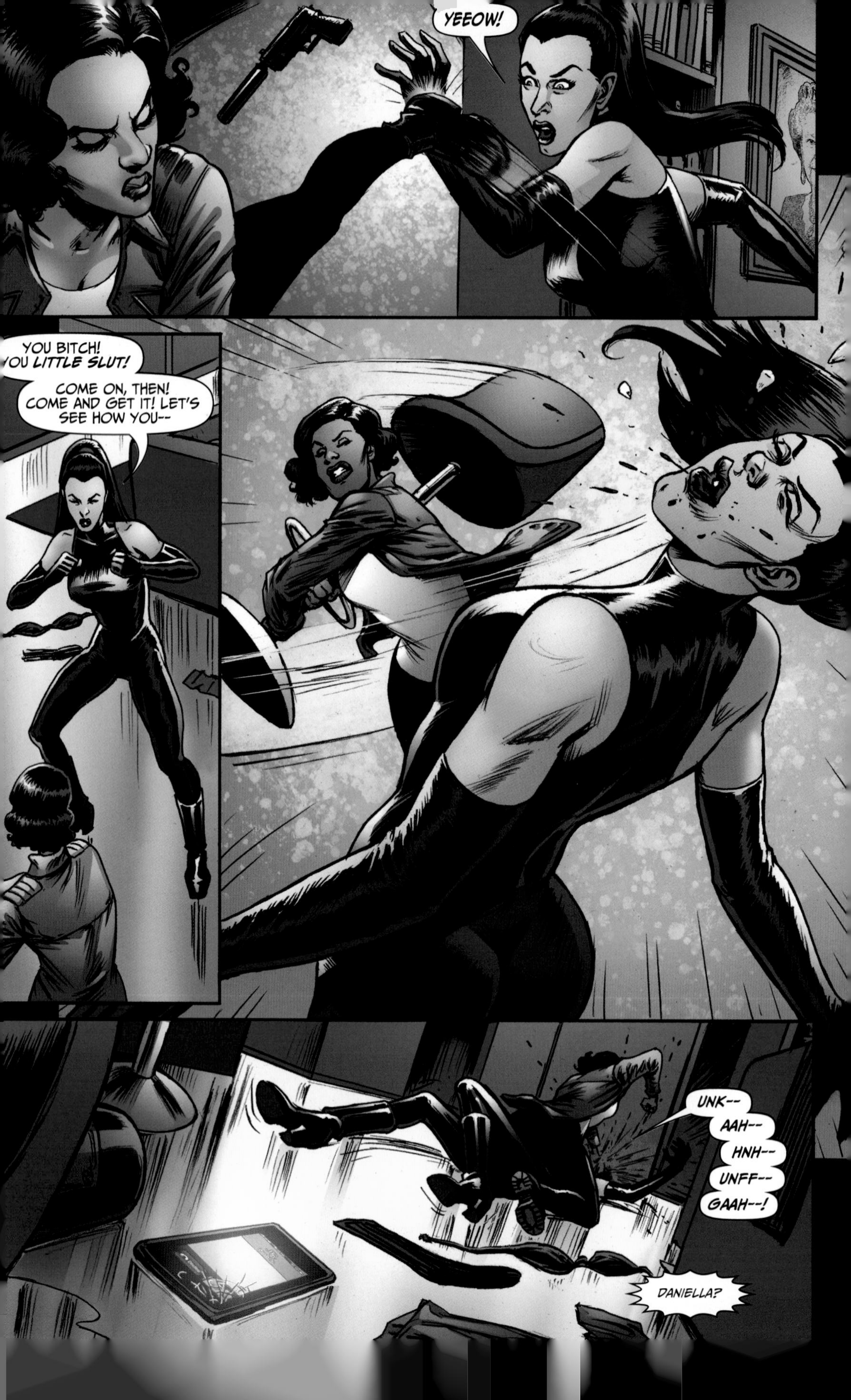
YEEOW!
YOU BITCH!
OU LITTLE SLUT!
COME ON, THEN! COME AND GET IT! LET'S SEE HOW YOU--
UNK--
AAH--
HNH--
UNFF--
GAAH--!
DANIELLA?

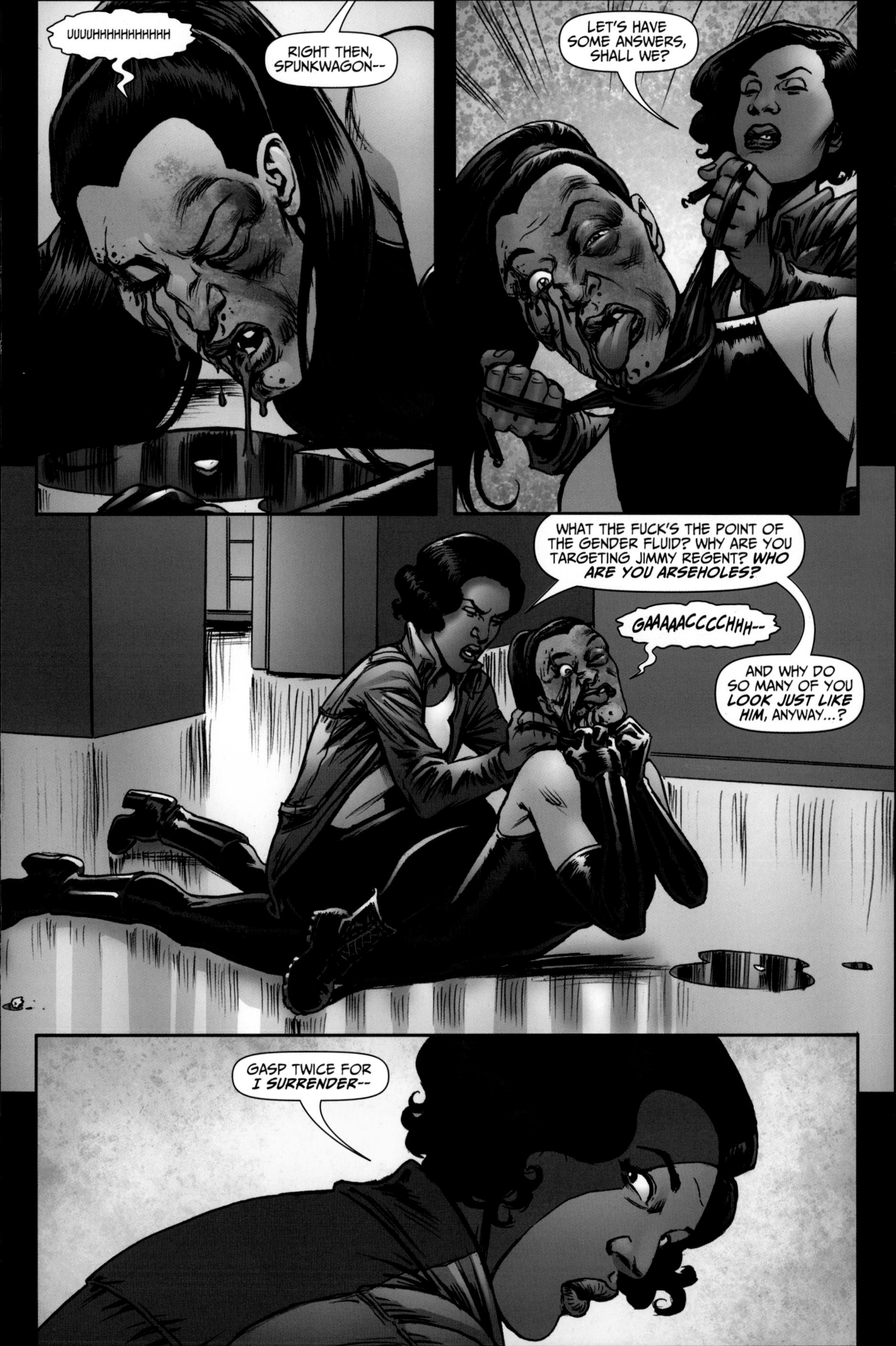
UUUUHHHHHHHHHHHH
RIGHT THEN, SPUNKWAGON--
LET'S HAVE SOME ANSWERS, SHALL WE?
WHAT THE FUCK'S THE POINT OF THE GENDER FLUID? WHY ARE YOU TARGETING JIMMY REGENT? ***WHO ARE YOU ARSEHOLES?***
GAAAAACCCCHHH--
AND WHY DO SO MANY OF YOU ***LOOK JUST LIKE HIM***, ANYWAY...?
GASP TWICE FOR ***I SURRENDER***--

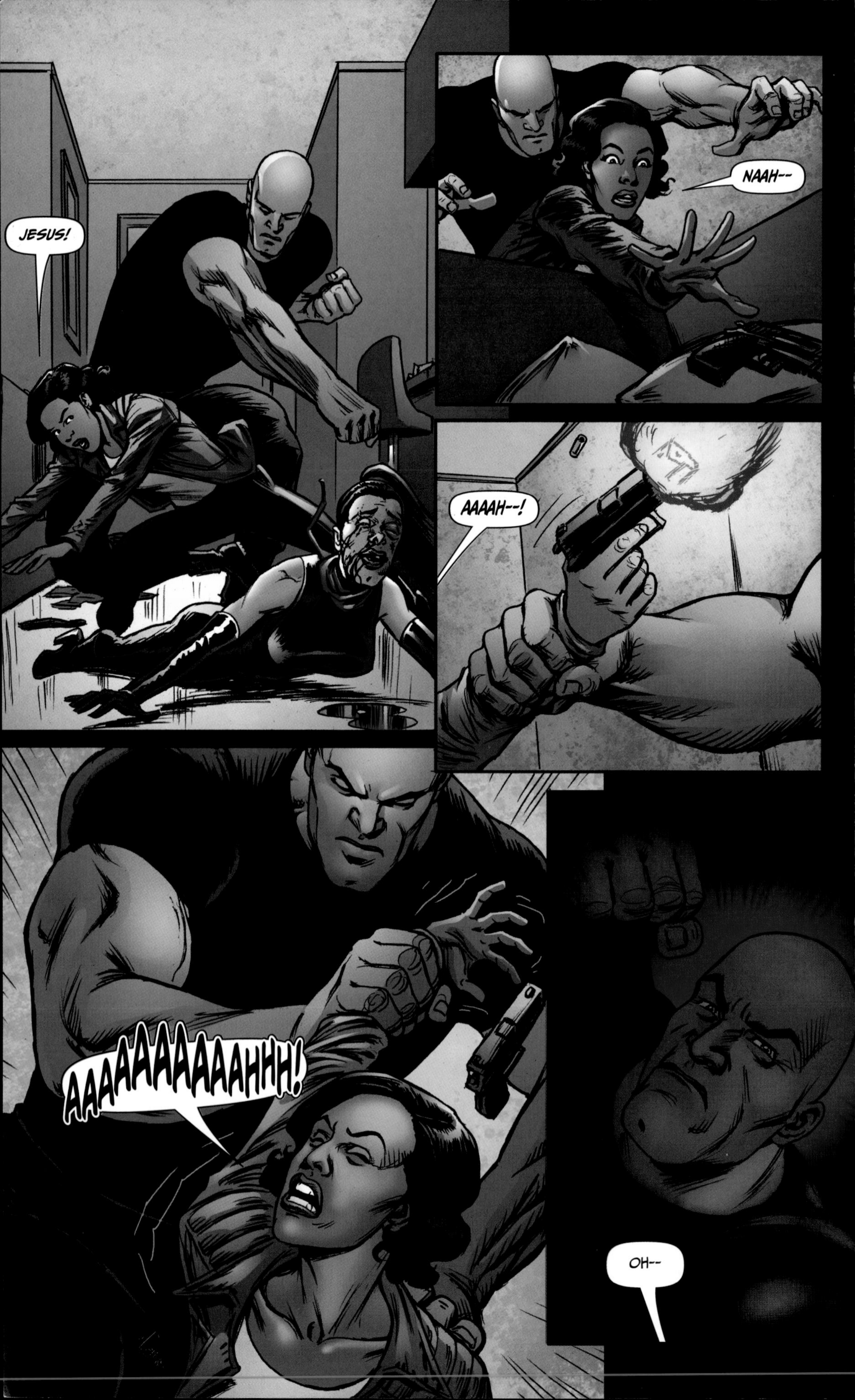
JESUS!
NAAH--
AAAAH--!
AAAAAAAAAAHHH!
OH--

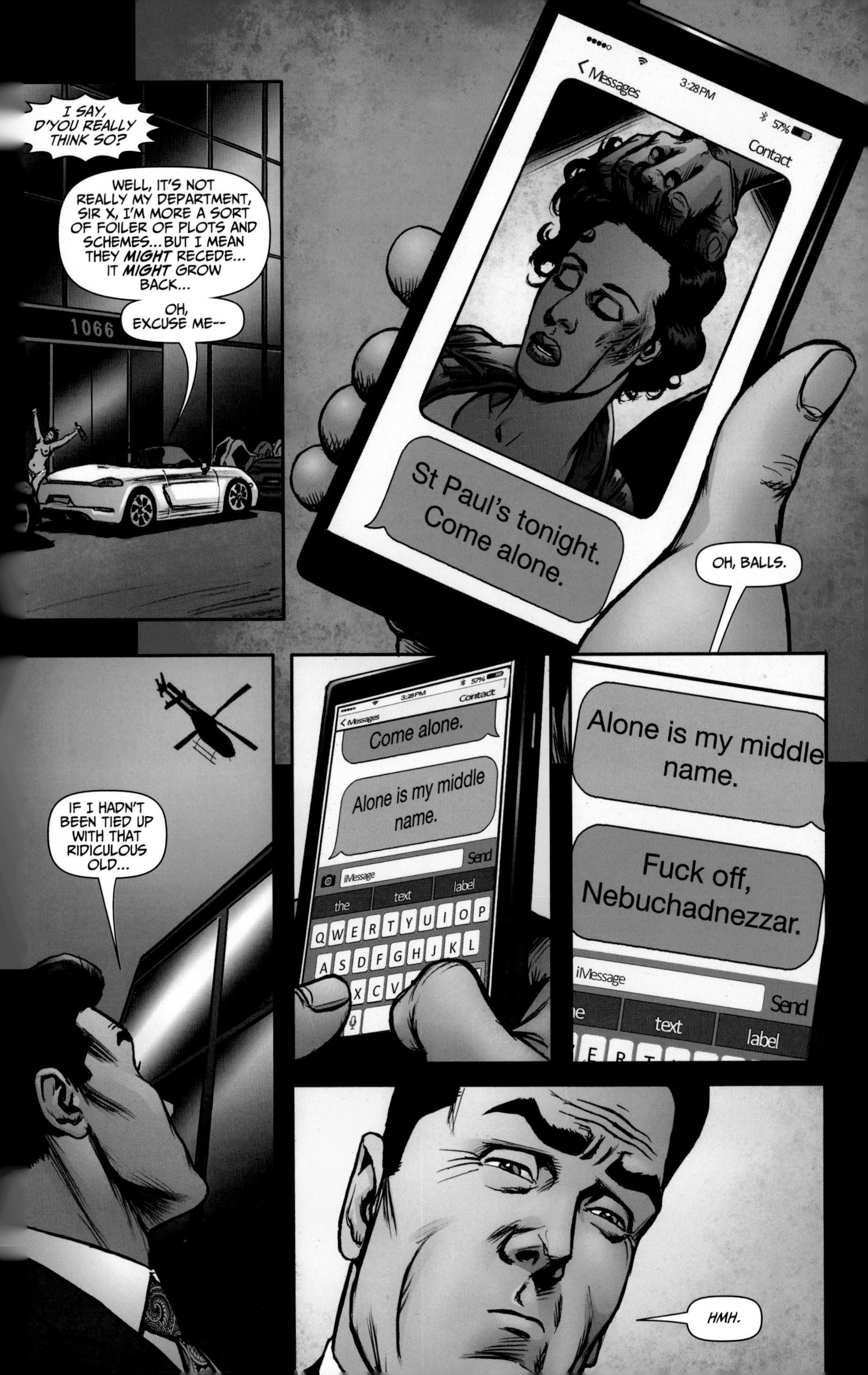
I SAY, D'YOU REALLY THINK SO?
WELL, IT'S NOT REALLY MY DEPARTMENT, SIR X, I'M MORE A SORT OF FOILER OF PLOTS AND SCHEMES... BUT I MEAN THEY MIGHT RECEDE... IT MIGHT GROW BACK...
OH, EXCUSE ME--
1066
Messages
3:28 PM
57%
Contact
St Paul's tonight. Come alone.
OH, BALLS.
IF I HADN'T BEEN TIED UP WITH THAT RIDICULOUS OLD...
Come alone.
Alone is my middle name.
Send
iMessage
Alone is my middle name.
Fuck off, Nebuchadnezzar.
iMessage
Send
HMH.

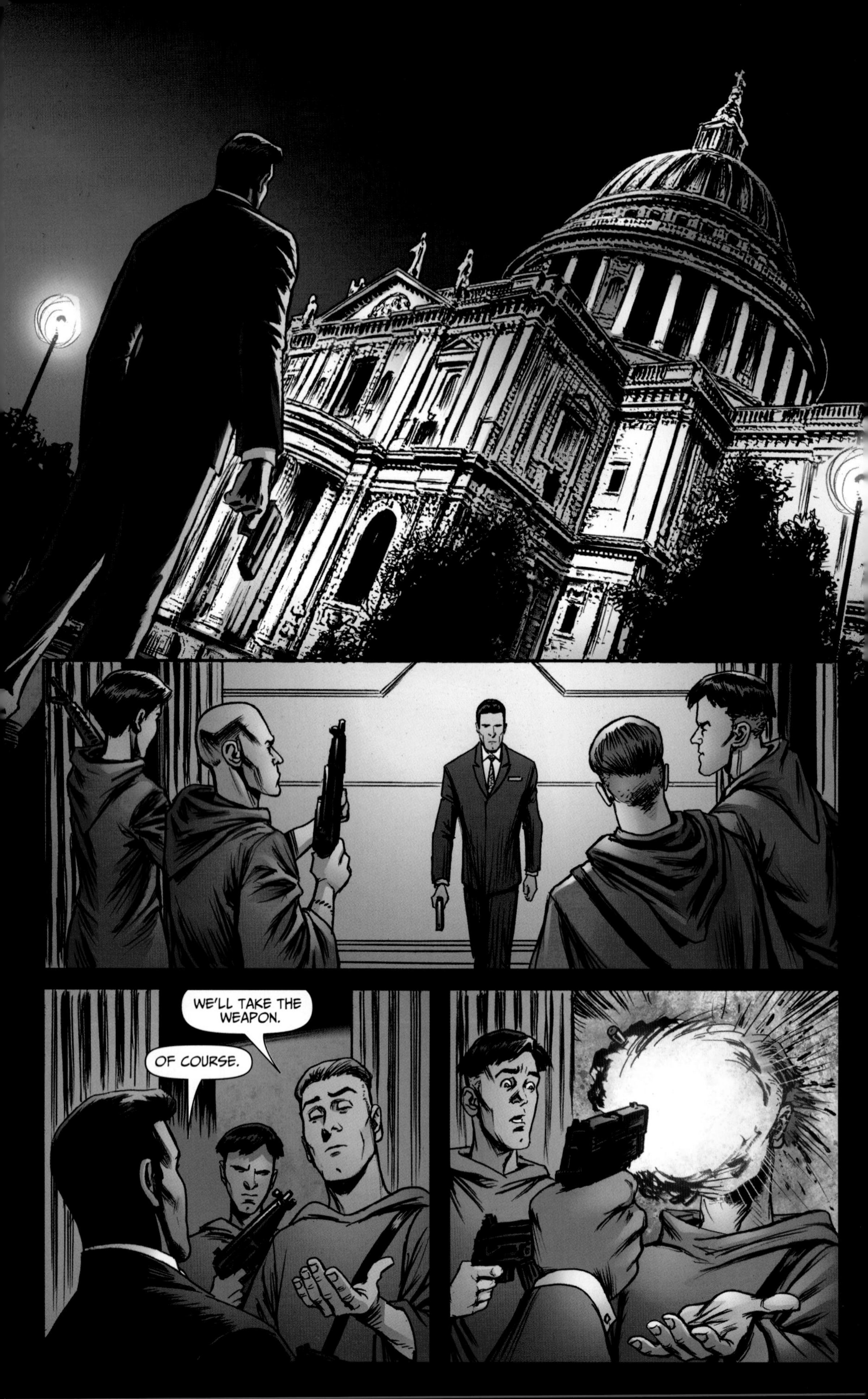
WE'LL TAKE THE WEAPON.
OF COURSE.

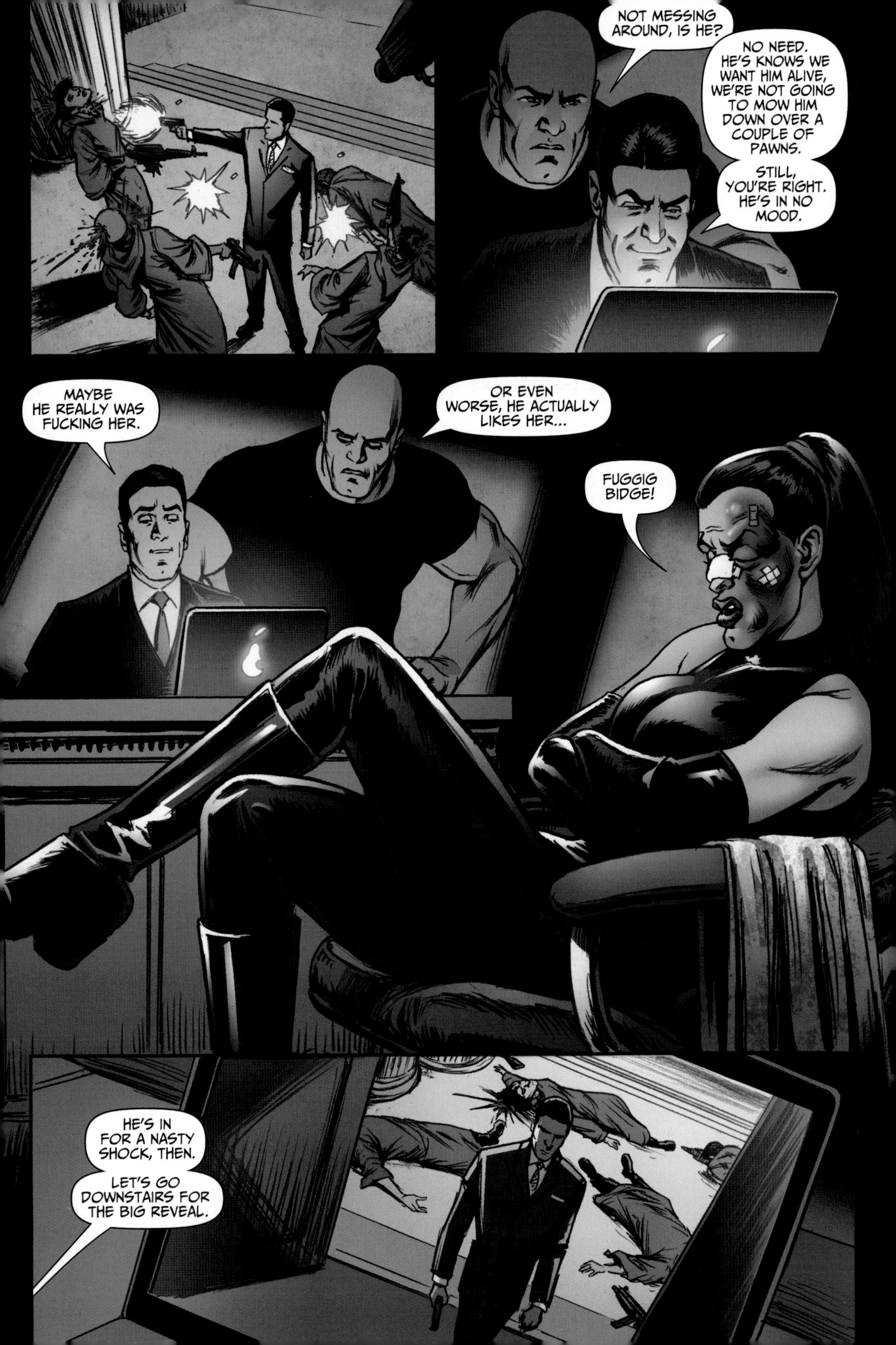
NOT MESSING AROUND, IS HE?
NO NEED. HE'S KNOWS WE WANT HIM ALIVE, WE'RE NOT GOING TO MOW HIM DOWN OVER A COUPLE OF PAWNS.
STILL, YOU'RE RIGHT. HE'S IN NO MOOD.
MAYBE HE REALLY WAS FUCKING HER.
OR EVEN WORSE, HE ACTUALLY LIKES HER...
FUGGIG BIDGE!
HE'S IN FOR A NASTY SHOCK, THEN.
LET'S GO DOWNSTAIRS FOR THE BIG REVEAL.

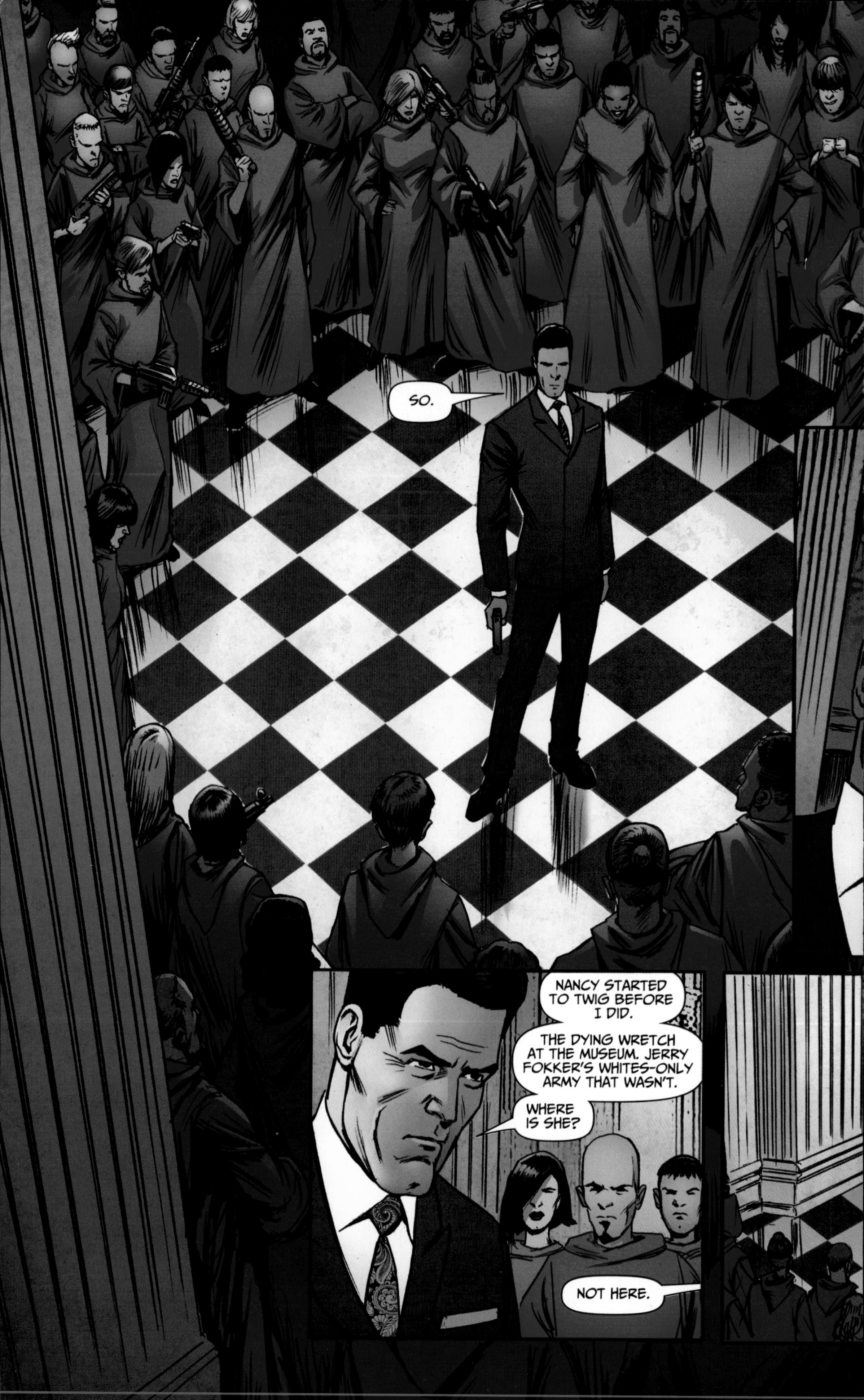
SO.
NANCY STARTED TO TWIG BEFORE I DID.
THE DYING WRETCH AT THE MUSEUM. JERRY FOKKER'S WHITES-ONLY ARMY THAT WASN'T.
WHERE IS SHE?
NOT HERE.

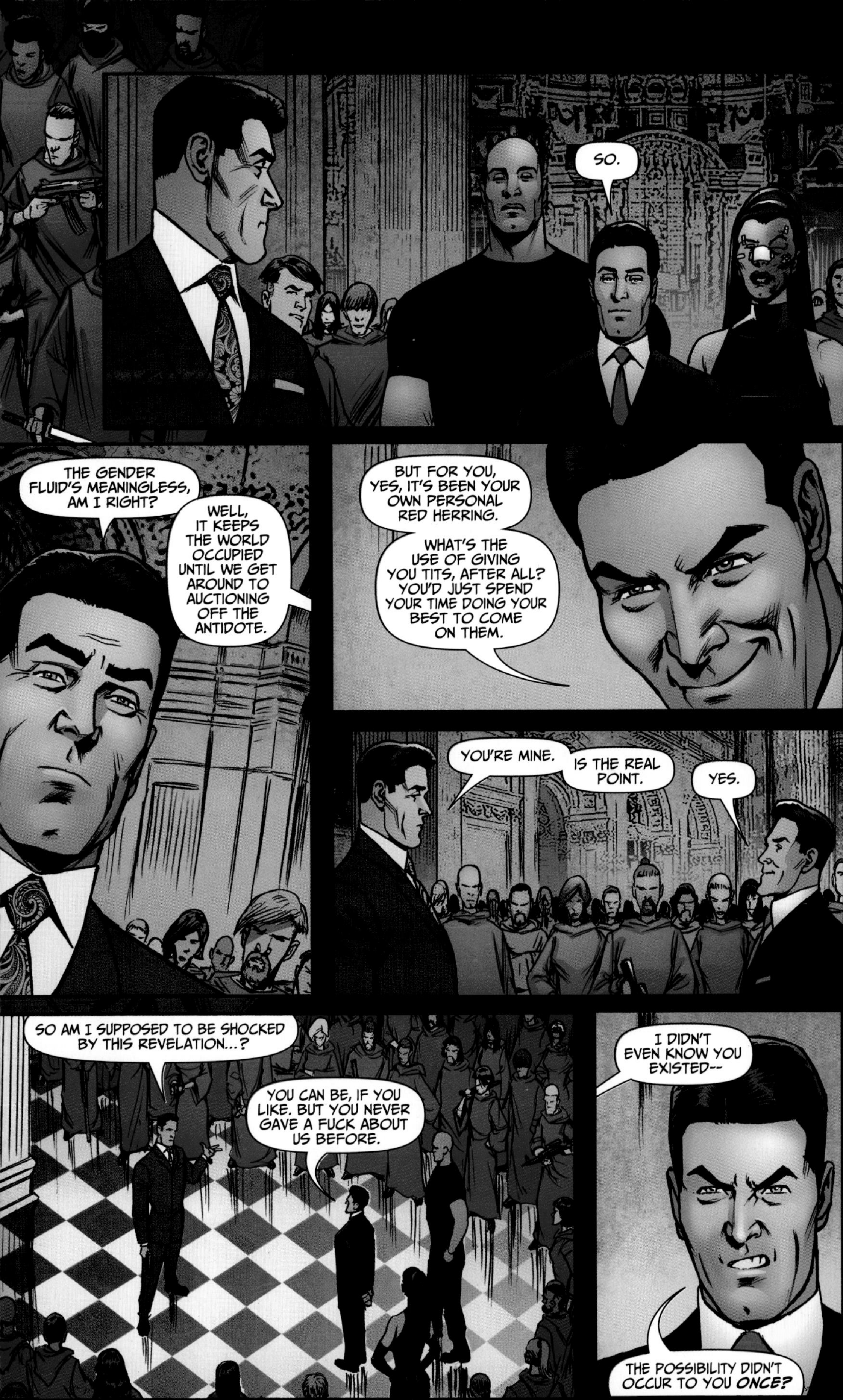
SO.
THE GENDER FLUID'S MEANINGLESS, AM I RIGHT?
WELL, IT KEEPS THE WORLD OCCUPIED UNTIL WE GET AROUND TO AUCTIONING OFF THE ANTIDOTE.
BUT FOR YOU, YES, IT'S BEEN YOUR OWN PERSONAL RED HERRING.
WHAT'S THE USE OF GIVING YOU TITS, AFTER ALL? YOU'D JUST SPEND YOUR TIME DOING YOUR BEST TO COME ON THEM.
YOU'RE MINE.
IS THE REAL POINT.
YES.
SO AM I SUPPOSED TO BE SHOCKED BY THIS REVELATION...?
YOU CAN BE, IF YOU LIKE. BUT YOU NEVER GAVE A FUCK ABOUT US BEFORE.
I DIDN'T EVEN KNOW YOU EXISTED--
THE POSSIBILITY DIDN'T OCCUR TO YOU *ONCE?*

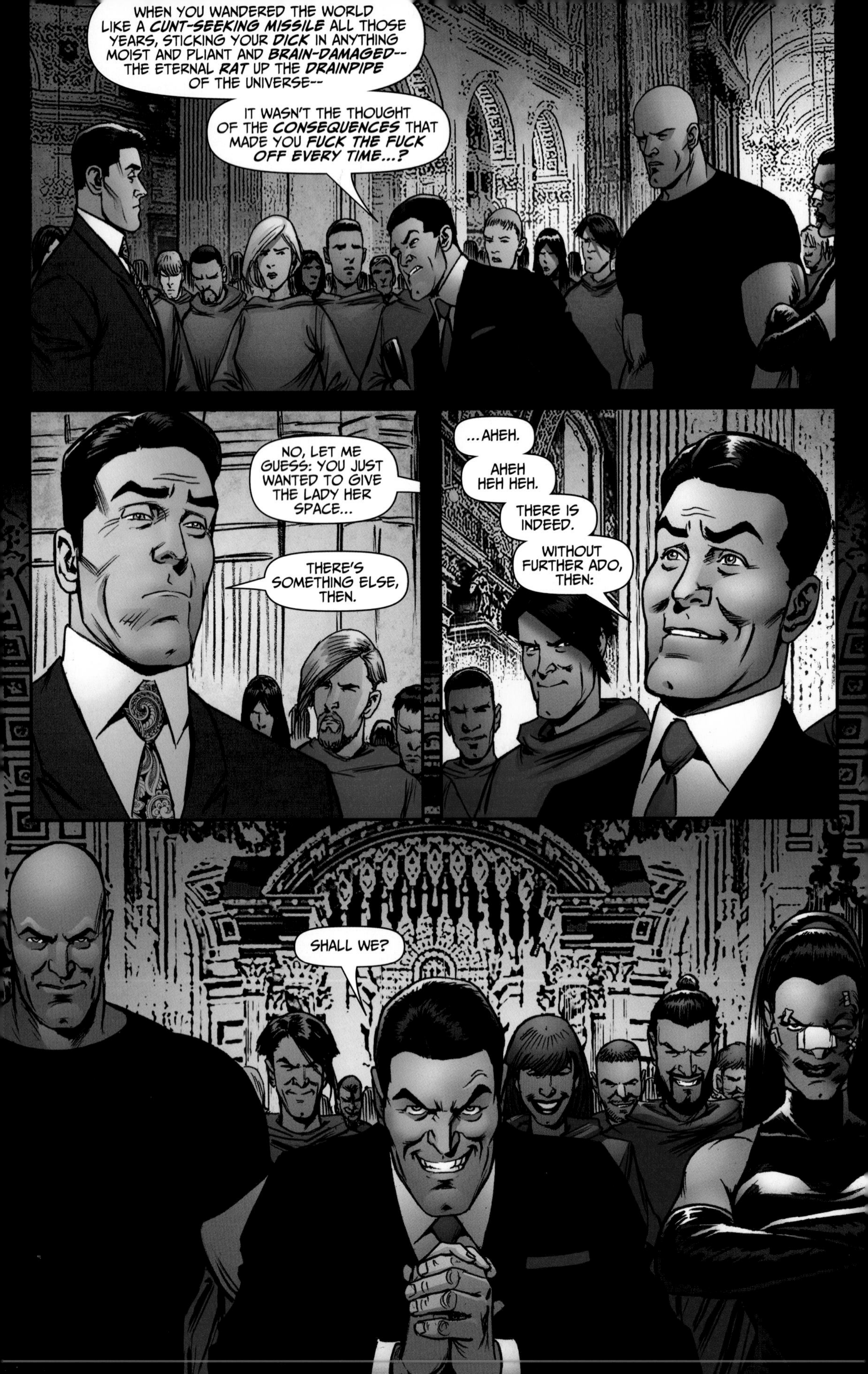
WHEN YOU WANDERED THE WORLD LIKE A CUNT-SEEKING MISSILE ALL THOSE YEARS, STICKING YOUR DICK IN ANYTHING MOIST AND PLIANT AND BRAIN-DAMAGED-- THE ETERNAL RAT UP THE DRAINPIPE OF THE UNIVERSE--
IT WASN'T THE THOUGHT OF THE CONSEQUENCES THAT MADE YOU FUCK THE FUCK OFF EVERY TIME...?
NO, LET ME GUESS: YOU JUST WANTED TO GIVE THE LADY HER SPACE...
THERE'S SOMETHING ELSE, THEN.
...AHEH.
AHEH HEH HEH.
THERE IS INDEED.
WITHOUT FURTHER ADO, THEN:
SHALL WE?

5

BETTER GET THE PUPPY

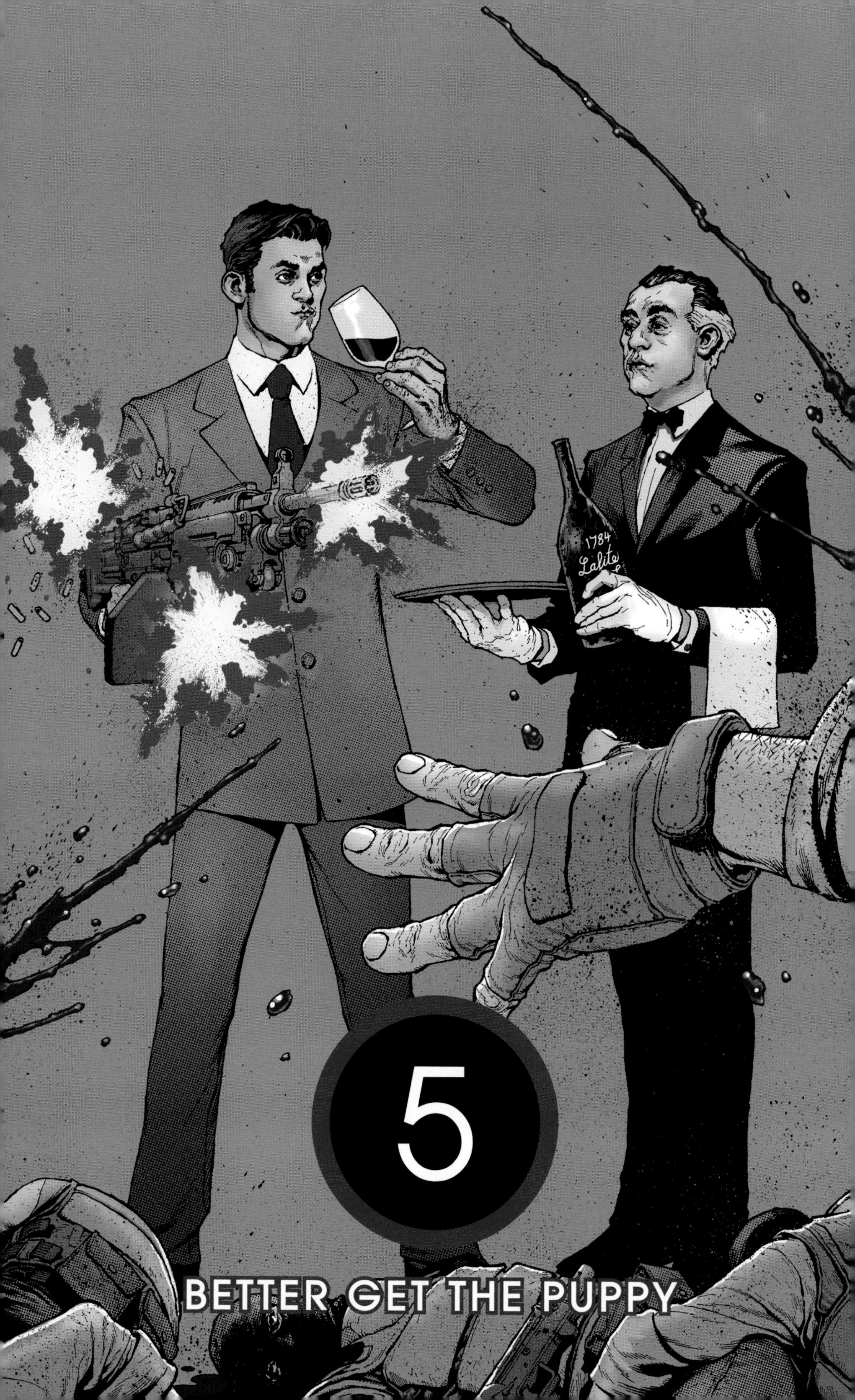

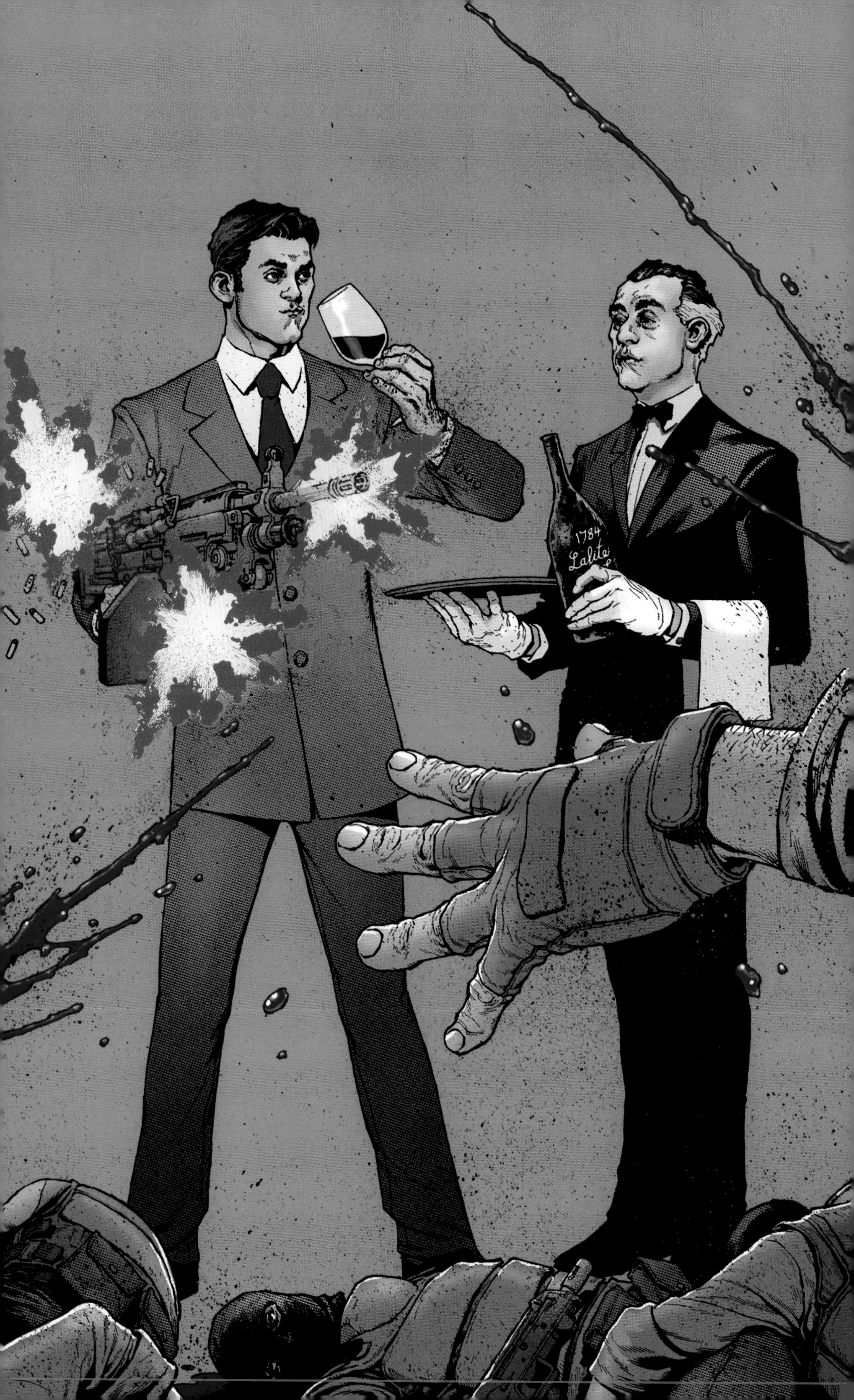
1784
Lalite

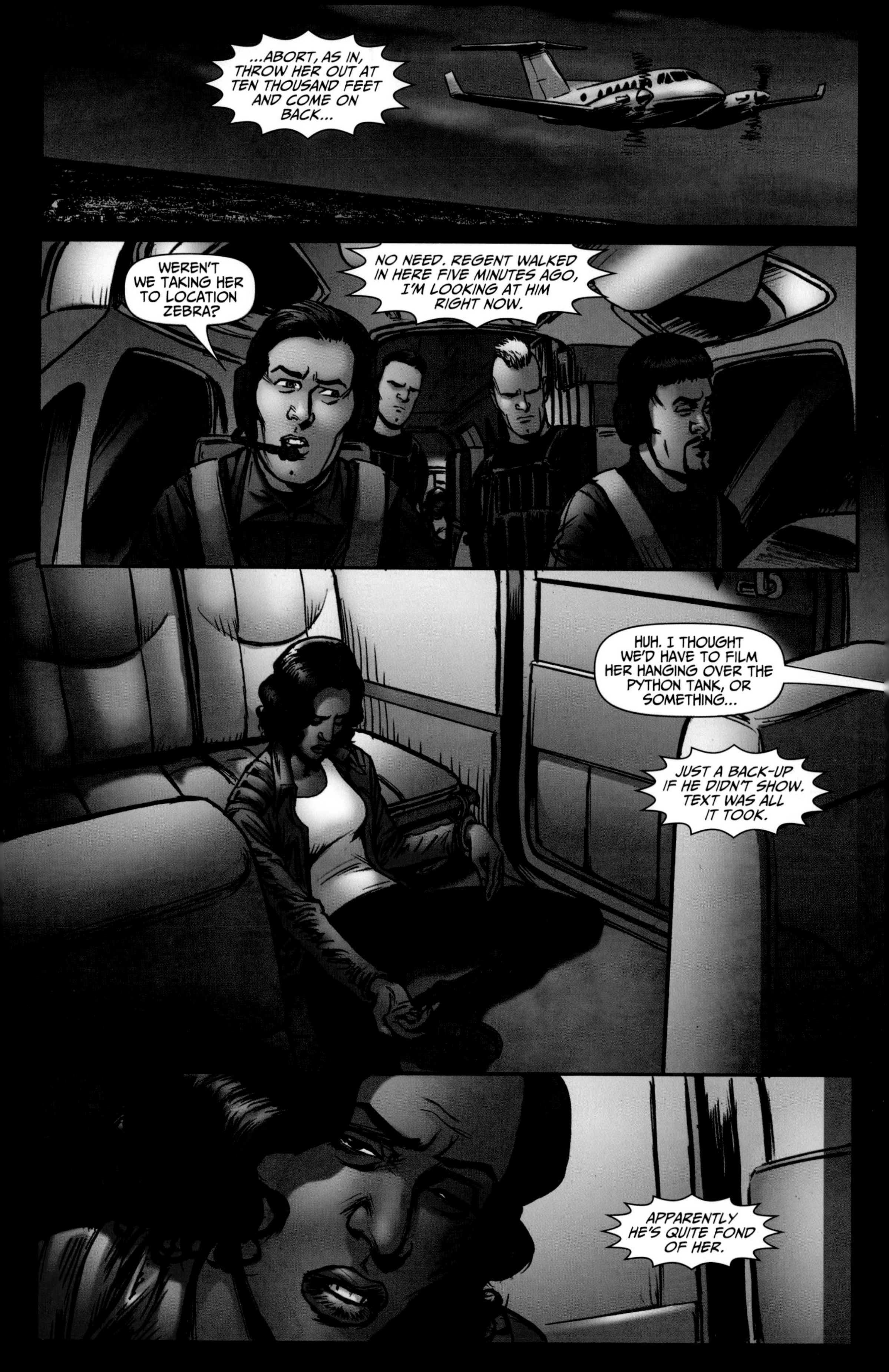
...ABORT, AS IN, THROW HER OUT AT TEN THOUSAND FEET AND COME ON BACK...
WEREN'T WE TAKING HER TO LOCATION ZEBRA?
NO NEED. REGENT WALKED IN HERE FIVE MINUTES AGO, I'M LOOKING AT HIM RIGHT NOW.
HUH. I THOUGHT WE'D HAVE TO FILM HER HANGING OVER THE PYTHON TANK, OR SOMETHING...
JUST A BACK-UP IF HE DIDN'T SHOW. TEXT WAS ALL IT TOOK.
APPARENTLY HE'S QUITE FOND OF HER.

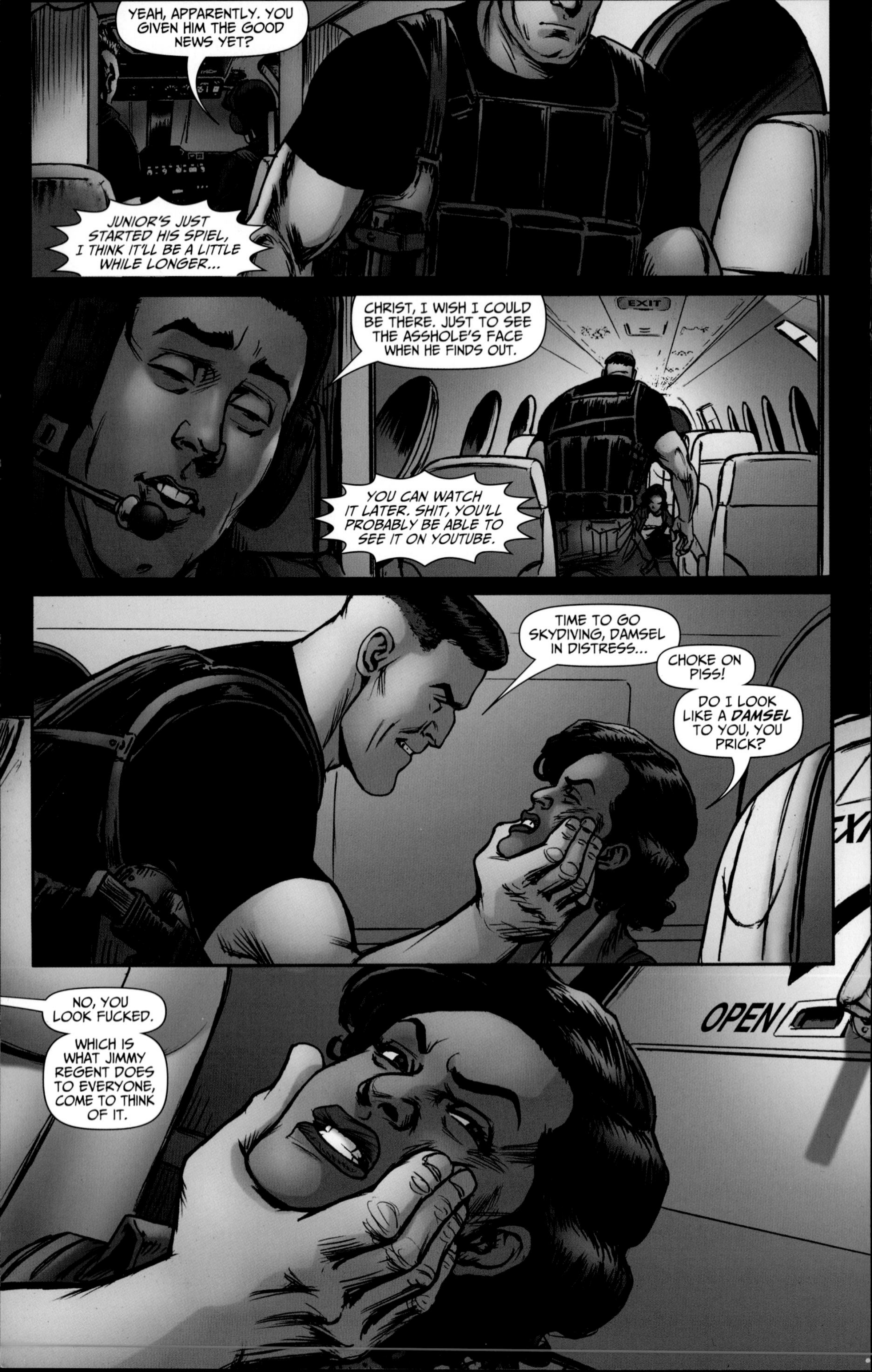
YEAH, APPARENTLY. YOU GIVEN HIM THE GOOD NEWS YET?
JUNIOR'S JUST STARTED HIS SPIEL, I THINK IT'LL BE A LITTLE WHILE LONGER...
CHRIST, I WISH I COULD BE THERE. JUST TO SEE THE ASSHOLE'S FACE WHEN HE FINDS OUT.
EXIT
YOU CAN WATCH IT LATER. SHIT, YOU'LL PROBABLY BE ABLE TO SEE IT ON YOUTUBE.
TIME TO GO SKYDIVING, DAMSEL IN DISTRESS...
CHOKE ON PISS!
DO I LOOK LIKE A DAMSEL TO YOU, YOU PRICK?
NO, YOU LOOK FUCKED.
WHICH IS WHAT JIMMY REGENT DOES TO EVERYONE, COME TO THINK OF IT.
OPEN

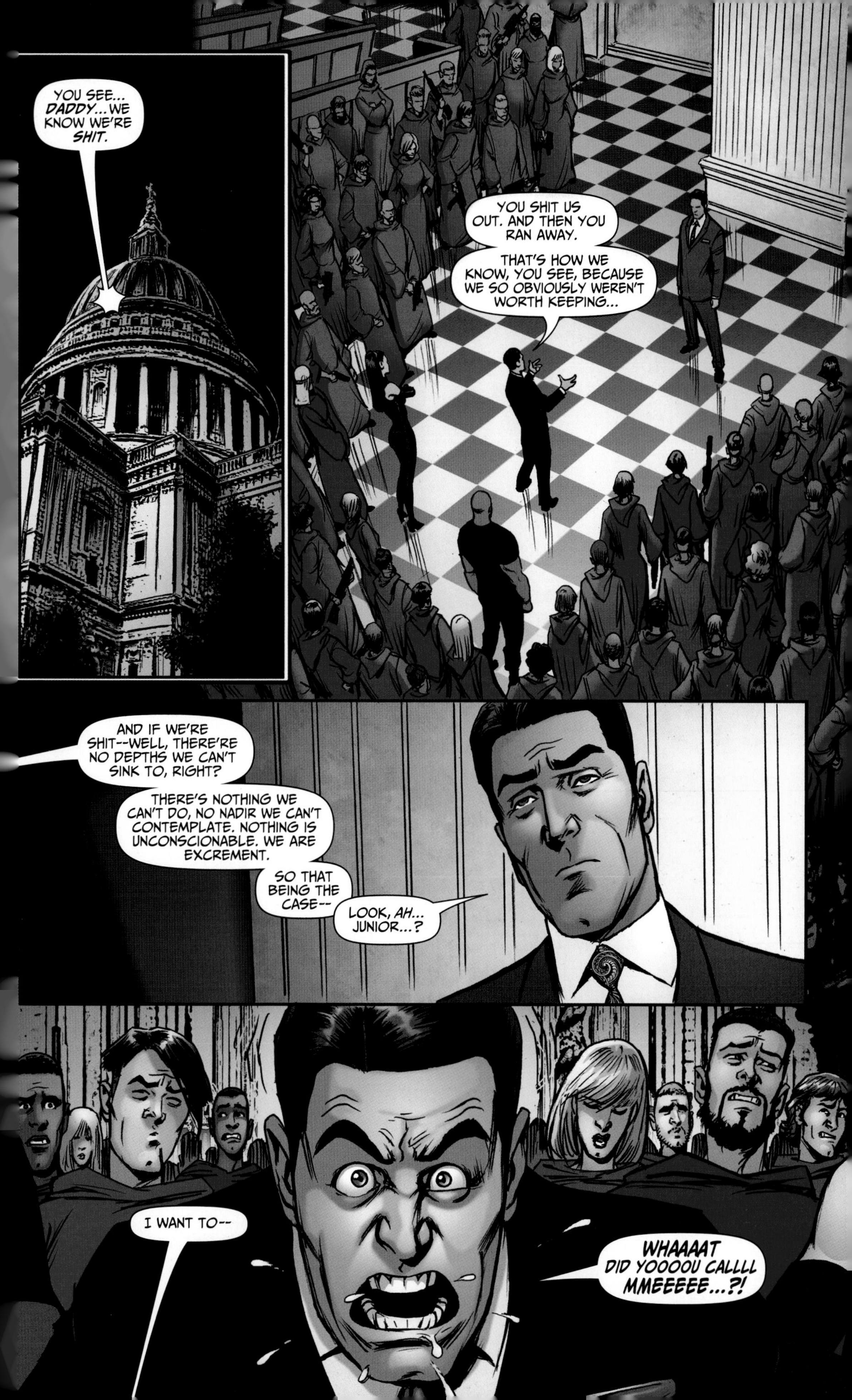
YOU SEE... DADDY...WE KNOW WE'RE SHIT.
YOU SHIT US OUT. AND THEN YOU RAN AWAY.
THAT'S HOW WE KNOW, YOU SEE, BECAUSE WE SO OBVIOUSLY WEREN'T WORTH KEEPING...
AND IF WE'RE SHIT--WELL, THERE'RE NO DEPTHS WE CAN'T SINK TO, RIGHT?
THERE'S NOTHING WE CAN'T DO, NO NADIR WE CAN'T CONTEMPLATE. NOTHING IS UNCONSCIONABLE. WE ARE EXCREMENT.
SO THAT BEING THE CASE--
LOOK, AH... JUNIOR...?
I WANT TO--
WHAAAAT DID YOOOOU CALLLL MMEEEEEE...?!

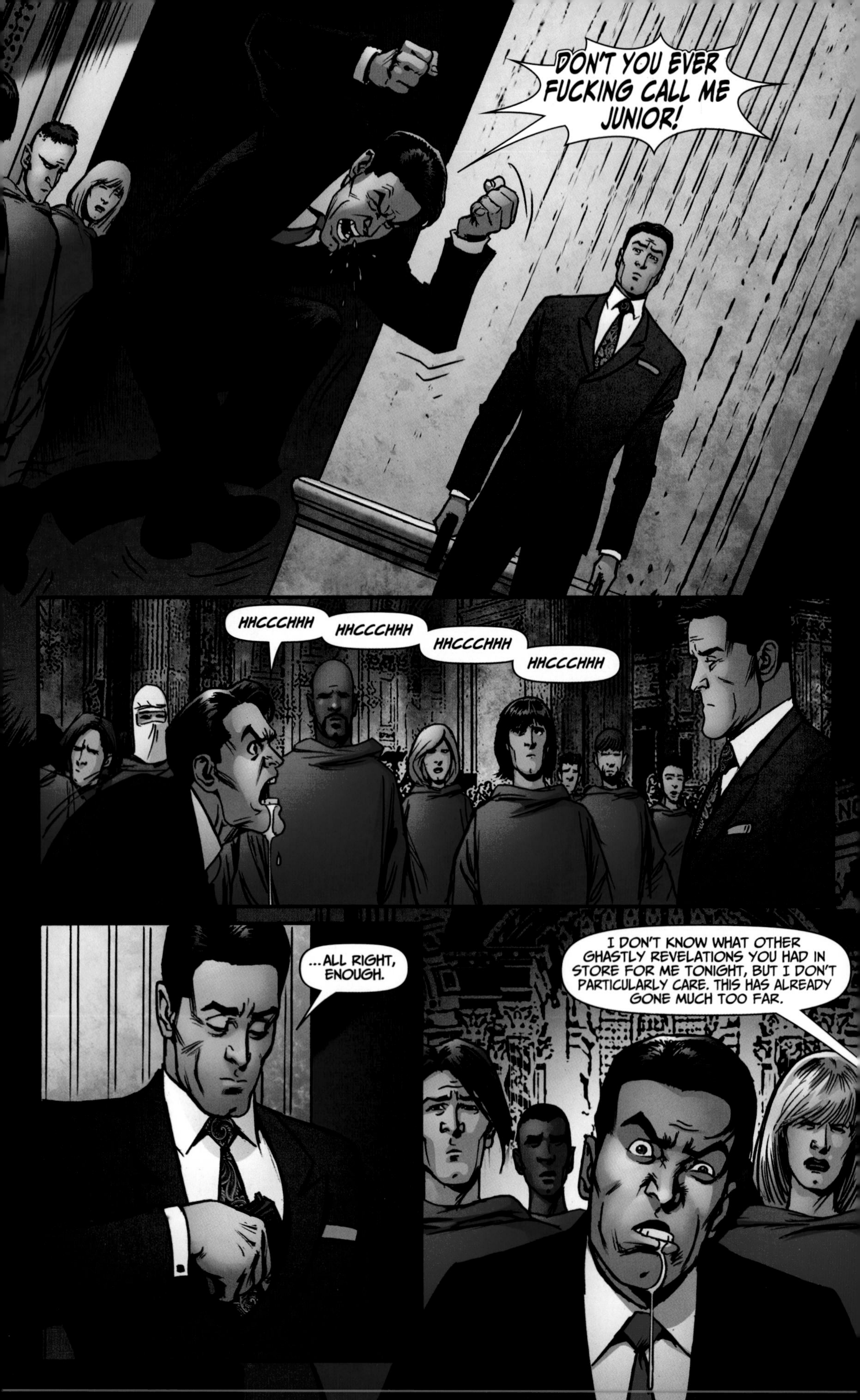
DON'T YOU EVER FUCKING CALL ME JUNIOR!
HHCCCHHH
HHCCCHHH
HHCCCHHH
HHCCCHHH
...ALL RIGHT, ENOUGH.
I DON'T KNOW WHAT OTHER GHASTLY REVELATIONS YOU HAD IN STORE FOR ME TONIGHT, BUT I DON'T PARTICULARLY CARE. THIS HAS ALREADY GONE MUCH TOO FAR.

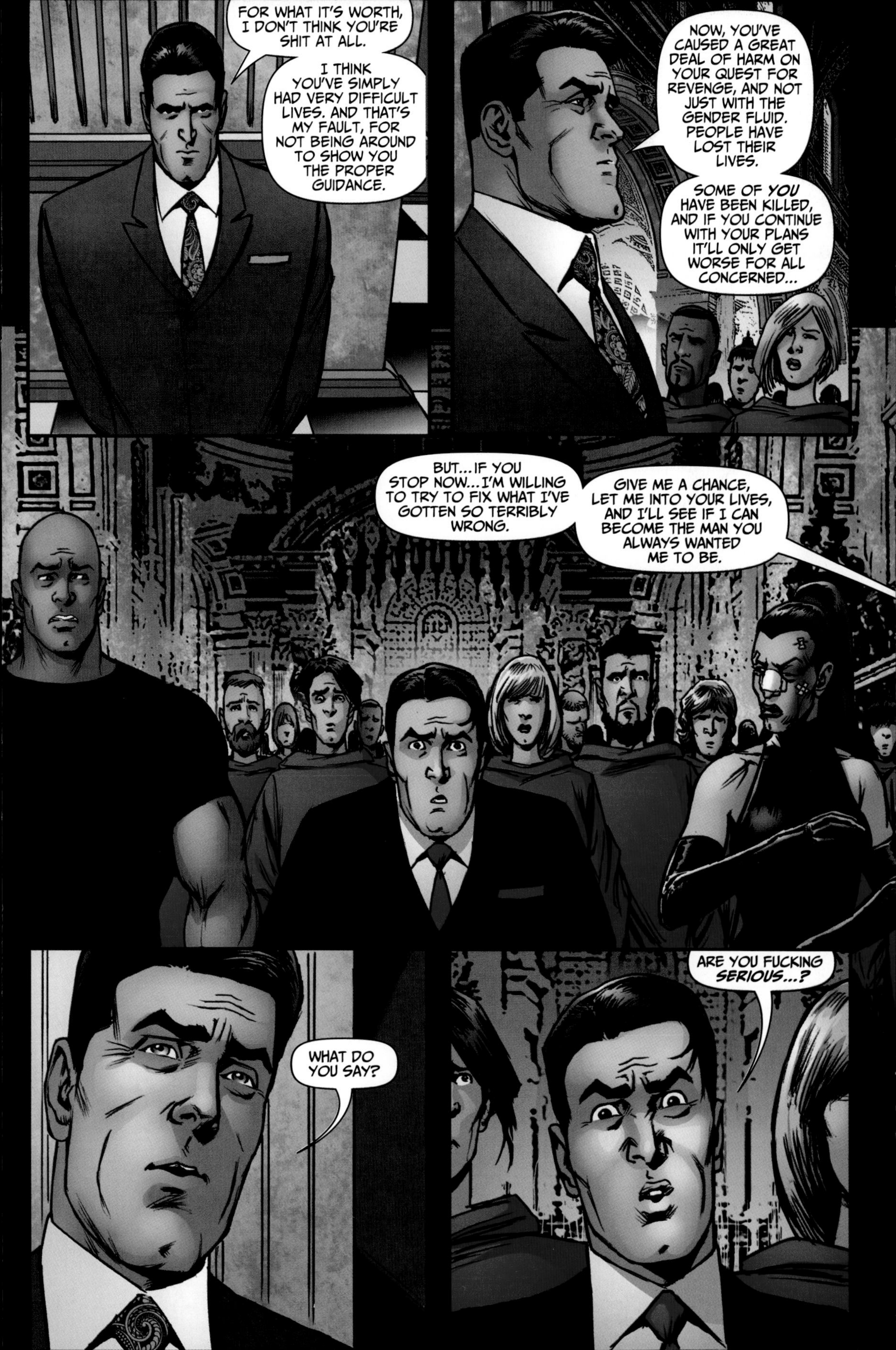
FOR WHAT IT'S WORTH, I DON'T THINK YOU'RE SHIT AT ALL.
I THINK YOU'VE SIMPLY HAD VERY DIFFICULT LIVES. AND THAT'S MY FAULT, FOR NOT BEING AROUND TO SHOW YOU THE PROPER GUIDANCE.
NOW, YOU'VE CAUSED A GREAT DEAL OF HARM ON YOUR QUEST FOR REVENGE, AND NOT JUST WITH THE GENDER FLUID. PEOPLE HAVE LOST THEIR LIVES.
SOME OF *YOU* HAVE BEEN KILLED, AND IF YOU CONTINUE WITH YOUR PLANS IT'LL ONLY GET WORSE FOR ALL CONCERNED...
BUT...IF YOU STOP NOW...I'M WILLING TO TRY TO FIX WHAT I'VE GOTTEN SO TERRIBLY WRONG.
GIVE ME A CHANCE, LET ME INTO YOUR LIVES, AND I'LL SEE IF I CAN BECOME THE MAN YOU ALWAYS WANTED ME TO BE.
WHAT DO YOU SAY?
ARE YOU FUCKING *SERIOUS...?*

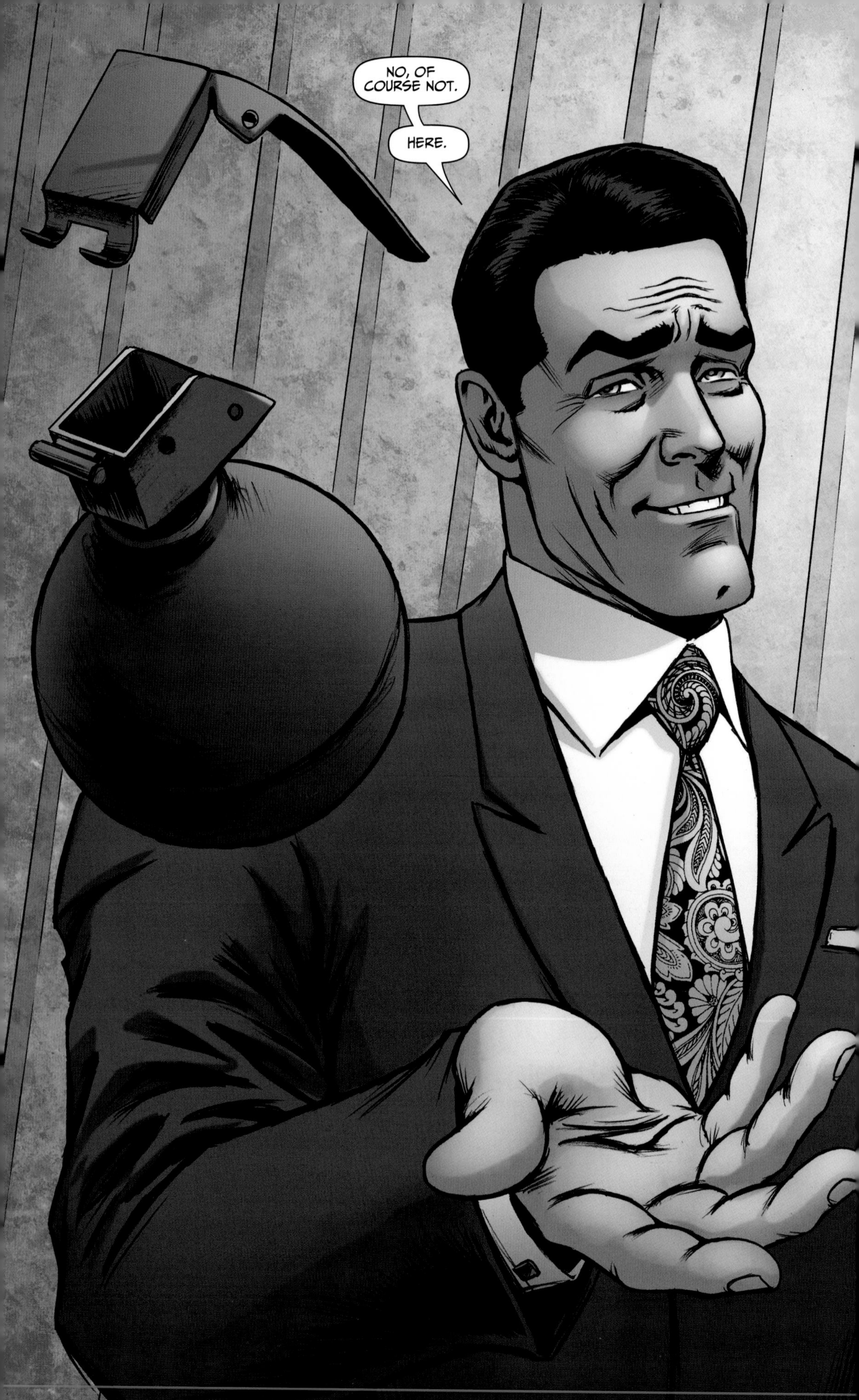
NO, OF COURSE NOT.
HERE.

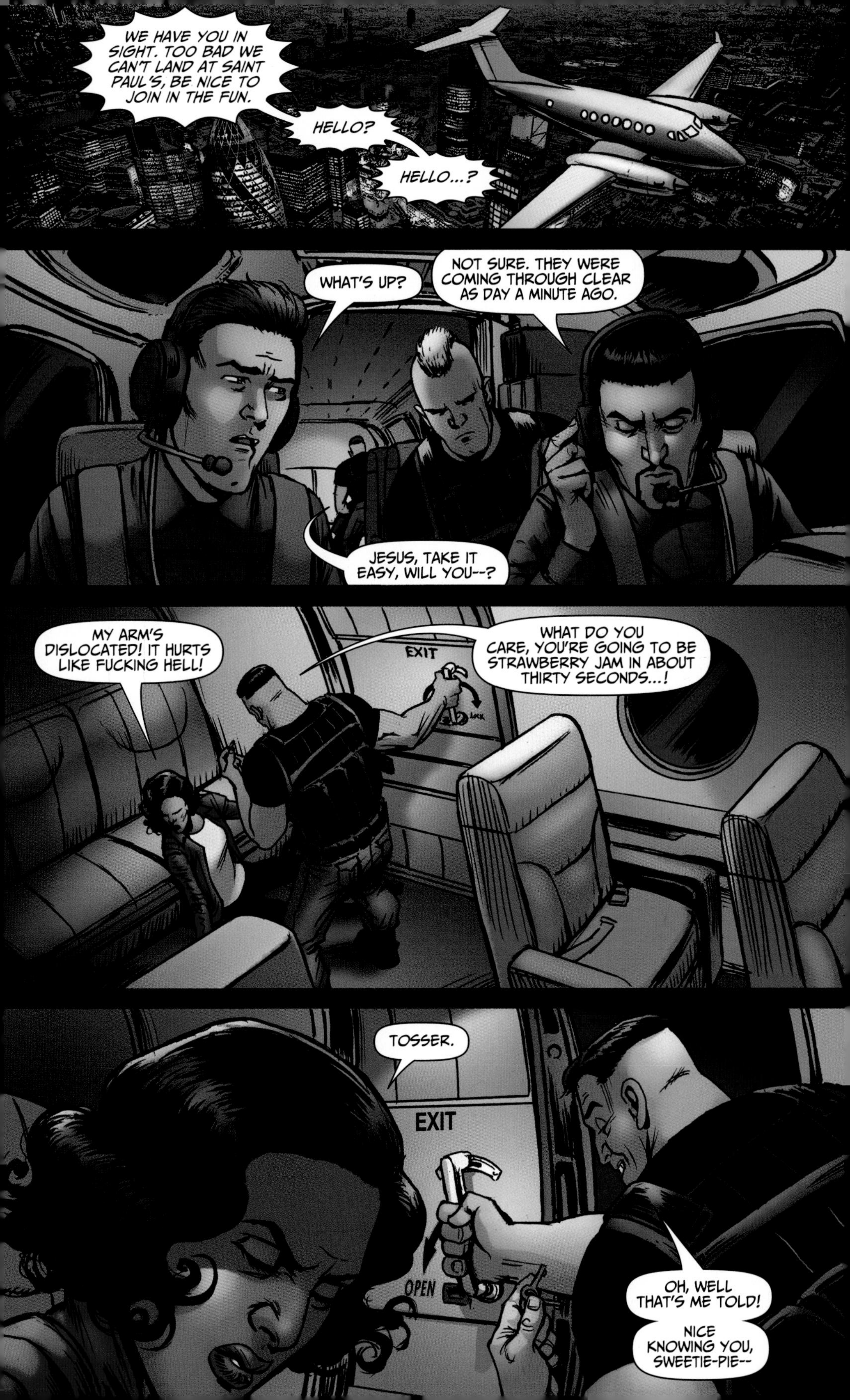
WE HAVE YOU IN SIGHT. TOO BAD WE CAN'T LAND AT SAINT PAUL'S, BE NICE TO JOIN IN THE FUN.
HELLO?
HELLO...?
WHAT'S UP?
NOT SURE. THEY WERE COMING THROUGH CLEAR AS DAY A MINUTE AGO.
JESUS, TAKE IT EASY, WILL YOU--?
MY ARM'S DISLOCATED! IT HURTS LIKE FUCKING HELL!
WHAT DO YOU CARE, YOU'RE GOING TO BE STRAWBERRY JAM IN ABOUT THIRTY SECONDS...!
EXIT
TOSSER.
EXIT
OPEN
OH, WELL THAT'S ME TOLD!
NICE KNOWING YOU, SWEETIE-PIE--

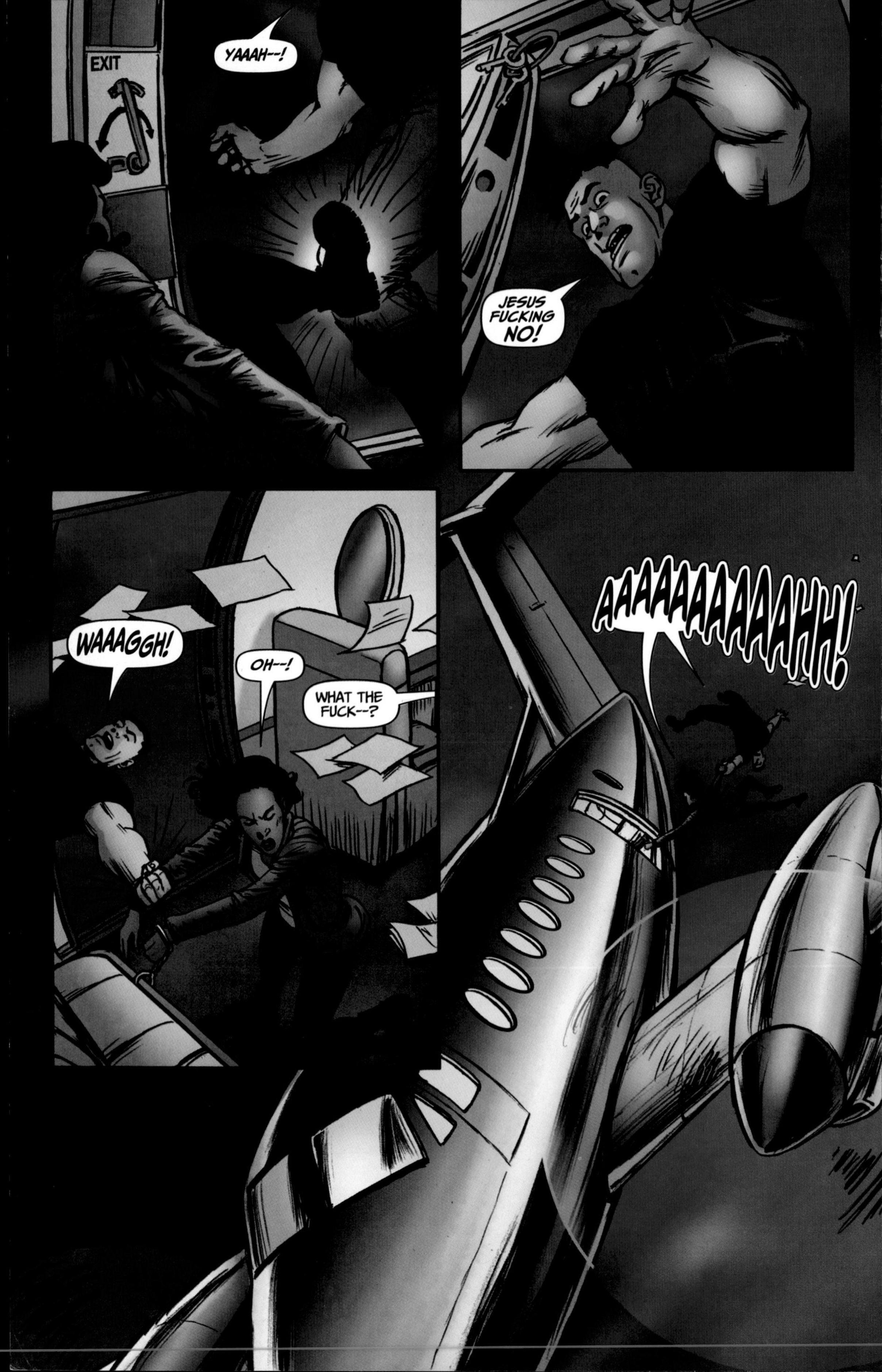
EXIT
YAAAH--!
JESUS FUCKING NO!
WAAAGGH!
OH--!
WHAT THE FUCK--?
AAAAAAAAAAAHH!

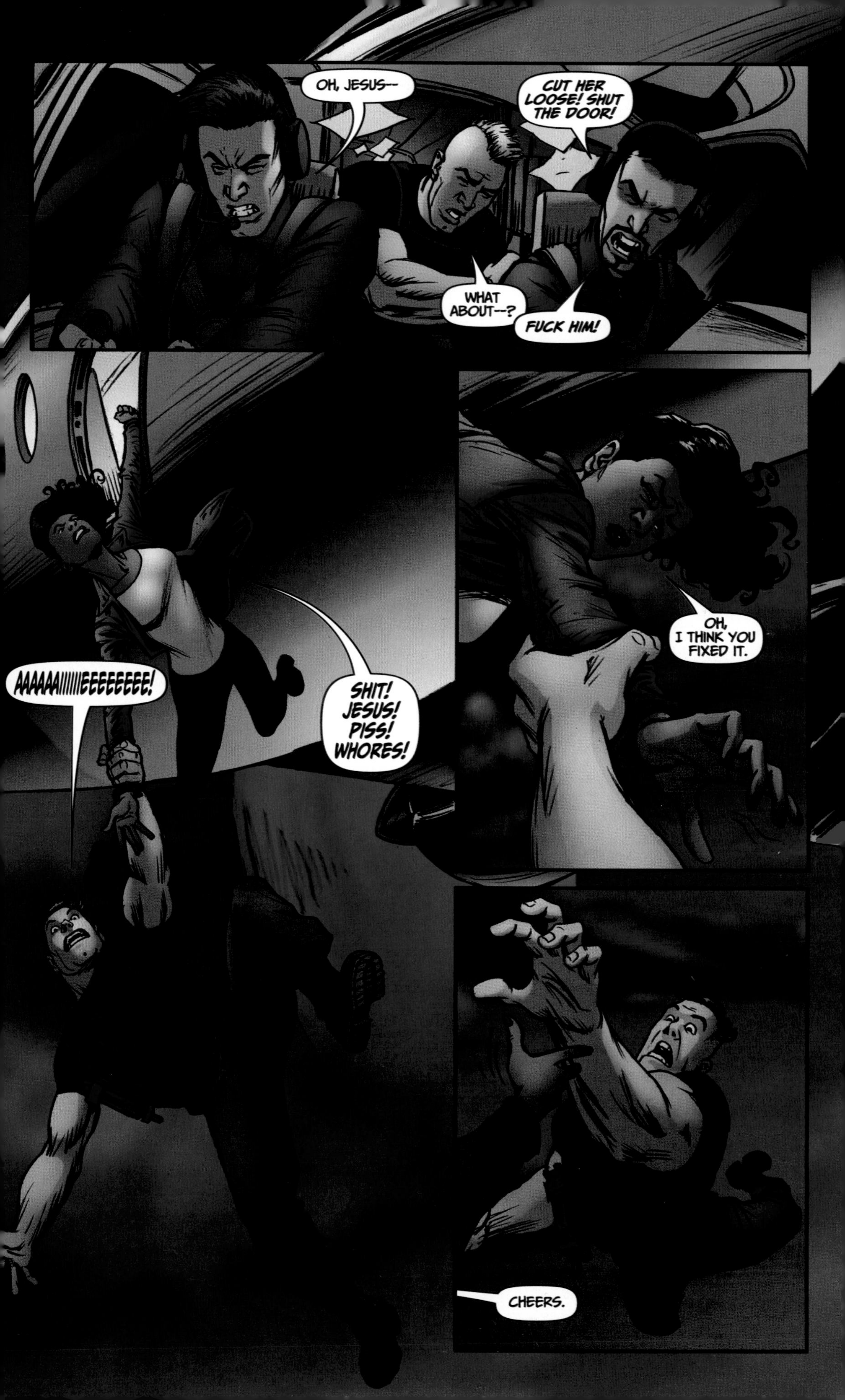
OH, JESUS--
CUT HER LOOSE! SHUT THE DOOR!
WHAT ABOUT--?
FUCK HIM!
AAAAAAIIIIIIEEEEEEEE!
SHIT! JESUS! PISS! WHORES!
OH, I THINK YOU FIXED IT.
CHEERS.

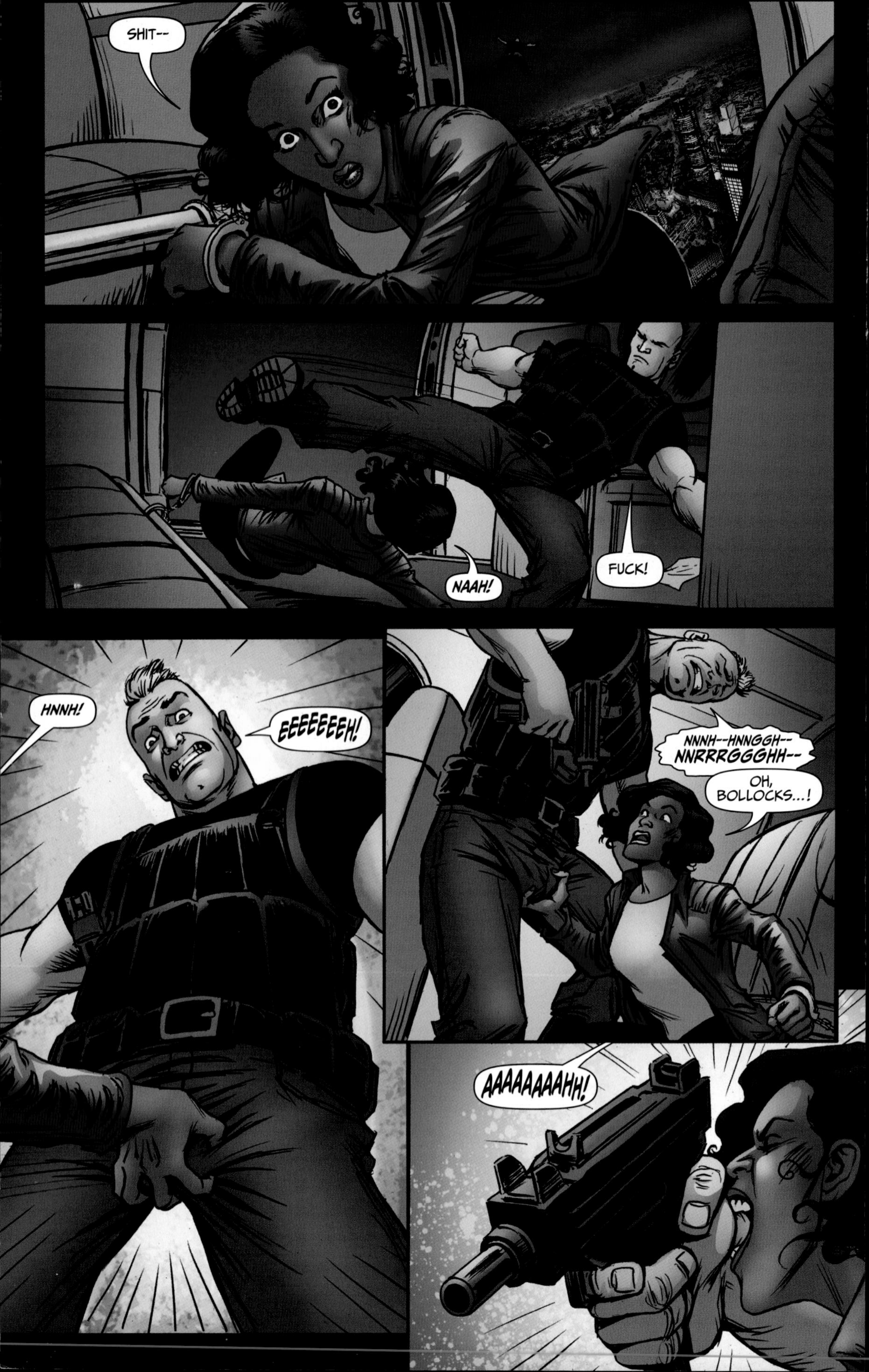
SHIT--
NAAH!
FUCK!
HNNH!
EEEEEEEH!
NNNH--HNNGGH--
NNRRRGGGHH--
OH, BOLLOCKS...!
AAAAAAAAHH!

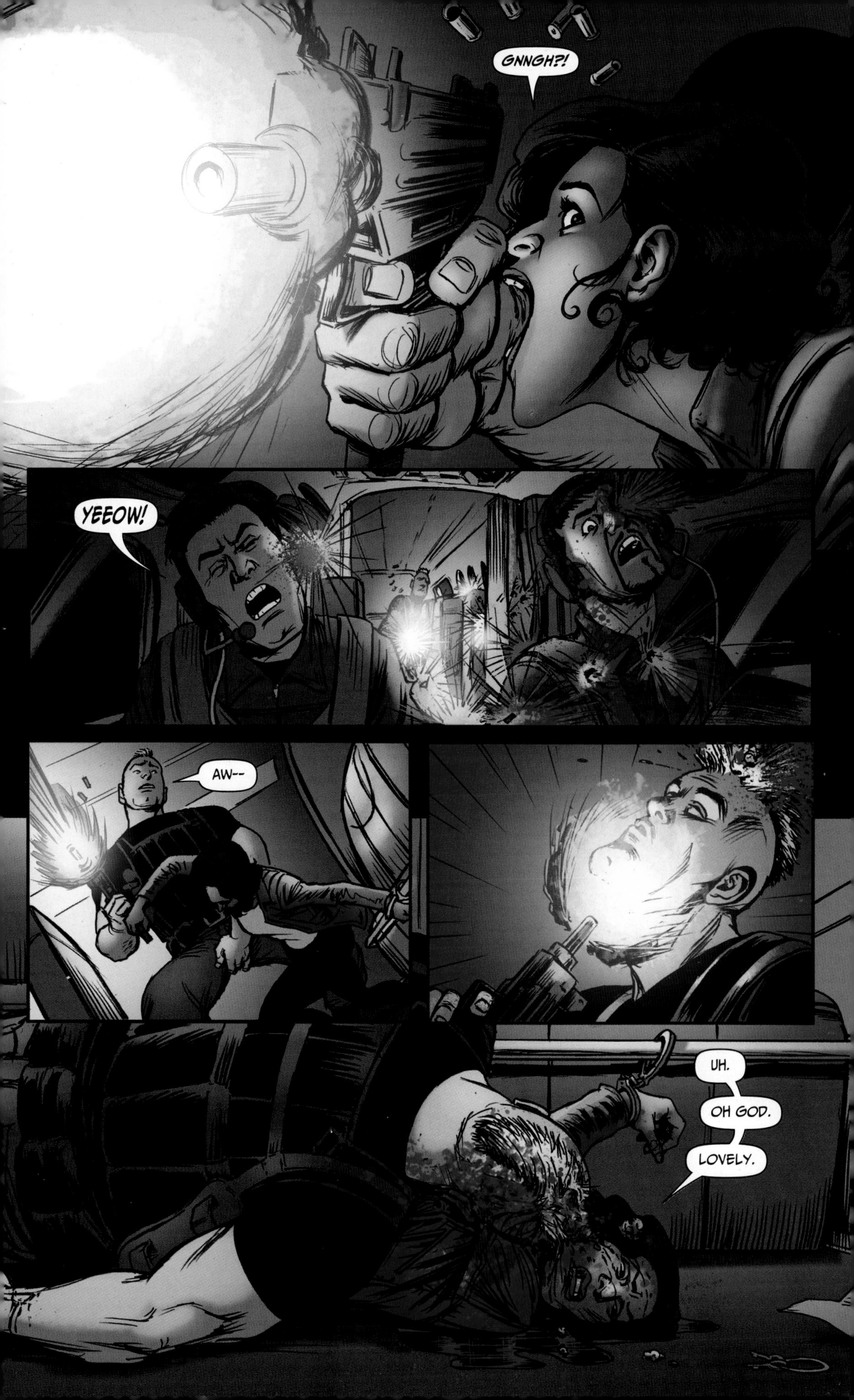
GNNGH?!
YEEOW!
AW--
UH.
OH GOD.
LOVELY.

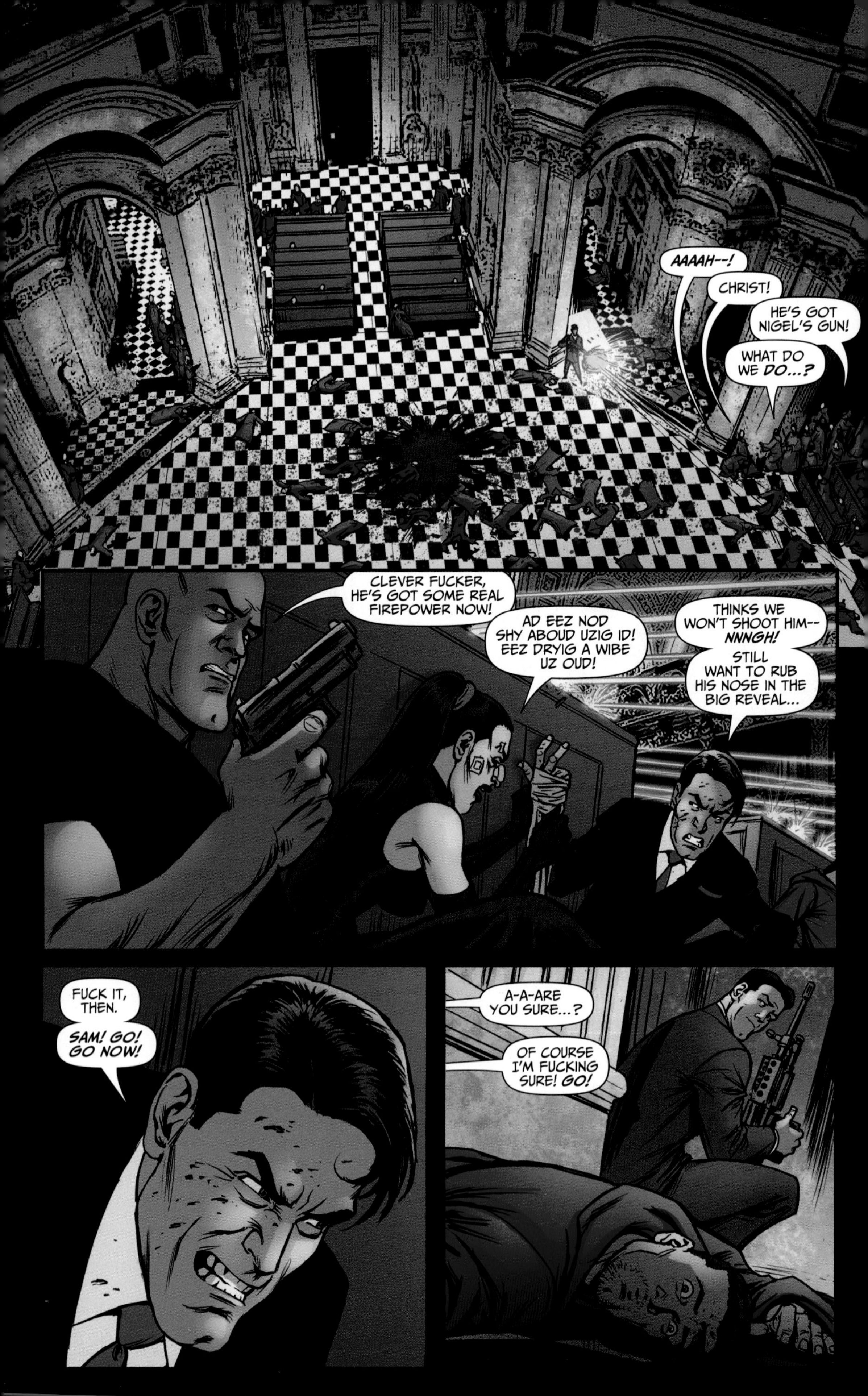
AAAAH--!
CHRIST!
HE'S GOT NIGEL'S GUN!
WHAT DO WE DO...?
CLEVER FUCKER, HE'S GOT SOME REAL FIREPOWER NOW!
AD EEZ NOD SHY ABOUD UZIG ID! EEZ DRYIG A WIBE UZ OUD!
THINKS WE WON'T SHOOT HIM-- NNNGH!
STILL WANT TO RUB HIS NOSE IN THE BIG REVEAL...
FUCK IT, THEN.
SAM! GO! GO NOW!
A-A-ARE YOU SURE...?
OF COURSE I'M FUCKING SURE! GO!

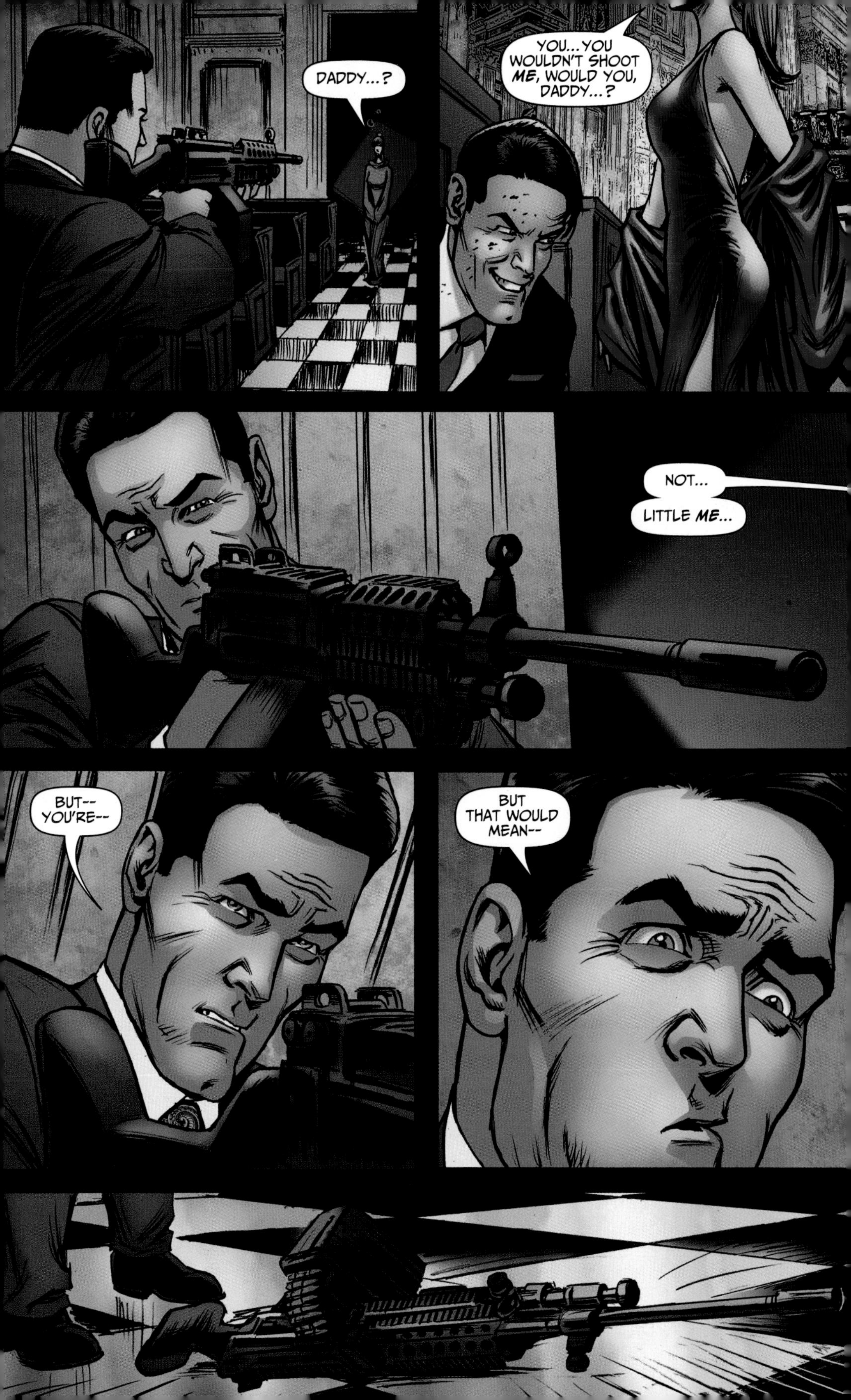
DADDY...?
YOU...YOU WOULDN'T SHOOT *ME*, WOULD YOU, DADDY...?
NOT...
LITTLE *ME*...
BUT-- YOU'RE--
BUT THAT WOULD MEAN--

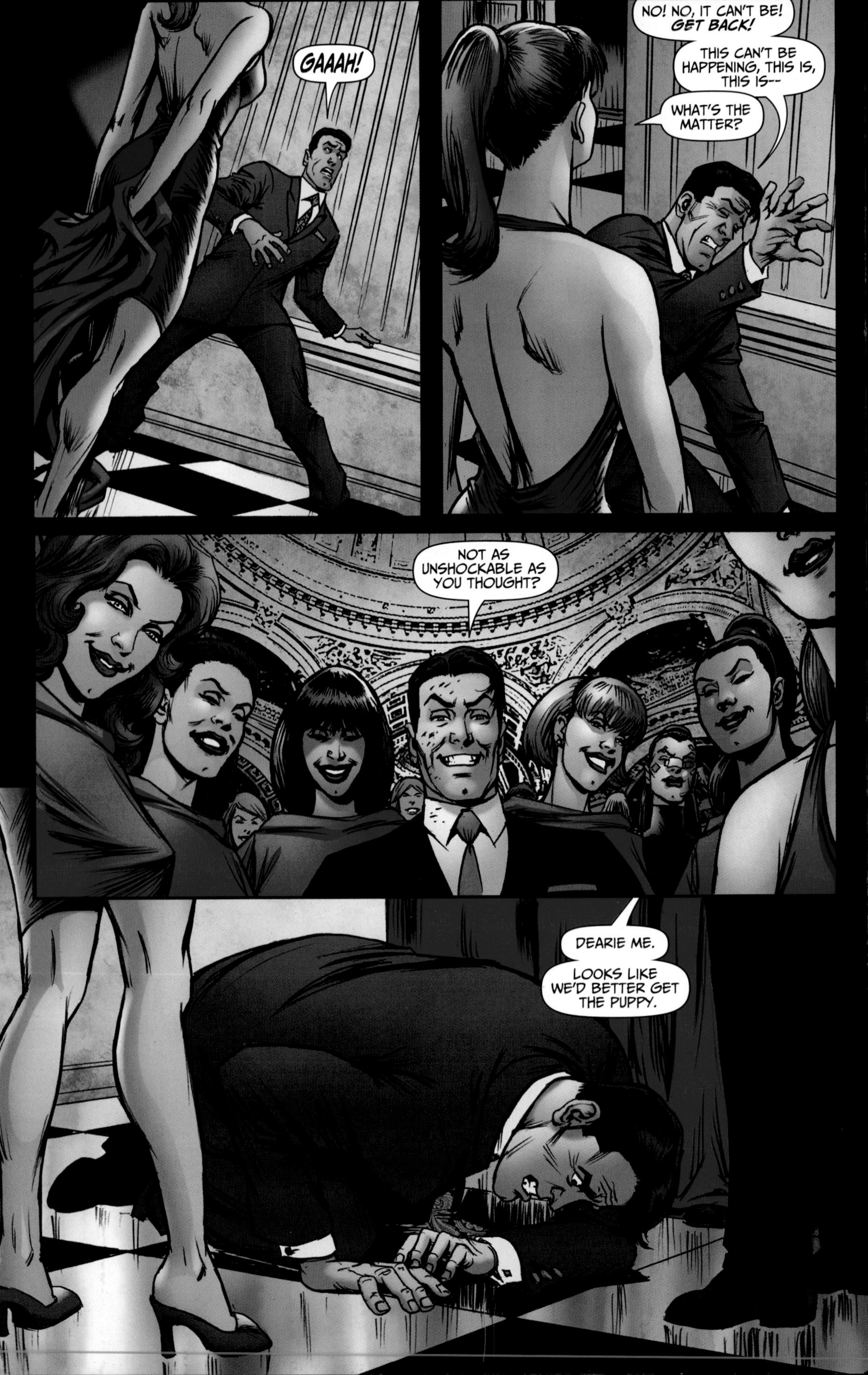
GAAAH!
NO! NO, IT CAN'T BE! GET BACK!
THIS CAN'T BE HAPPENING, THIS IS, THIS IS--
WHAT'S THE MATTER?
NOT AS UNSHOCKABLE AS YOU THOUGHT?
DEARIE ME.
LOOKS LIKE WE'D BETTER GET THE PUPPY.

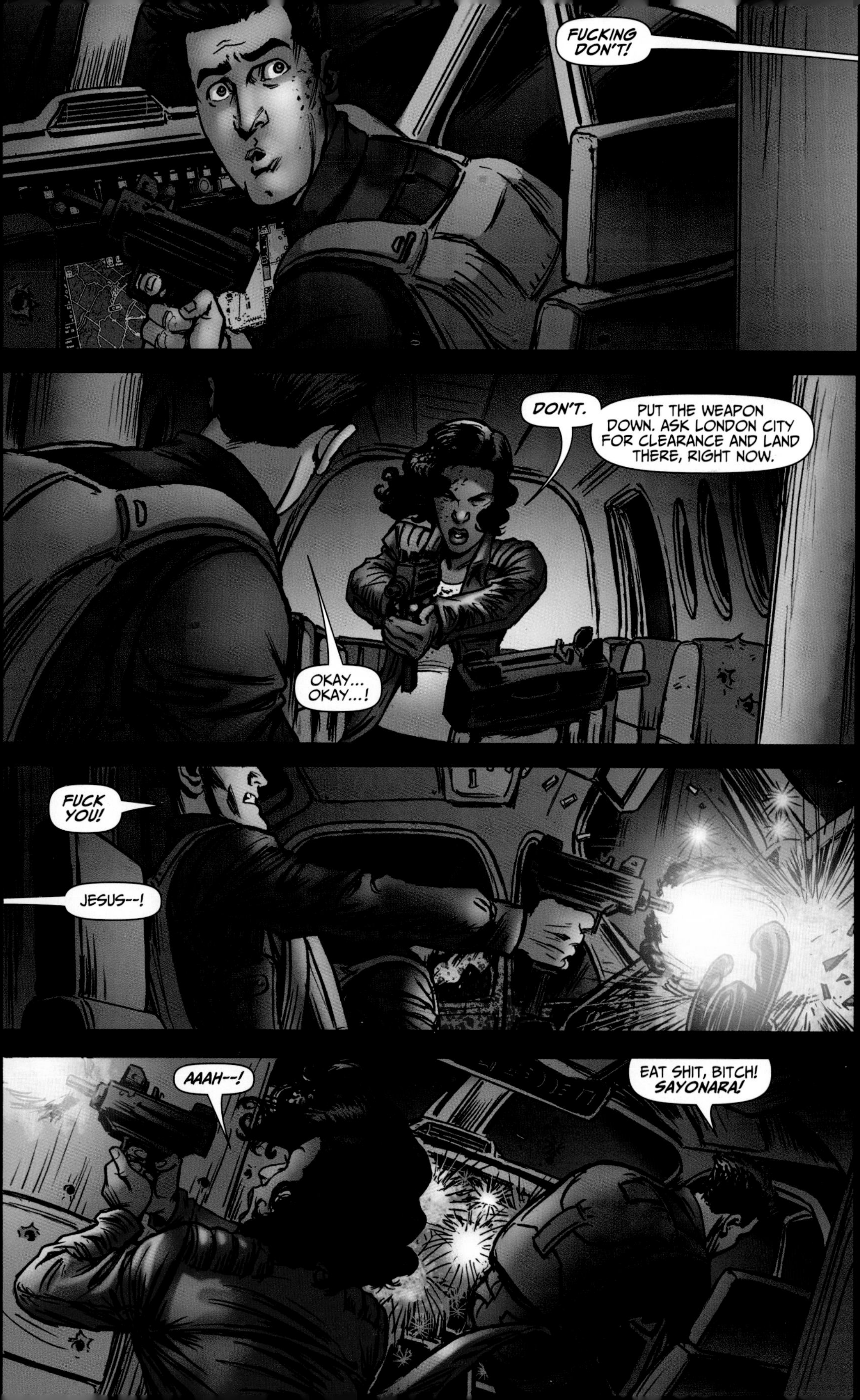
FUCKING DON'T!
DON'T.
PUT THE WEAPON DOWN. ASK LONDON CITY FOR CLEARANCE AND LAND THERE, RIGHT NOW.
OKAY... OKAY...!
FUCK YOU!
JESUS--!
AAAH--!
EAT SHIT, BITCH! SAYONARA!

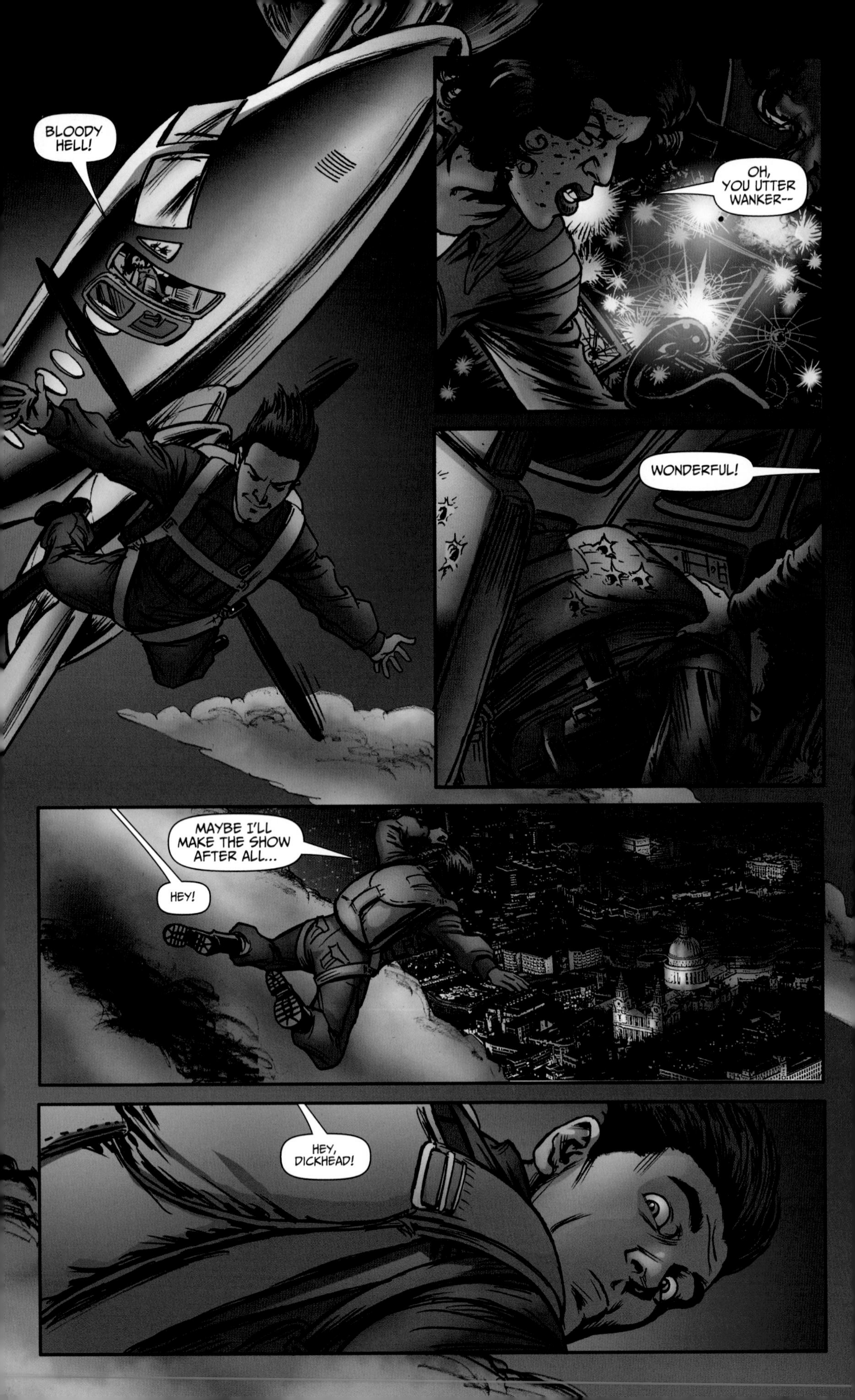
BLOODY HELL!
OH, YOU UTTER WANKER--
WONDERFUL!
MAYBE I'LL MAKE THE SHOW AFTER ALL...
HEY!
HEY, DICKHEAD!

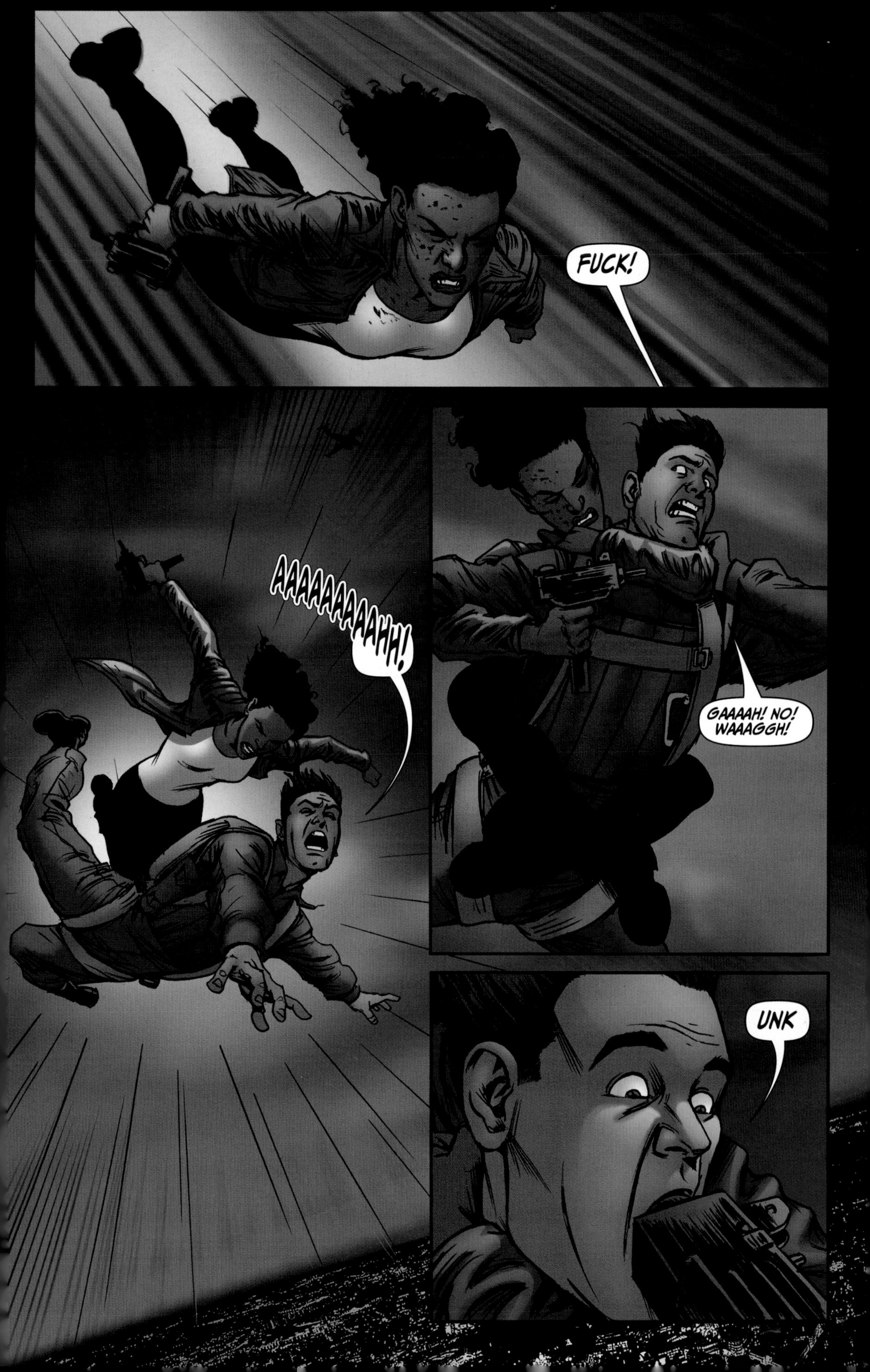
FUCK!
AAAAAAAAAAHH!
GAAAAH! NO! WAAAGGH!
UNK

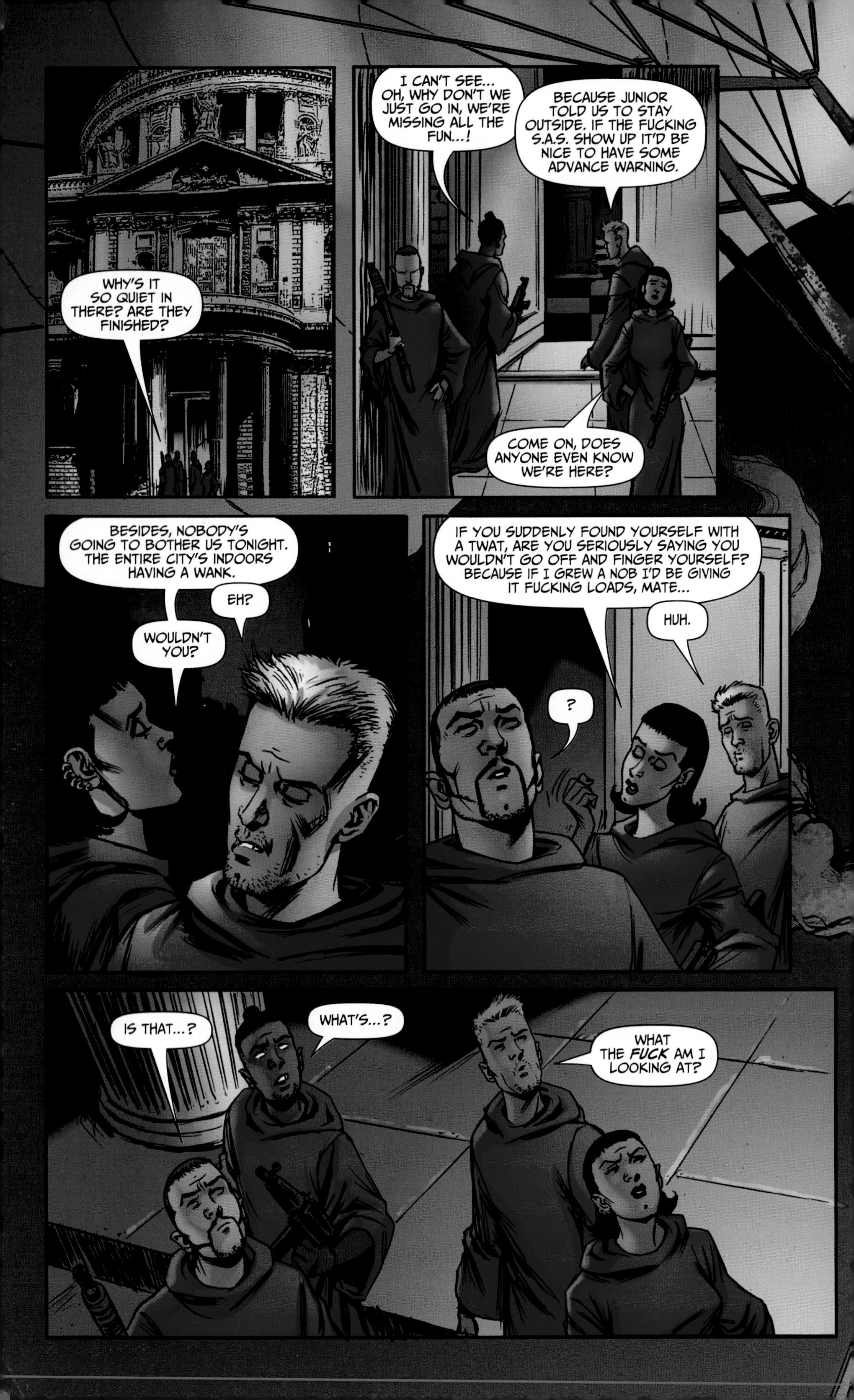
WHY'S IT SO QUIET IN THERE? ARE THEY FINISHED?
I CAN'T SEE... OH, WHY DON'T WE JUST GO IN, WE'RE MISSING ALL THE FUN...!
BECAUSE JUNIOR TOLD US TO STAY OUTSIDE. IF THE FUCKING S.A.S. SHOW UP IT'D BE NICE TO HAVE SOME ADVANCE WARNING.
COME ON, DOES ANYONE EVEN KNOW WE'RE HERE?
BESIDES, NOBODY'S GOING TO BOTHER US TONIGHT. THE ENTIRE CITY'S INDOORS HAVING A WANK.
EH?
WOULDN'T YOU?
IF YOU SUDDENLY FOUND YOURSELF WITH A TWAT, ARE YOU SERIOUSLY SAYING YOU WOULDN'T GO OFF AND FINGER YOURSELF? BECAUSE IF I GREW A NOB I'D BE GIVING IT FUCKING LOADS, MATE...
HUH.
?
IS THAT...?
WHAT'S...?
WHAT THE *FUCK* AM I LOOKING AT?

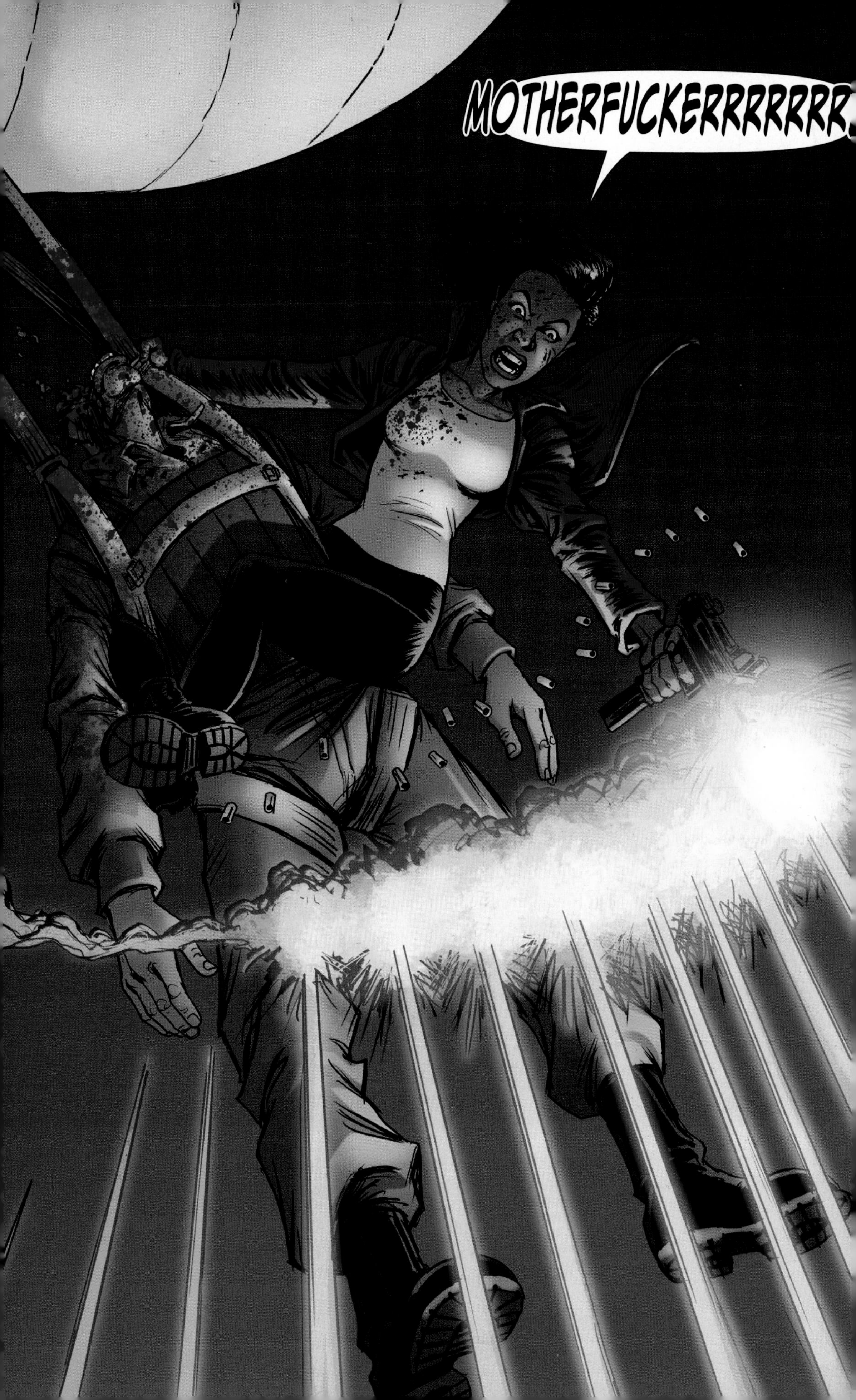
MOTHERFUCKERRRRRRR

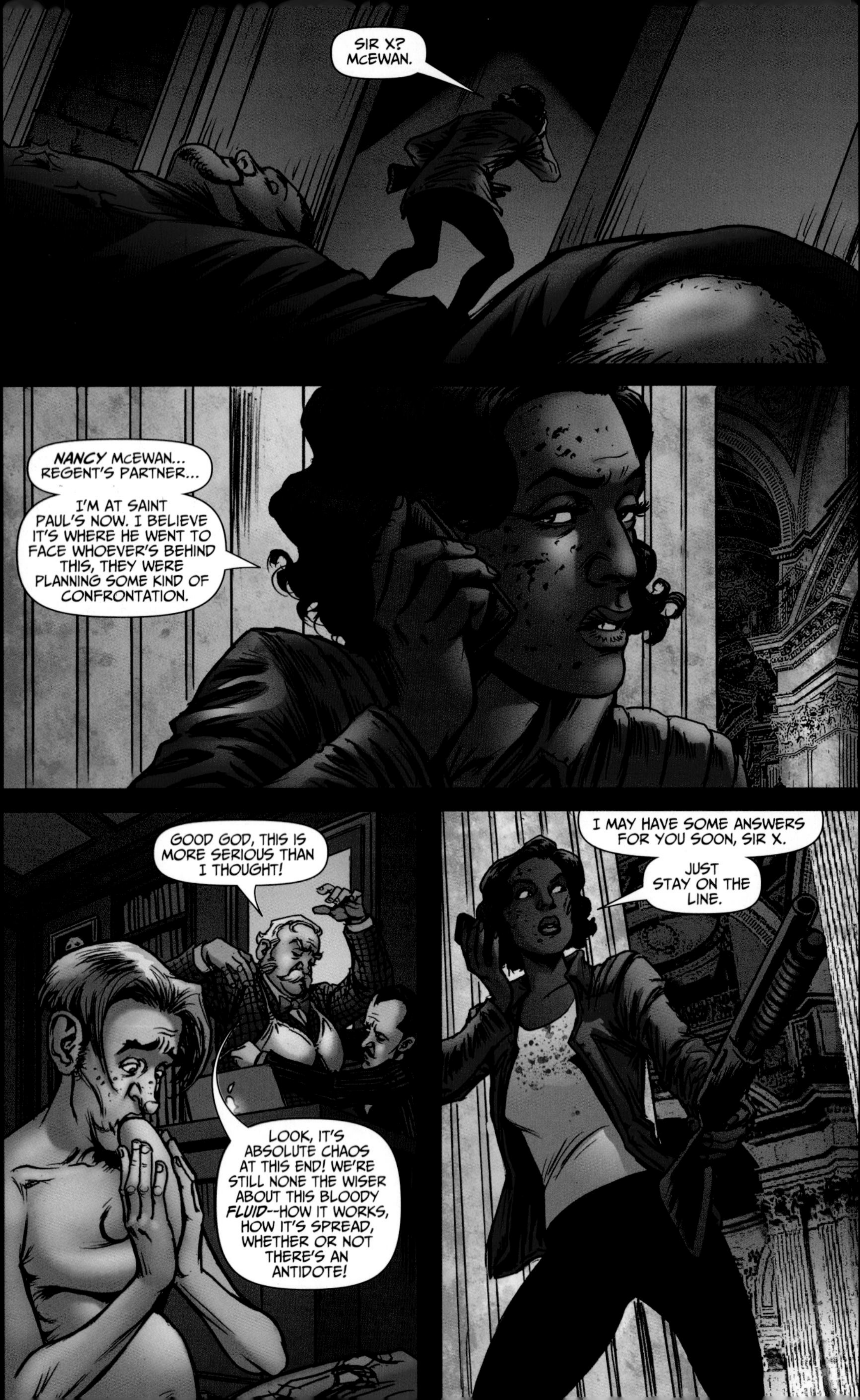
SIR X? McEWAN.
NANCY McEWAN... REGENT'S PARTNER...
I'M AT SAINT PAUL'S NOW. I BELIEVE IT'S WHERE HE WENT TO FACE WHOEVER'S BEHIND THIS, THEY WERE PLANNING SOME KIND OF CONFRONTATION.
GOOD GOD, THIS IS MORE SERIOUS THAN I THOUGHT!
LOOK, IT'S ABSOLUTE CHAOS AT THIS END! WE'RE STILL NONE THE WISER ABOUT THIS BLOODY FLUID--HOW IT WORKS, HOW IT'S SPREAD, WHETHER OR NOT THERE'S AN ANTIDOTE!
I MAY HAVE SOME ANSWERS FOR YOU SOON, SIR X.
JUST STAY ON THE LINE.

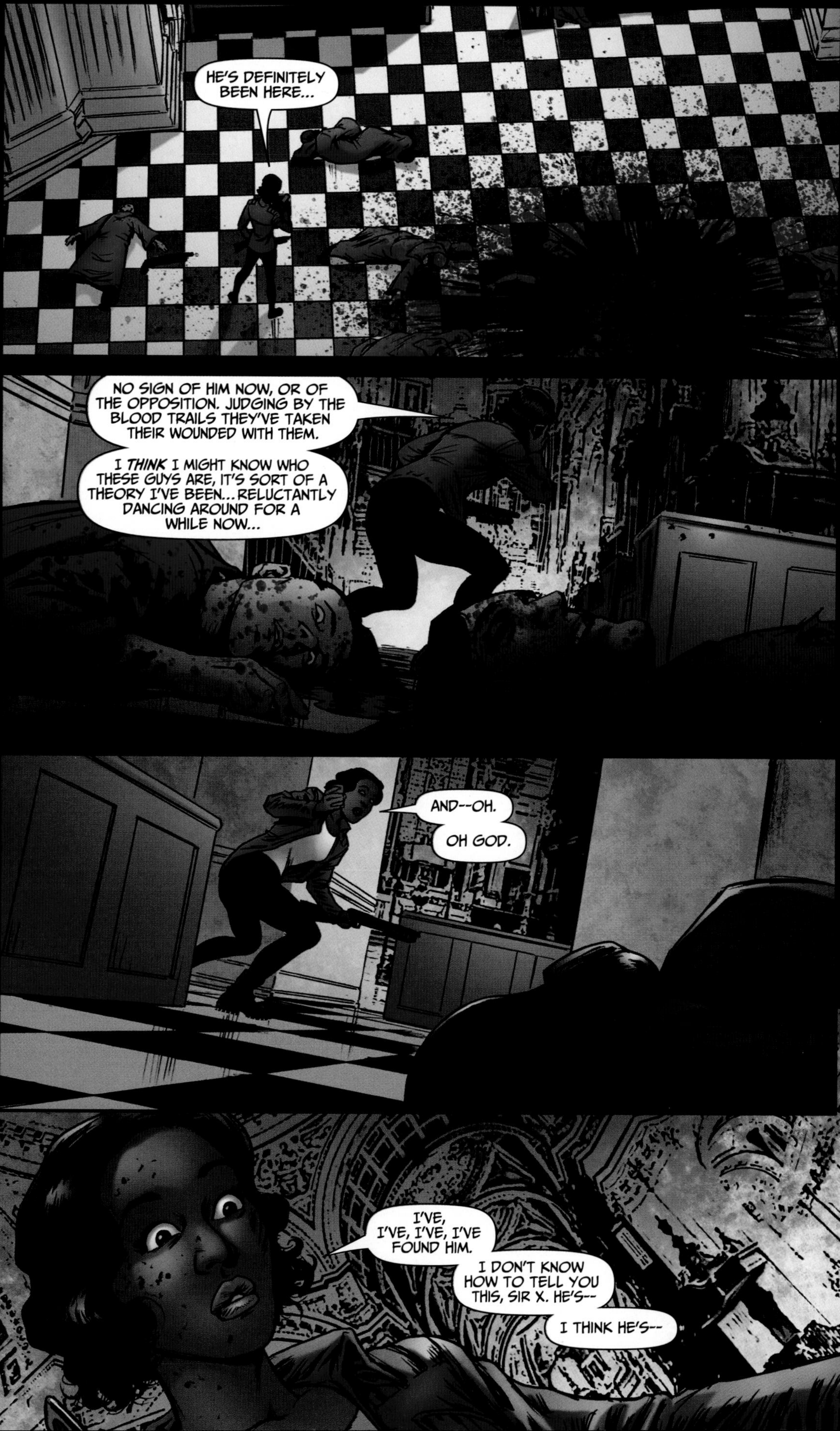
HE'S DEFINITELY BEEN HERE...
NO SIGN OF HIM NOW, OR OF THE OPPOSITION. JUDGING BY THE BLOOD TRAILS THEY'VE TAKEN THEIR WOUNDED WITH THEM.
I *THINK* I MIGHT KNOW WHO THESE GUYS ARE, IT'S SORT OF A THEORY I'VE BEEN...RELUCTANTLY DANCING AROUND FOR A WHILE NOW...
AND--OH.
OH GOD.
I'VE, I'VE, I'VE, I'VE FOUND HIM.
I DON'T KNOW HOW TO TELL YOU THIS, SIR X. HE'S--
I THINK HE'S--

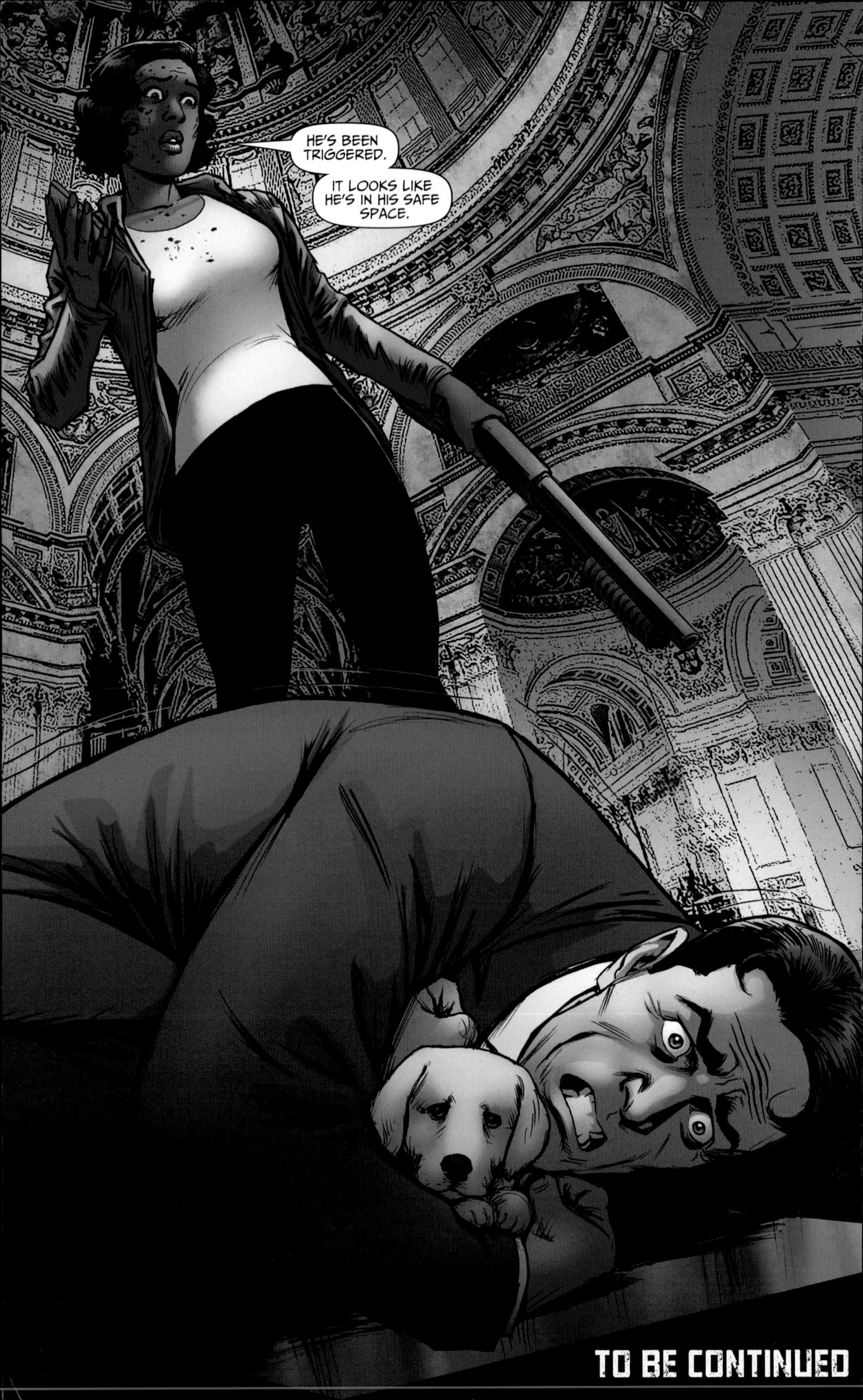
HE'S BEEN TRIGGERED.
IT LOOKS LIKE HE'S IN HIS SAFE SPACE.
TO BE CONTINUED

JIMMY'S BASTARDS

COVER GALLERY

AFTERSHOCK

Issue 1
RUSS BRAUN & JOHN KALISZ
Cover B

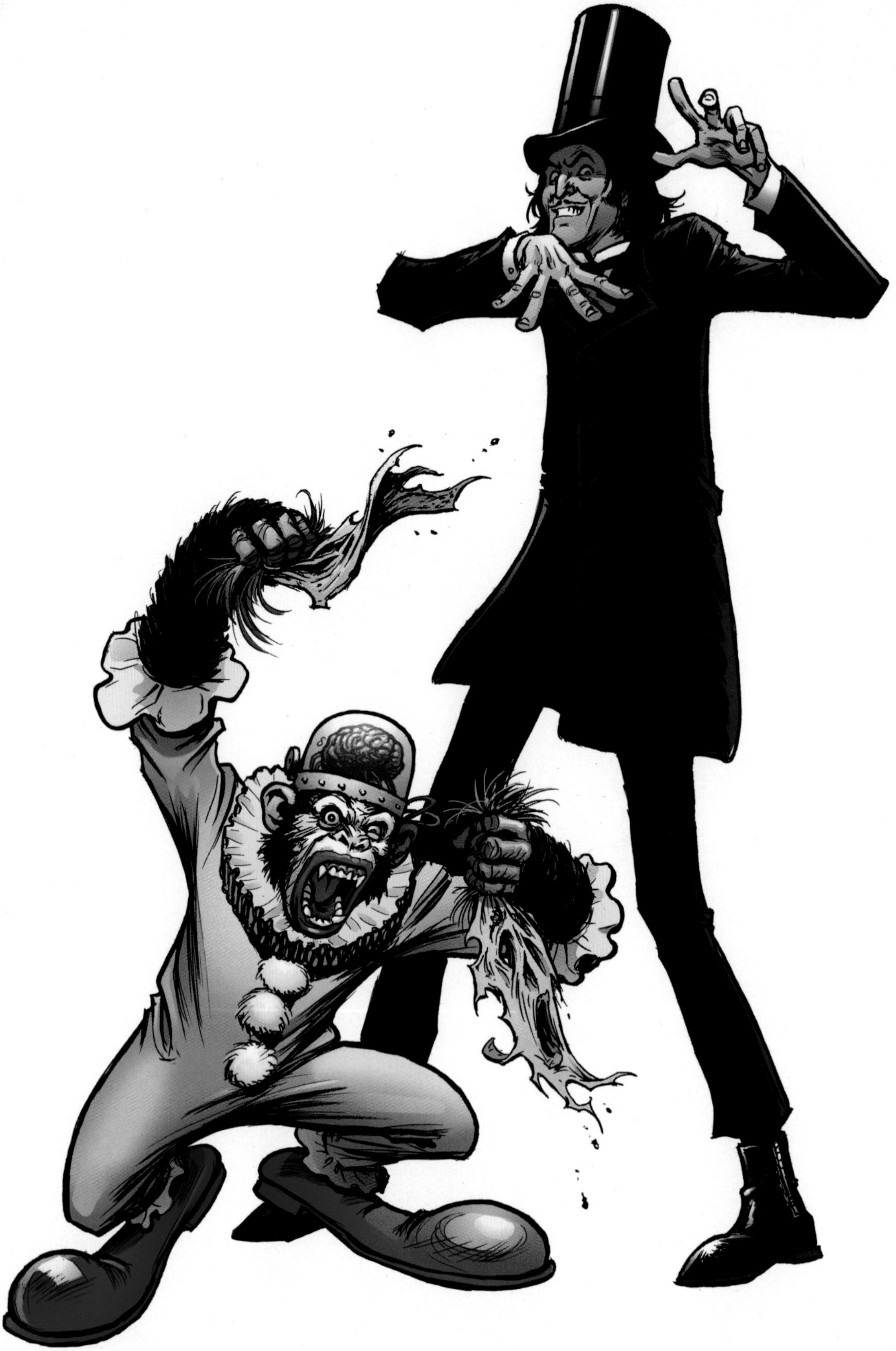

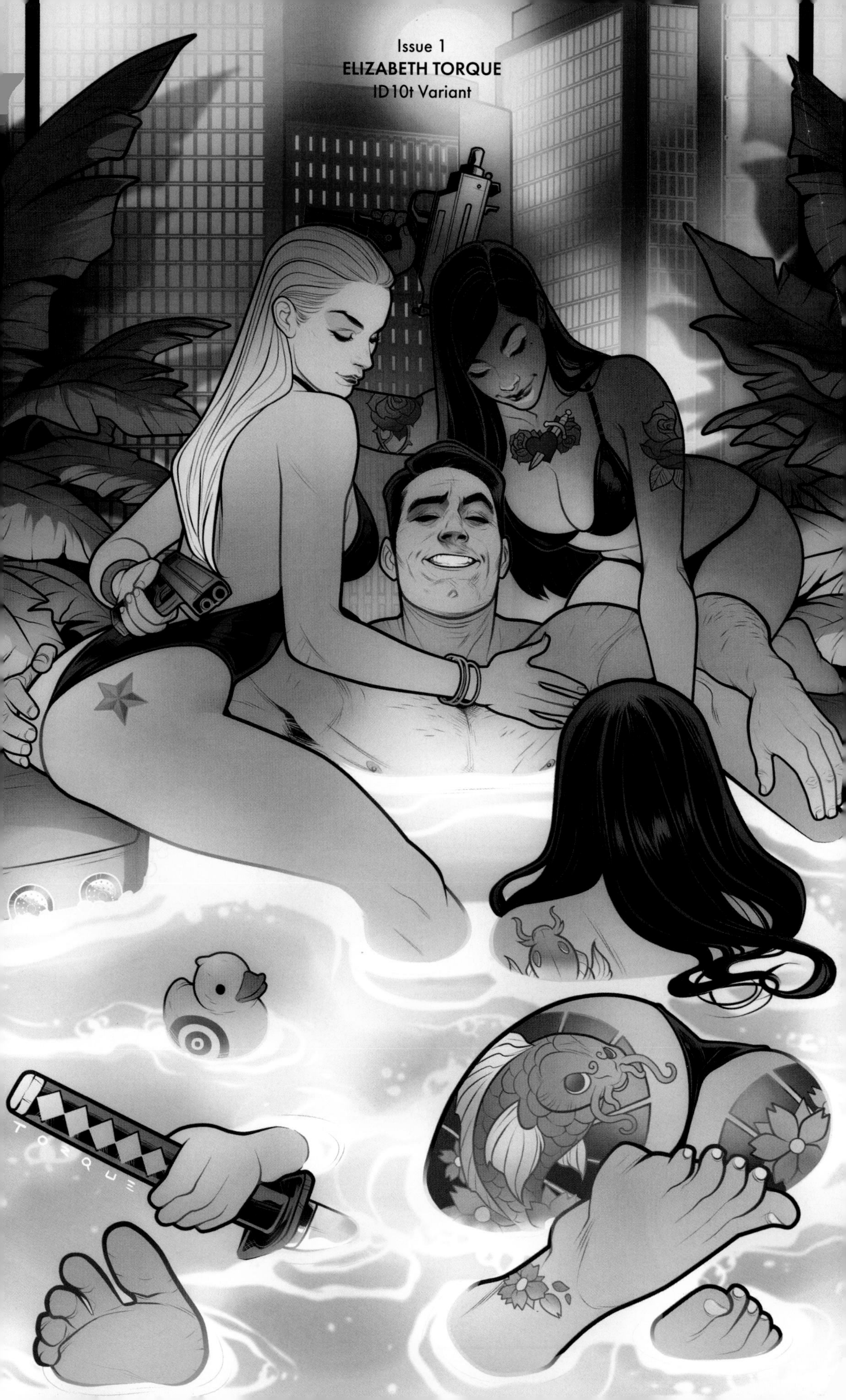
TORQUE

Issue 1
ELIZABETH TORQUE
ID10t Variant

Issue 1
ANDREW ROBINSON
Comic Mint Variant

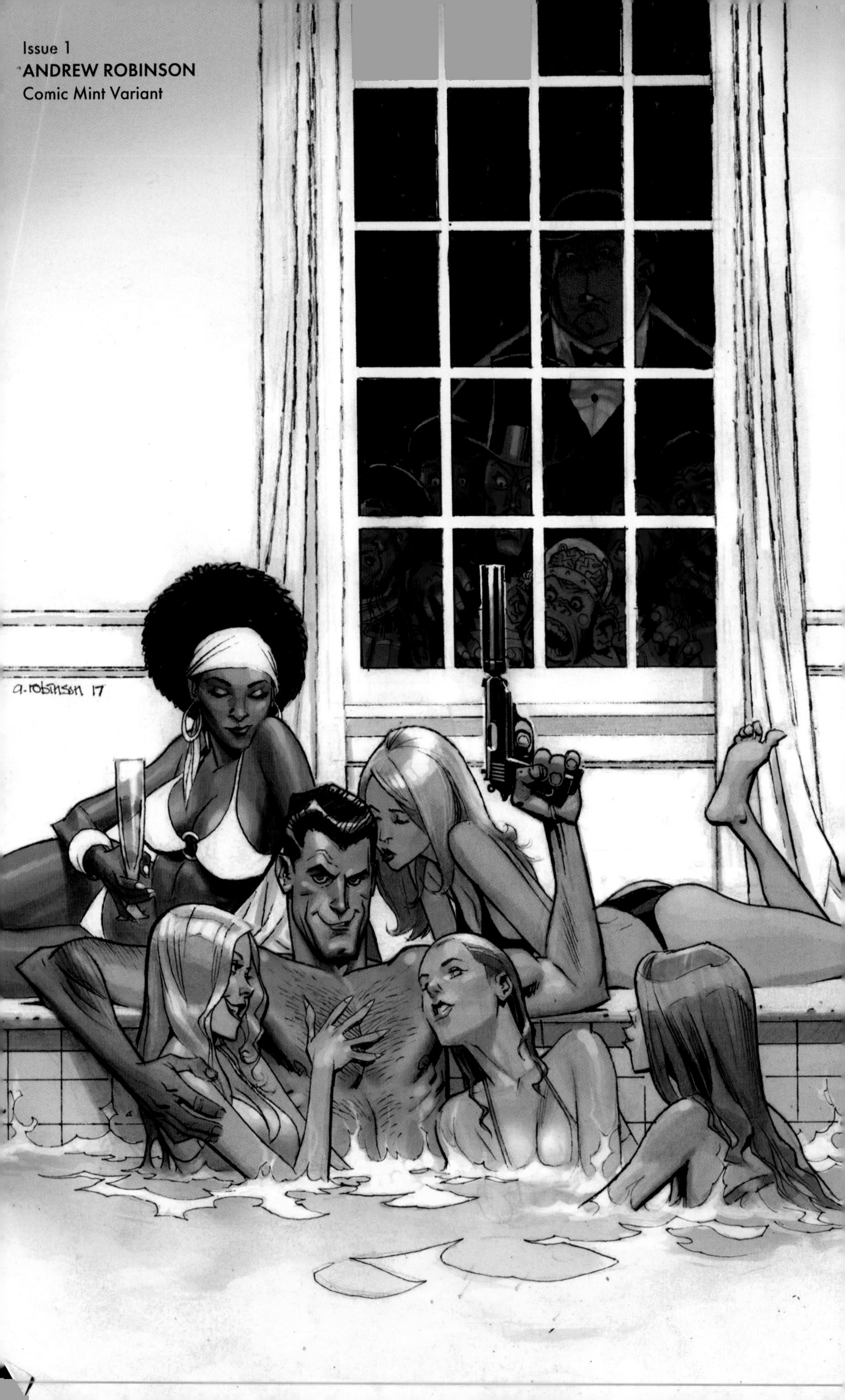
a. robinson 17

Comic Mint Foil Variant

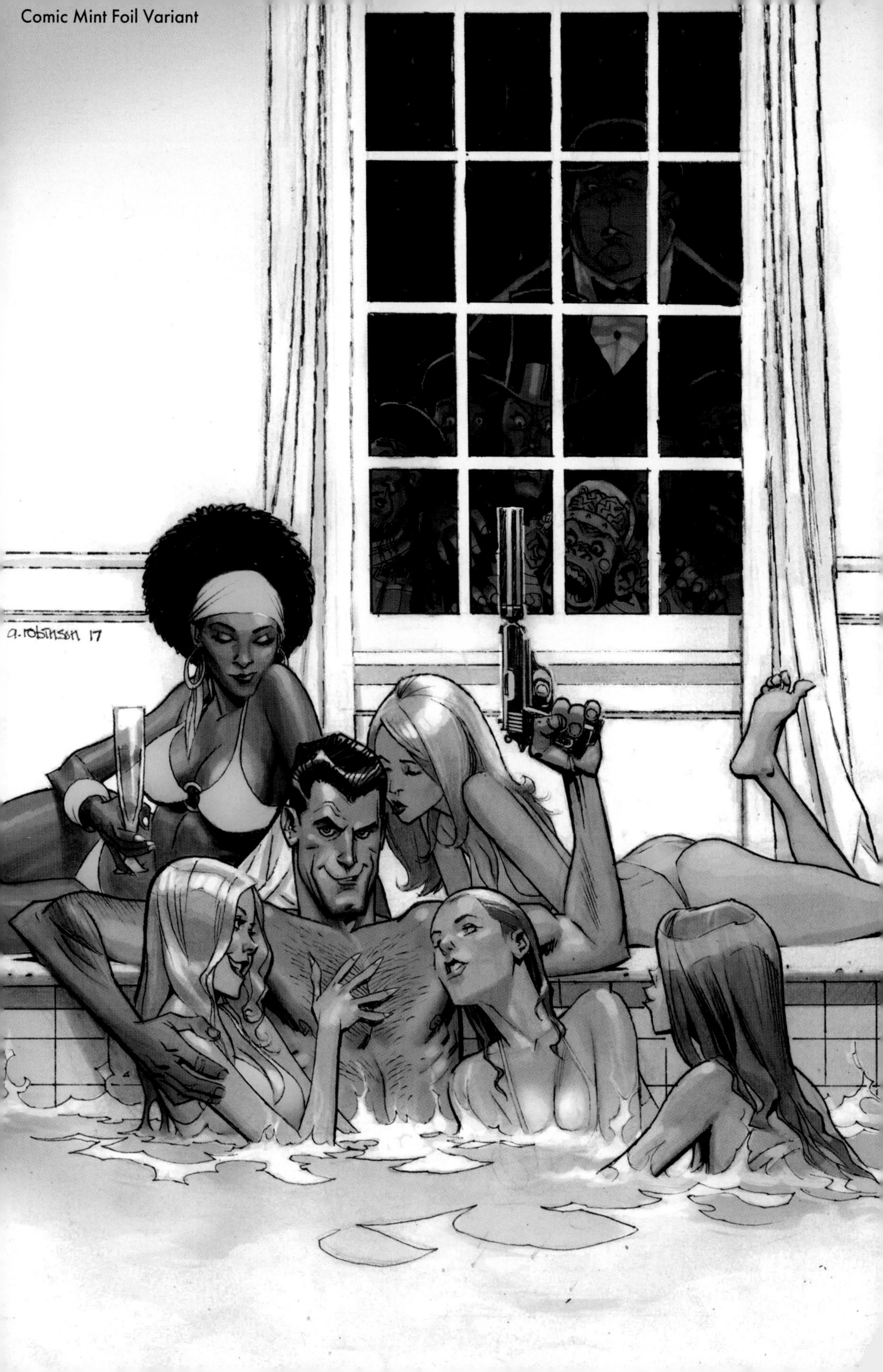
a.robinson 17

Issue 1
CULLY HAMNER
Heroes & Fantasies Variant

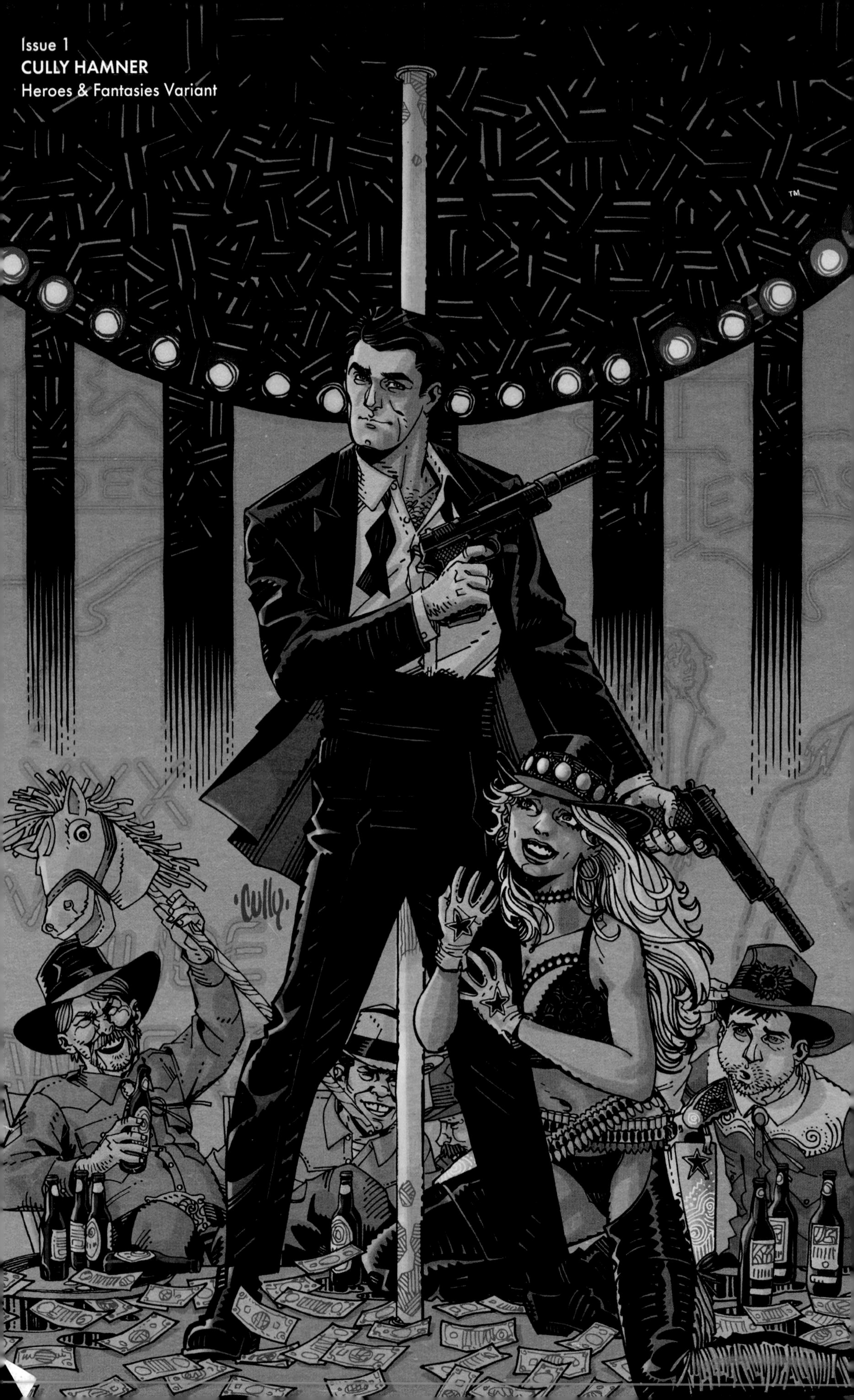

Issue 1

CULLY HAMNER

Heroes & Fantasies Black & White Variant

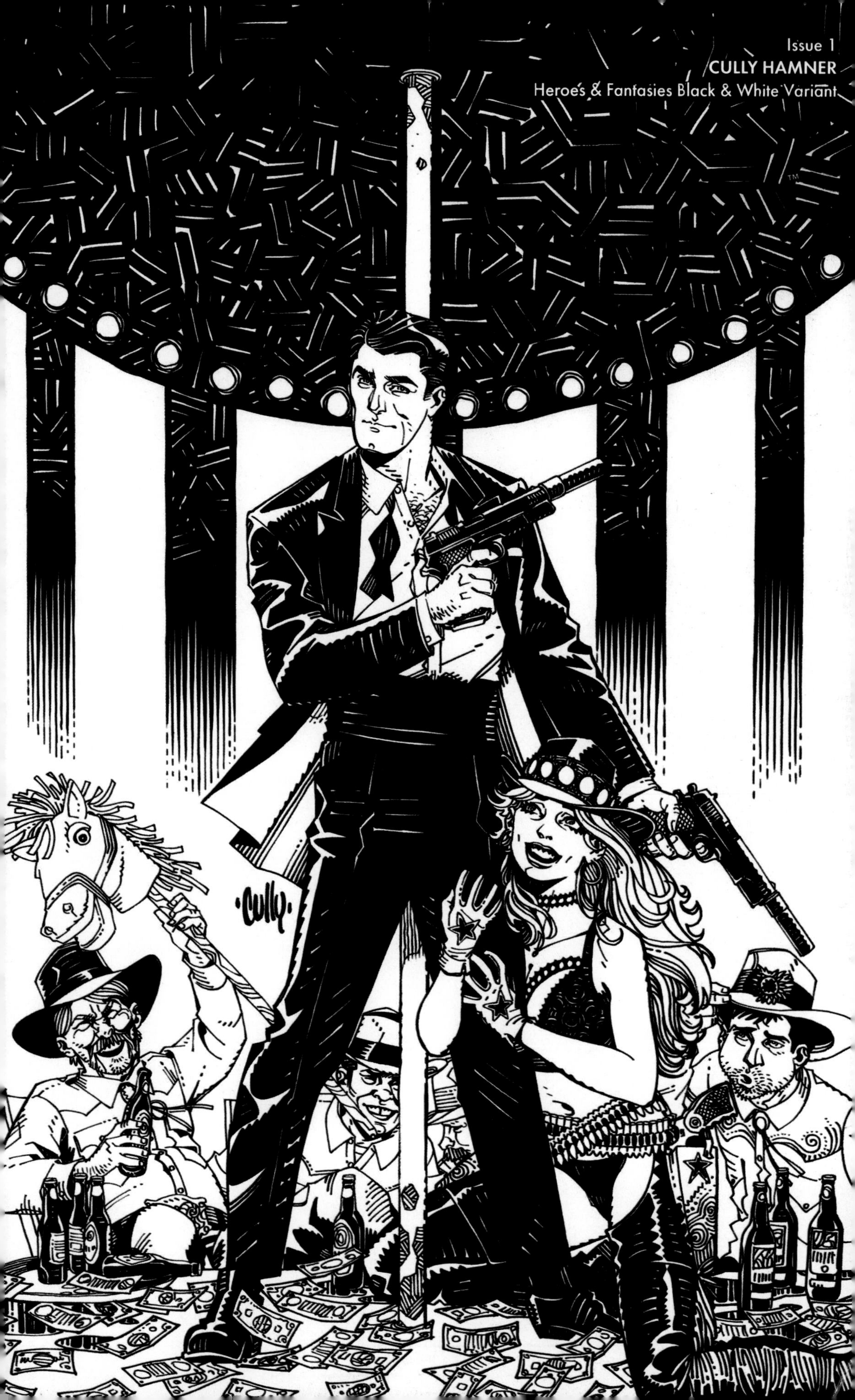

CULLY

Issue 1

MIKE ROOTH

Most Good Hobby Variant

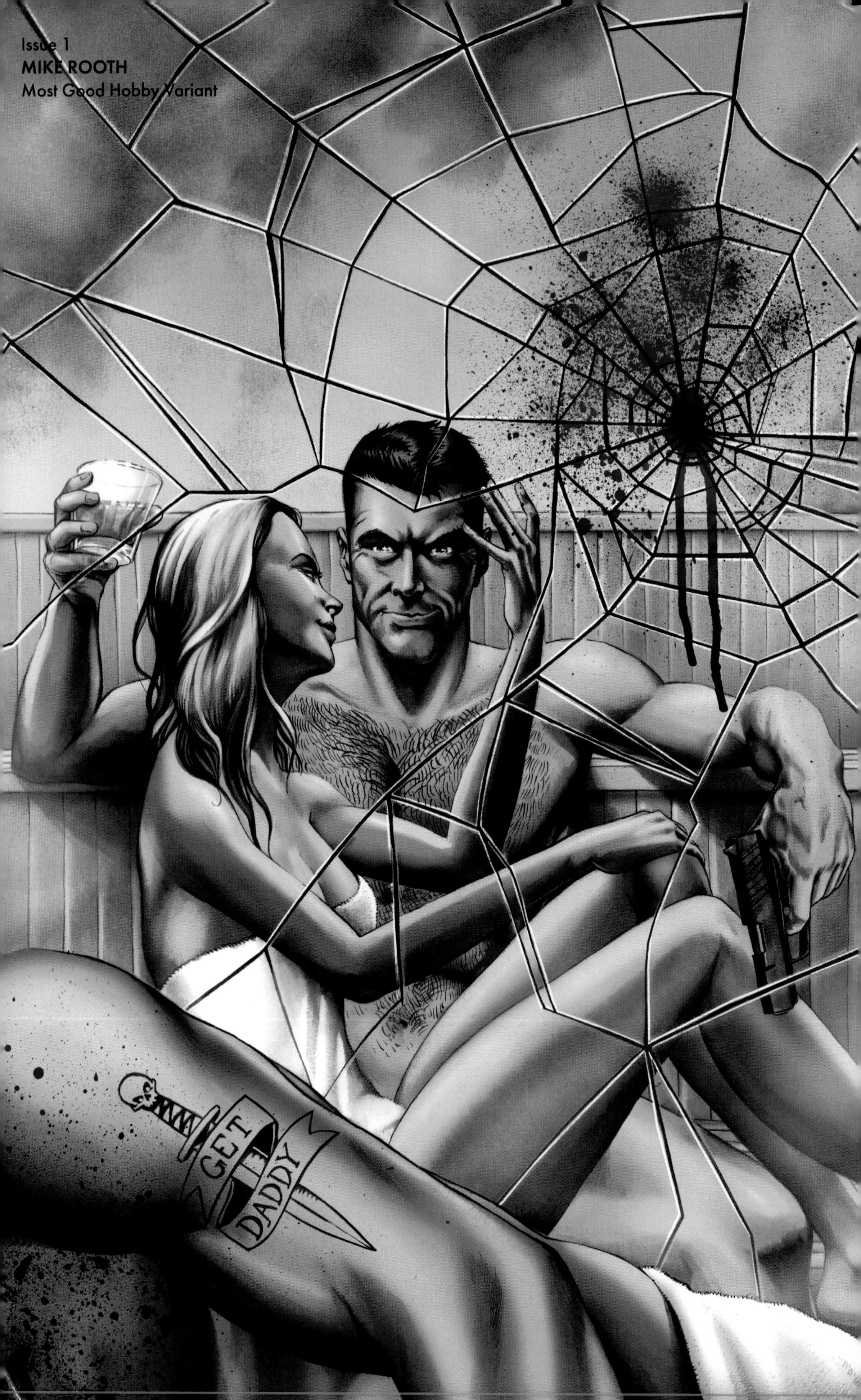
GET
DADDY

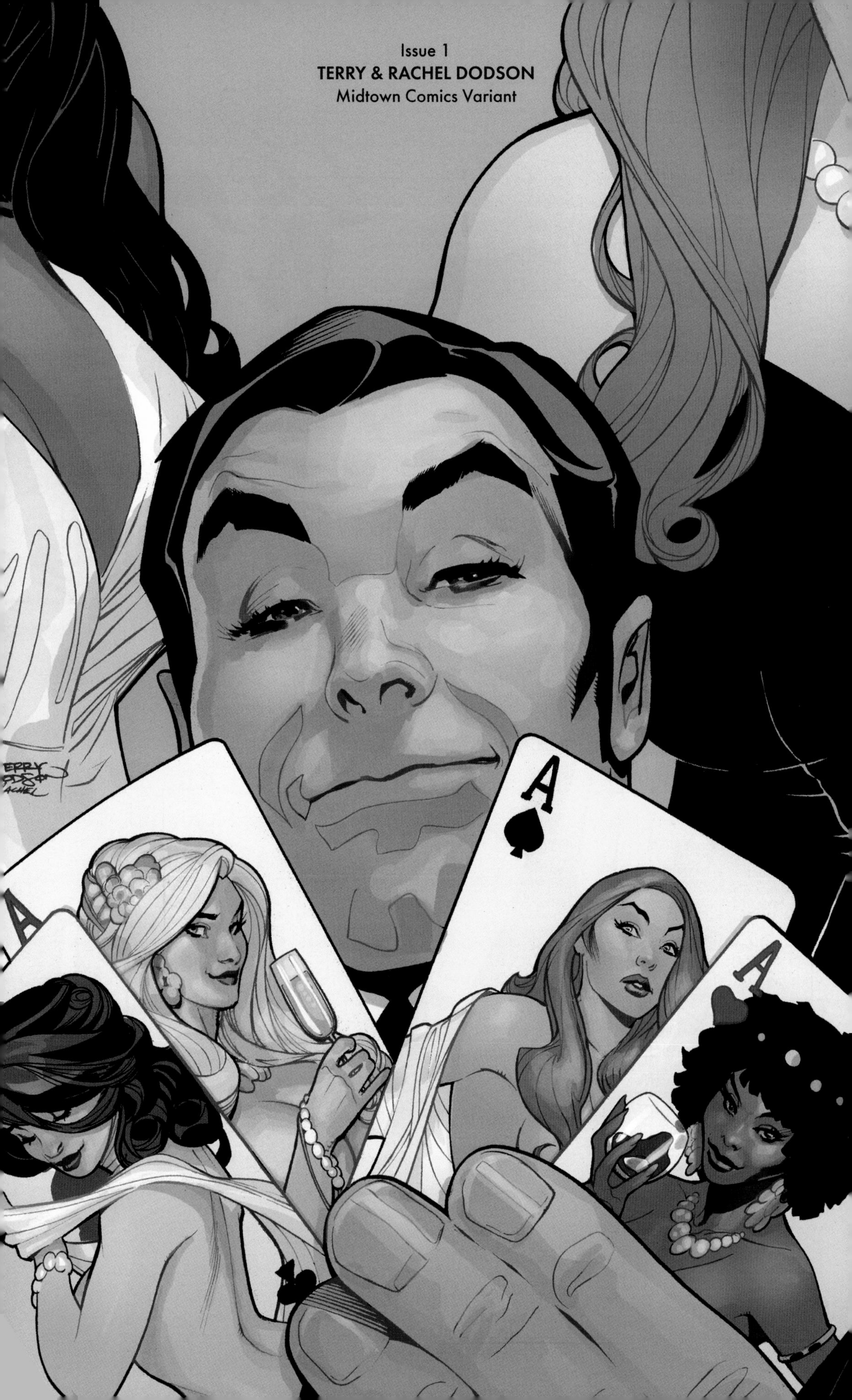

Issue 1
TERRY & RACHEL DODSON
Midtown Comics Variant

Issue 4

PHIL HESTER & MIKE SPICER

Kowabunga Comics Variant

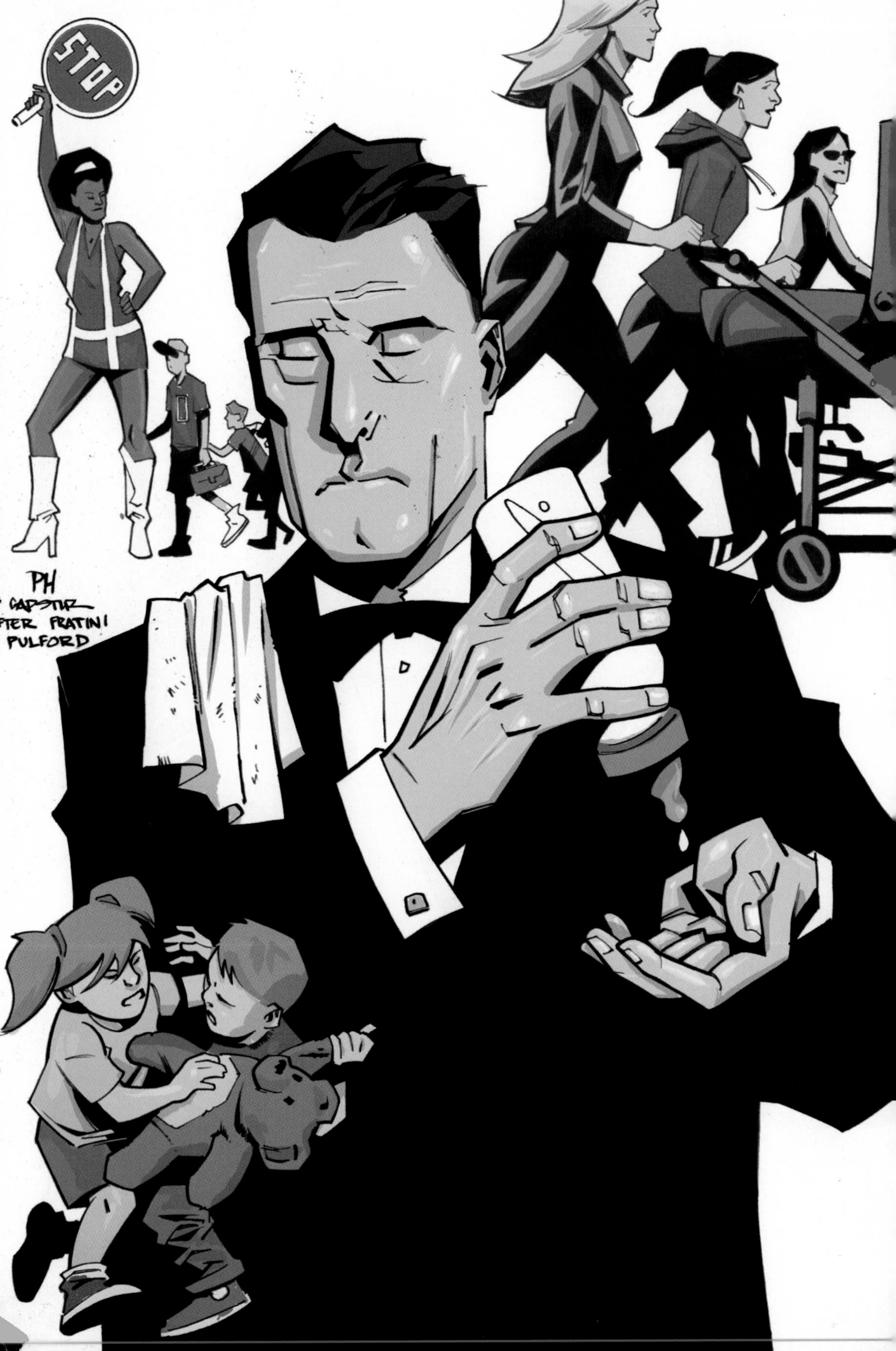
STOP
PH
& GAPSTUR
AFTER FRATINI
& PULFORD

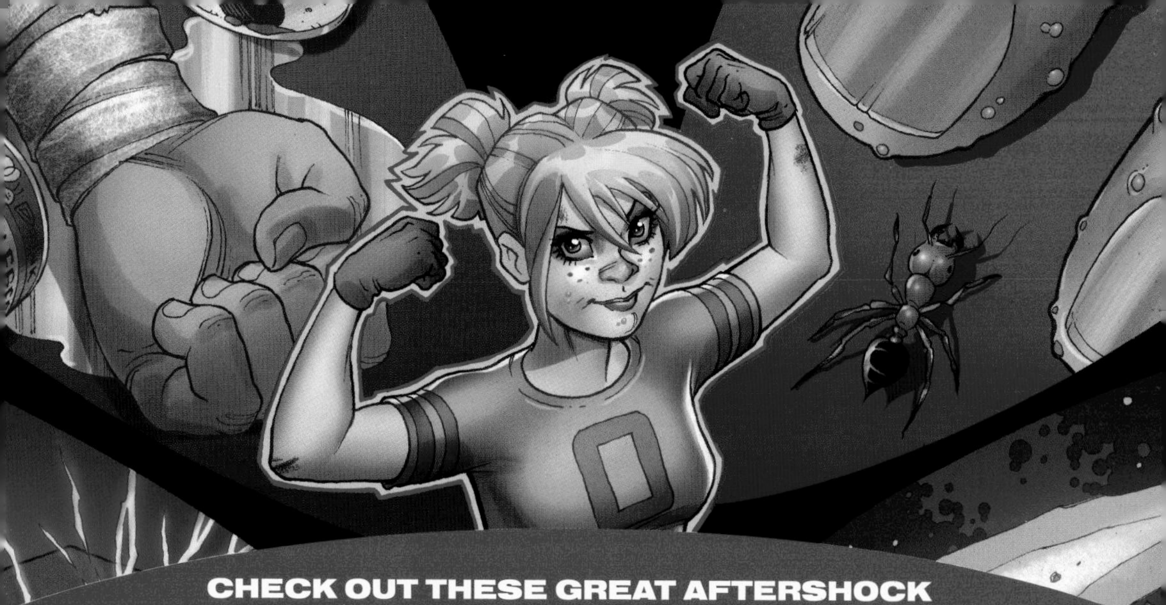

ABOUT THE CREATORS OF JIMMY'S BASTARDS™

GARTH ENNIS writer

Garth Ennis has been writing comics since 1989. His credits include *Preacher*, *The Boys*, *Crossed*, *Battlefields* and *War Stories*, and successful runs on *The Punisher* and *Fury* for Marvel Comics. Originally from Belfast, Northern Ireland, he now lives in New York City with his wife, Ruth.

RUSS BRAUN artist

Russ has been drawing comics for over twenty-five years, with a seven-year break for a stint with Walt Disney Feature Animation. Known for his expressive characters and storytelling, readers have enjoyed Russ' work on numerous titles, including *Batman*, *Animal Man* and *Swamp Thing* for DC, *Fables*, *Fairest* and *Jack of Fables* for Vertigo, and *Son of Satan* and *Where Monsters Dwell* for Marvel. Russ is best known, however, for his frequent collaborations with Garth Ennis on *The Boys*, *Battlefields* and *War Stories*, and most recently, *Sixpack & Dogwelder*.

JOHN KALISZ colorist
🐦 @jkalisz

John Kalisz has been coloring comics for over twenty years, working on just about every major character or book in comics at one point or another...from *Avengers* to *Zatanna* and everything in between.

ROB STEEN letterer

Rob Steen is the illustrator of the *Flanimals* series of children's books written by Ricky Gervais and the Garth Ennis children's book *Erf*. He is also the colorist of David Hine's graphic novel *Strange Embrace* and letterer of comic books for AfterShock, Marvel, Dynamite, Image and First Second.